MY IDEA OF FUN

MY IDEA OF FUN

The Autobiography

LEE SHARPE

ORION

First published in hardback in Great Britain in 2005 by
Orion Books
an imprint of the Orion Publishing Group Ltd
Orion House, 5 Upper St Martin's Lane,
London WC2H 9EA

1 3 5 7 9 10 8 6 4 2

A CIP catalogue record for this book is available
from the British Library.

ISBN: 0 75287 206 0

Printed in Great Britain by
Clays Ltd, St Ives plc

www.orionbooks.co.uk

CONTENTS

Where did it all go wrong?

Lee Sharpe, eh? What does my name conjure up in your mind? Football memories, of me dancing round corner flags, doing daft little slinky dances when I scored, playing football with a smile on my face? The original Boy Wonder, hat-trick at Highbury when Man U beat Arsenal 6–2, in the England team at nineteen, sweet left foot, lots of pace, you didn't want your team to be playing against me when I was flying. The first popstar footballer of the Premiership age, every teenage girl's pin-up when Alex Ferguson was dragging United out of the years of underachievement, and football was becoming sexy – they wouldn't be Blu-Tacking pictures of Steve Bruce on their bedroom walls, would they?

So what happened to me? Aged just thirty-three, with my old mate Roy Keane still powering the furnace of United's midfield, how come I was finished with football, fetching up on *Celebrity Love Island*, thrilling a watching nation with my skill at lolling round a swimming pool? Where did it all go wrong? Everybody interested in football wants to know, and everybody thinks they know. They've all heard the stories, know someone who knows someone who saw me at it. I lived too fast, too young, that was it. Pure and simple. Flew too high and burned out. Manchester in the early 1990s: E, acid, coke, house music, the Hacienda, all that scene and everything that went with it. People would see me out in the clubs, dancing, grinning and they just knew I had to be on something. Everybody could see it. You can't have that much fun on a couple of bottles of cider. Poor Alex Ferguson, the caring, nurturing father figure, tried everything with me; he was at his wits' end. Pulled poor, innocent Ryan Giggs out of a party at my house just in time, before I had a chance to drag Giggsy down into my pit of corruption. Fergie even had me living in his house for a while, to try to get me on the straight and narrow – that's how far his dedication stretched for the young men in his care. United put out the story that I had viral meningitis – head problems, you see, nudge, wink – when everybody knew it was drugs. The manager tried everything, but none of it worked; I was too wild, too out of control, and so in the end, reluctantly, with a sorrowful shake of his head, he had to sell me.

United left me behind and went on to win leagues, the Treble, steamrollering success, and I became a fond memory for the fans, a breath of crazy, happy days before it all got very serious, industrial, a business. I went to Leeds but nobody remembers too much what I did there; the club had its brief seasons of near success with its glittering young team, but I wasn't part of it. Not dedicated enough, see. Had my chance with two managers of huge talents in George Graham and humble, straightforward David O'Leary, but blew it again. Ended up a lost soul at Bradford, not making the most of it, not working my way back to form and fame. Should have done better. Fetched up at places like Exeter for a few games, for God's sake.

Where did it all go wrong? I threw it all away. It was all my fault. I compare myself to Giggsy and grimace, wish I'd got my head down, put the poker face on, dedicated myself, worked harder. Instead, I had stars in my eyes, stopped doing the graft, fell into the Madchester drug scene, lived for then, paid later. I feel sorry for Alex Ferguson, actually, the trouble I gave him, poor man. Could have given him a heart attack. At least my blighted career stands as a warning for those who came after me: keep on the straight and narrow and listen to your elders, the good people in football. They know best.

Ha.

It weren't quite like that.

CHAPTER 1

Born smiling

When I was nine or ten, playing football in the Cubs' team in Halesowen, Birmingham, before the start of every football season my mum and dad would unveil a brand-new, shiny pair of football boots and a spotless ball – awesome gifts. I used to take them tenderly up to my room at night, tuck them under the covers, settle down and sleep with them. I think it was love.

My dreams, as I grew older, were never very complicated: I was going to be a footballer. I spent secondary school playing for teams in the year above, and doodled through lessons practising my autograph. That meant I left without an O-level to my name but, I thought, with all the skills I'd need. My mum used to worry: 'What are the chances,' she'd say, 'of you really being a professional footballer?' She wanted me to have something to fall back on, in case it didn't work out. I didn't give that much thought, and my dad backed me up, which was surprising, because he was always the safe, steady one, more cautious by nature than my mum: 'Someone's got to be,' he used to say. 'Why can't Lee be one of the few? He's good enough.' She used to shake her head, worry about her boys, lost in fantasy.

I daydreamed about stepping out for one of the big clubs at the great grounds, the stands packed with passionate fans, roaring their team on, chanting my name. I don't think I was ever stuck on the idea of 'winning things' – of hoisting a cup above my head, carrying a medal home, finishing top of the league; I'm not sure I ever gave that stuff a thought. My imagination was dazzled by the game itself: scoring goals, skipping past full-backs, using the natural pace I always had as a boy, going on mazy dribbles, breathing the joy of the crowd and celebrating with them. I'd be in awe of the games they showed on TV, wingers in full flow, strikers banging in goals, and I loved the little cameos they'd play over and over again on *Match of the Day*, those quirky moments: Alan Birchenall of Leicester and Tony Currie of Sheffield United falling in a heap, then giving each other a little kiss before they stood up; players suspending hostilities for a second to give each other piggy backs, cuddle a ref, climb on a wall to celebrate a sweet bit of play. Stealing a bit of time to laugh and enjoy themselves.

I ended up supporting Aston Villa – it was a case of siding with my granddad, my mum's dad, who supported the Villa and got me to support them too as a put-down to my dad. He was always needling my dad, starting with size, because my granddad was a huge man, a lorry driver, 6' 4", while my dad's only 5' 8". My dad's a Birmingham City fan and he did take me to a few games at St Andrews, but my granddad said: 'You're not supporting the team that duck egg supports! You'll support the Villa.'

So I thought, cool, I'll support the Villa, if Granddad does. I never went to many games, though; I was born on 25 May 1971, so when I was fourteen, fifteen, football-supporting age, it was the mid-1980s, when there was a lot of trouble at matches, and my mum was never keen on me taking the three-bus odyssey from our house to Villa Park with mayhem and madness kicking off everywhere. I was ten when Villa won the League Championship, and eleven when they won the European Cup the following year; magical performances, so unexpected, and at that age I took it all in like a sponge. Even then, I was a Gary Shaw or Tony Morley fan, loving the trickery and skill, rather than an admirer of Ken McNaught's prowess as a stopper, or Des Bremner fetching and carrying in midfield. For me, football was Trevor Francis, not John McGovern; Kenny Dalglish, not Joey Jones; the showmen, not the workhorses. And, along with being a dazzling football superstar when I was older, I naturally thought I'd have a good standard of living, a nice house, flash car, girls fluttering around – I was never the most difficult soul to please; not then, not now.

Birmingham in the 1970s might not evoke a picture of heaven for everybody, but it was for me growing up, a happy, wonderful childhood. I had a warm, loving family, my mum and dad could not have done more for us, I always had good mates and our estate was a playground, full of laughs and endless, flowing games of football. It might not have been the same toothy grin which, for some reason I can still never work out, would later drive so many football managers to distraction, but I think I was born with a smile on my face.

My mum and dad – Gail and Leo – were school sweethearts really; they married at nineteen and had me, their oldest, at twenty-one. I was born in inner Birmingham but when I was tiny we moved out to a semi-detached three-bedroom house on a newish estate in Blackheath,

Black Country territory. My dad was – still is – a metal-spinner, an old, skilled, Brummie trade, which he's done since he left school at sixteen. He worked for years for a big company locally, then, when I was ten or eleven, made the big, brave move of setting up on his own and having a few blokes working for him. He called his company ATOL Spinnings, for A Touch of Luck, so he must have been fingers-crossed about it at the time. My mum is the more adventurous type – they reckon I take after her more than my dad with my freewheeling, what-will-be-will-be approach to life. She stayed at home when I – and my younger brother John and sister Nicola when they came along – were kids, but she always had work or her own little business ventures on the go: industrial cleaning, ironing on some incredible scale. Years later, she'd have her hands full running the Lee Sharpe fan club for thousands of besotted adolescent girls, but we'll get to that.

We weren't rich but we were reasonably well off. They always looked after us kids. We were well dressed, never had ripped clothes or shoes hanging off us. I don't remember ever going short of anything; we always had what we wanted at Christmas and birthdays. When I was still only eighteen months old we moved to a different estate, which became my stamping ground as I grew up. One of my main muckers there, Ross Hadley, is still my mate now, and by the time we were six or seven Ross and I would be roaming all over the estate. It wasn't massive, and it was safe; my mum just used to tell us to be careful as we went out to play in the morning, and she wouldn't see us again until teatime. Sometimes our mums would make us a packed lunch and we'd cycle round the estate pretending we were travelling round the world; we'd stop and say we were in a different country, and eat a sandwich or two to celebrate our arrival, toast it with a can of Coke.

We played anywhere, sledging down a bank at the back of the estate when it snowed, leaping off a low wall on our bikes down by some garages, and I had plenty of time to act out my football dreams, in the streets or on grass verges, mammoth games, lasting hours on end, till the dark was creeping over us and our tummies were nagging us to finally take them home. We played football wherever, developing a feel for the ball, a taste for tricks, going past or beating the lad trying to stop you, smacking a goal in without a thought, having marathon skills competitions out in the park by a tree: who could keep it up longest, who could volley, shoot, score. I'm not sure tracking back or man-marking played any part in those magical sessions, but imagining ourselves performing heroics, basking in the roars of the crowds in the great grounds of the Midlands, certainly did.

I played my first proper match, for the Cubs, at eight. Couldn't wait. Could hardly sleep. So nervous beforehand, as I always would be before matches, at any level. We lost 10–1. I don't think I was too bothered about that; we played a team older and bigger than us, so we got slaughtered. More important to me was the thrill of putting my first proper team kit on: bright red top, red shorts, yellow socks, yellow numbers on the back. Quality gear, right from the start. With the kit on, I felt a foot taller, stronger, faster, a proper footballer. Within twelve months, our team had grown up, a few decent players joined us and soon we were the best in the area, beating everyone. My mum and dad shipped us everywhere; they grumbled about being a taxi service taking me and, later, John to football,

Nicola to dancing or gymnastics, but they loved it really. They were always there, always encouraging, always proud. Mostly, though, at that early age, I'd be staying with Nan and Granddad at weekends, and my granddad would take me to the Cubs football on Saturday mornings.

I idolised him, loved, worshipped him. Looked so far up to him it hurt my neck. I was a granddad's boy, as I think a lot of little boys are. I spent so much time with them when I was growing up, I've found out in recent years it caused a few rows between Mum and Dad because my dad complained he hardly saw me. It started when I was only six or seven; they were helping my mum out really. She used to take me to the edge of the estate on Fridays and put me on the bus to Halesowen, the next town along, about five miles away. Nan and Granddad would be waiting for me at the other end, standing there with a little present, a new Action Man outfit or a couple of toy cars, and we'd go up to the Labour Club or the social club where they'd play bingo, watch a cabaret, have a few pints and I'd run around and play hide-and-seek with some of the other kids outside. When I was a little bit older, we kids all used to traipse round the streets, down a gully to a chippie, get roe or fish and chips, ask for them to be wrapped in newspaper, then walk back and eat them together sitting outside the club, like a real, proper posse.

Granddad used to drive his lorry to supermarkets, delivering food around the country, so I used to go with him in the holidays sometimes, sit up in his cab like a grown-up, like his mate. Mum would get me up early and walk me to the edge of the estate. He'd roll up in his wagon at six o'clock and they'd throw me into the cabin. He had a bed made up for me in there. I'd go straight back to sleep, then wake up hundreds of miles down the road, unloading cargo somewhere up north, or in Wales.

His nickname was the Duke – he looked a bit like John Wayne – and he had plenty of aggression to match his size; he used to get road rage before they invented the phrase. Loved a pint, too. In the days before the clampdown on drink-driving, he'd have twelve or fifteen pints in an evening, then drive home. God knows how many cigarettes he'd smoke, woodbines with no filters. He used to take me into pubs with him and sit me up on the bar, buy me a Coke and tell me to behave myself while he and his mates had a few pints. He even bought me a little suit from the market, used to dress me in that and tell landlords I wasn't a kid, I was a dwarf, so they'd let me in.

We moved nearer their flat, in Halesowen, when I was eleven, a bigger house for us in a nicer area. When I started secondary school, I had to walk past their flat to get the bus to school, so I stayed the odd night there at first, because I was knocking around with a few lads who lived down there and thought I might as well leave my uniform with my nan and kip there. I ended up pretty much living with them for eighteen months; it might seem strange, but I was so close to them, I just never went home. They used to spoil me rotten: Nan used to wake me up in the morning with a cup of tea in bed, my school uniform used to be in the airing cupboard so it was all warm when I put it on, they fussed and pampered me. It was the good life, and I never complained. My dad probably did, a lot, although I didn't know it at the time. You can understand it from his point of view – I used to see him and my mum all the time, but I never stayed at home because life was so sweet at my nan and granddad's.

I think it would be fair to say I was not the most assiduous swot ever to grace the classrooms of Hagley High School; I was in the top sets but treated all the subjects the same – did bugger all on any of them. I spent the days waiting for the time when I just knew starstruck girls would be queuing up for my autograph, then I used to go out on the sports field and make a name for myself, whatever the sport. Football, of course, but I had an eye for cricket, and loved basketball. I was quick, taller than I look at first, I loved games and I had a natural athleticism, which served me well whatever we were doing. I ended up with the archetypal footballer's reports: 'Could do better if only he tried' in every subject, but 'a pleasure to have around, excels' for PE. I can't say I had too much of a problem with that. I always enjoyed school, though, and was never in any trouble; I was a happy-go-lucky young lad. I wasn't a rebel or cheeky to the teachers; I was brought up to respect them and all my figures of authority, particularly the men: my dad, my granddad, the teachers.

When I was eleven, my Cubs side played one of the strong Sunday league junior clubs in the area, Stourbridge Falcons. They were the kind that attracts – or hoovers up, depending on how you look at it – all the best kids around and goes about hammering all the other little sides into the ground. We took them on and beat them 1–0; I was a left-winger even back then, using my pace to get past people, or playing up front behind a striker and running at defenders, which I loved. Sure enough, after the game, along comes the pushy coach, asking me and two other lads to play for them. One was Darren Goodall, a very good right-winger, who ended up on West Brom's books; the other was Mark Davey, a really tough no-nonsense left-back, a bit of a kicker, which was great for me. I played left-wing in front of him for years, and if anybody kicked me, Mark used to seek out double portions of vengeance and kick a real lump out of them.

Stourbridge Falcons was a good club and a good standard. I used to take full-backs on and put crosses in, and I scored quite a few goals too. We had one of those really over-developed lads playing centre-forward, Craig Toy, the kind who strikes terror into lanky pubescent defenders everywhere because he's got rippling muscles and hair where they're not sure you're supposed to have it. He looked a bit like George Michael, designer stubble and everything, at twelve. He wasn't a great player but he put himself about, scared the centre-halves to death, won everything in the air, and I'd read his flick-ons, run on to them, gallop through and have plenty of one-on-ones with keepers, usually putting them away with my left foot, no problem. I always loved scoring – the elation, the joy, the ultimate football experience – although I'm not sure I followed up the goals with my own specially minted celebrations, not quite yet.

We did well, were always one of the top teams in that part of the Midlands, but I still never played much for the district, and that was my first taste of football politics: that who you know, or someone's idea of who you are, can too often determine whether you're going to be in a team, rather than how good you are and how well you're performing. The teacher who ran the district team was friendly with the manager of another Sunday league club, and everyone from that club seemed to get picked, while we didn't. I used to get on very well with the games teacher at my school, Mr Shannon – I always kept in touch with him, throughout my professional career; he's stayed at my house in recent years the odd time he's been up watching matches in the north. He knew the teacher running the district team for the year above, so I ended up getting picked for that, when I was supposedly not good enough for the team representing my own age group. Strange, but a fair preparation for the games people play. Football's a simple game, they always say, and that's true, but the men involved in it, their egos, hang-ups, prejudices, whatever it is, can make it very complicated, and, if you're not careful, it can leave you feeling pretty sour, too.

One ordinary day, when I was twelve, I was on my way home from school to see Nan and Granddad, and was surprised to see my dad and brother waiting for me as I stepped off the bus. Dad's face was ashen: 'We've got some bad news,' he said. 'Your granddad's died.'

My world ended, right there. I'd stayed with them the night before, and in the morning, really early, three, four o'clock, Granddad had got up and gone to work. He was driving tarmac lorries at the time, moving the black stuff to where motorways were being repaired. He'd stopped smoking on doctor's orders a couple of years earlier, but he was still pretty strong, working away. That morning he hadn't felt too well; thought he had a bit of flu coming on. Nan told him to phone in and take the day off but he lived for his work and said he'd go but come home early and have a lie-down.

He was just doing a routine job, they said, bending down to undo a valve on the truck. He had some water on his heart, had a huge heart attack out of the blue and died right there, gone. It was a freak, really. He was only just sixty, and we've always wondered how much longer he'd have been with us if he'd only taken that day off work. I was distraught. I missed him so much, couldn't believe the emptiness of life without him. I used to mope on the sofa in front of the telly at home, and moan: 'I wish I was dead too. I want to see my granddad,' and Mum used to tell me not to be so silly.

I suppose twelve might be one of the worst ages for dealing with death; you're old enough to know what's happened, but not emotionally mature enough to understand. I remember Mr Shannon saying to me: 'In five years at secondary school, I never saw you without a smile on your face – except for that little while, after your grandfather died.'

I couldn't believe he was gone. I'd have loved to knock about with him when I was a teenager or an adult, and I always regret that, while he stood, strong and silent, freezing on the touchline with a flask of tea watching me race about for the Cubs, he never saw me galloping down the line, scoring goals for Man U, at Old Trafford, or Highbury, or Villa Park. He'd have loved it. We've got on with life, of course we have, but we all still miss him, even now.

At fourteen, I met my own childhood sweetheart: Debbie Totney. Gorgeous. She started at our school in the second year. I think I was pretty much besotted the first time I saw her. We got chatting before too long, then we started going out, in a lovestruck-teenagers kind of style, kissing at the bus stop, going to each other's house after school for tea, that kind of thing. Debbie lived with her mum because her parents were divorced. On Fridays her mum would go to the pub with her boyfriend, so a few mates of mine and Debbie's friends would go round to the house for a party.

We might have a few lagers – big drinkers at fourteen, fifteen – play music, fool about, then her mum would come back at eleven, twelve o'clock and have a drink with us all. She'd go up to bed and we'd get the sleeping bags and blankets out and all sleep downstairs in the living room. In the morning, all the lads would get up early and catch the train together to go and play for the school team. Good days. My mum was convinced Debbie and I were made for each other and we'd end up getting married, and we did go out together, on and off, all the way through school and beyond, until I got to Man U where it all came to a sloppy, heartbreaking end.

At fifteen, a few of the lads who'd played together for a while formed our own team as part of another strong local outfit, Stourport Wednesday. Mark Davey's dad, John, started it; he was the manager, a real bawler and shouter, ranting and raving on the line, a great football man, bursting with fire and enthusiasm. He loved me and my pace; he used to stand there, screaming: 'Get the ball to Sharpey! Give it Sharpey!' They'd throw it over to me on the left wing and I'd try to push it past or dribble round the full-back and get crosses in, or stride through and score a few goals: tremendous. A few of us went on to play for the senior first team too, open-age football at a good Sunday league standard, and I did all right there. I was never really intimidated, I just wanted to get hold of the ball and play. Meaty blokes in opposing sides were always trying to kick me, to teach the quick, skilful kid a lesson, but it never bothered me. They'd tell me they'd break my legs, neck, kick my head in, and generally I'd shrug and say: 'Go on then, whatever.' If they whacked me I just used to get up and laugh – and that's what I've always done with kickers.

I've never been one to retaliate, but the physical side of football has never worried me either. Back then I had Mark Davey behind to look after me, who did really enjoy munching people, then in professional football I was never short of team-mates ready to mix it if the opposition were playing dirty. I used to get up, smile, say nothing, and take them on again next time – which winds up cloggers more than anything.

In the fifth year at school, I ended up playing in the sixth-form team, the Under 19s, when I was only fifteen, and Mr Shannon used to ladle responsibility on me, in a way I always remember. He'd take me to one side before a big game, and say: 'You can win this for us, Lee, with your ability. I can't say that to every boy because it would make some go under, but I know you can handle it. So you go out and win it for us.'

I'd stand there, grin, mumble: 'Well, all right, if you say so,' but inside he inspired me, filled me with confidence by showing he had belief in my ability, and telling me so. Positive motivation, I think they call it, and I used to stride out there feeling good in myself, and go and attack teams. The bigger the game, the more motivated I was. Because I mostly played for decent sides, even as a teenager we'd have top-of-the-table, end-of-season deciders, maybe with a bit of a crowd, an air of hostility and needle, and I always enjoyed those games, used to try to rise to the occasion.

I suppose a bit of fame spreads for you if you're good at sport as a kid, first in school, then in the area, a few write-ups in local papers, and at fifteen, Birmingham City decided they fancied having a look at me and signed me on schoolboy forms. A scout had watched me play for Stourbridge Falcons against another strong youth team,

North Star, from the other side of Birmingham. They gave us the full treatment, invited my dad, his brother Jack and me to watch a game, against Luton Town, I think, from an executive box at St Andrews, selling us the Blues as the place for me to build myself a future. My dad was made up, of course.

It was a different story when I got there. I went training one night a week, then every morning in the school holidays with the apprentices, but I never liked it. It was cliquey; lads who knew each other from their own clubs stuck together and I didn't particularly like them, felt on the fringes of it all. I played a few games then Kevin Reeves, the former Manchester City striker who was in charge of youth development, called my dad and me into his office to tell us he was letting me go. He said I had more skill than anybody else on their schoolboy books, but didn't believe I had the aggression to be a top-flight professional. Apparently, Dad told Mum that my face dropped so far he could have cried for me, but that's not how I remember feeling. I hadn't liked it there and didn't really want to go into full-time training, or an apprenticeship, with all these lads around who fancied themselves and weren't friendly. I think about what Kevin Reeves said now, and see it as an admission of failure on his part. I was the raw material – I loved the game, tried to play it creatively and with a bit of joy, I worked hard, gave it everything in training, stood up to physical stuff – so I think I was a player to work with. I think it's the job of the clubs to teach you the extra aggression you need in the professional game. Torquay, who'd finished bottom of the Fourth Division the year before I eventually went there, were to inject that aggression into me with cunning brutality, so I'd have thought Birmingham City might have managed.

I wasn't bothered; what will be will be – things happen for a reason, I believed that then and live by that philosophy now. The trial at Torquay popped up just a couple of days later. It was busy at school-leaving time, with clubs deciding who to take on to stock their apprenticeship schemes. Mark Davey and a couple of lads from his district team had gone down there and done well enough in trials to be invited back and he put a word in for me, said his mate had just been let go by Birmingham. Simple as that, word of mouth, which gave me my chance of a toehold at the bottom of football's ladder, a smiling lamb heading to the slaughter at the hands of two murderous taskmasters: Sean Haslegrave, the ultimate midfield terrier as a player, and a guy who would be a big man in my life, Derek Dawkins, the man they call the Dude.

Torquay, with nothing to lose, invited me down for a three-day trial. As it turned out, I played a full match on each of those three days; I was on my knees by the end. The first, on the Monday, was a trial game against another youth team. I found it no problem; soon I was flying down the wing. Mark played behind me and we got our game going, him winning it, playing it into my path, me taking people on and getting crosses in. People watching said they could tell we'd played together for a while, which was cool. He was unfortunate not to be taken on by Torquay; he'd have made a good professional – and we'd have had a great laugh together.

It seems unbelievable now, but the following day the first team had a match, a local derby against Exeter in a kind of South-West end-of-season cup they played in, and they just threw me straight into it. Most of the first team had packed up and gone away for the summer, there weren't many left-footed players around, so they slung me in, aged sixteen, having played a game the day before. True to my forgetfulness about the detail of matches, the statistical side of football which leaves me cold, I can't remember much about it, not the score, nothing really, except that I must have done OK, showed in places I could play a bit, and there were a few pats on my back when we all trooped off.

The following day, Wednesday, there was yet another trial game on, against some other local youth team, and there was me in the starting line-up, knackered, battered, begging for mercy, but I got through it. The three days over, they called me in: yes, they would offer me an apprenticeship, two years; they'd train me up and I'd have a chance of making something of myself in the game. OK, I said, chuffed but not showing it, I'll have a chat with my dad, and let you know.

I can remember the interminable length of the train journey back from Torquay to Birmingham, me stiff, bruised, wrecked, and the following day I had a trial lined up at West Brom, who were going to have a look at me as a centre-forward. I turned up so hangdog they only put me on for the second half. As I remember it, it was a scrappy game, there was no chance to do very much, then it was over. Afterwards, Dad and I were in some dingy dressing room – it was more of a boiler room, I think, old bandages everywhere, kit drying, saggy old benches – when a West Brom bloke came up and said: 'If Torquay have offered you a contract, I'd snap it up with both hands.'

My dad said he nearly chinned him. Wolves offered me a trial soon afterwards; they'd let all their young lads go, I'd done quite well in a game there at some point, so they were asking me back. The trials, though, weren't starting until

July, and Torquay's players would be back for pre-season training by then; I'd need to be giving them an answer, starting my apprenticeship there, before I'd even had my trial at the Wolves. Dad and I sat down to talk about it. Torquay had only managed to stay in the League the year before with a last-minute goal in the last match of the season; it was miles away from home, while Wolves were a legendary club where we lived, even though they were having hard times, half the ground was condemned and only Steve Bull seemed to be keeping them alive. Dad never pushed me, he didn't even really give me advice, he just wanted to be there as a sounding board, to help me chew over the options. The clincher was this: Torquay's was a solid offer. If I waited for Wolves, it might never happen. I was leaving school and Torquay were giving me the chance to go straight down there to a two-year apprenticeship, a chance to make my way in professional football, what I always said I'd do when I left school.

So that was it, I was off to the south coast. I'm not sure I even turned up for all my exams, I certainly didn't revise, but I left school smiling and with the good wishes of the sports teacher at my back. It was only Torquay, but to borrow a phrase that would become notorious at one of the big clubs I'd play for later in my career, I was living the dream. I was off to be a footballer. Like the man said, I snapped up that Torquay contract with both hands.

CHAPTER 2

Beside the seaside

I might never have made it at all, though, might have packed it in completely halfway through sprinting up the seventeenth hill of some tortuous day in the bleak uplands of the savage regime of Sean Haslegrave and the Dude, if I hadn't had a few little tweaks of luck at the right time and friendly, cosy digs to go back to. The apprenticeship at Torquay was a boot camp punctuated by grim, godforsaken football matches against adult, clogging sides down country roads so far from anywhere we young lads used to sit in the minibus and say we could be dead and nobody would ever find us. My mate, Craig Whiston, a good player, a centre-half I'd known from Birmingham Sunday league football, packed it in after a couple of months, his boyhood dreams shattered by the mindless, ridiculously hard training, the dark butchering which passed for football, the endless, abusive dressing-room bollockings and rancid digs. He said life was too short, and went home.

I remember the feeling of empty dread when my mum and dad left me there. We pulled up at the address we'd been given, hauled my case upstairs, they gave me a hug, we all stood about uselessly for a bit, then they got in the car and drove away. I went up to my bedroom to start unpacking my case and suddenly wondered what the hell I'd done, come all the way here on my own, three hours away from my mum and dad, my brother, sister, girlfriend, all my mates, to a place where I didn't know anyone or what to expect, and I just sat in my lonely room and burst into tears. No doubt my mum was not even back on the main road before she was doing the same.

Then the landlady poked her little head around my door. Irene Thompson; she's Scottish, from Fife. She only needed one experienced glance to take in my universe of teenage desolation, then she said, gently: 'We're having a bite to eat downstairs. Do you fancy coming down?'

So I picked myself up and moped downstairs, met the kids, Lee and Kelly, her husband Bill, a real character, and they cheered me up straight away, they were so nice. Bill worked on the rigs for two or three months at a time, while Irene looked after the kids and the three or four young footballers usually boarding with them. She always told us to make ourselves at home; she knew instinctively we needed a proper welcoming place to come back to once the taskmasters of Plainmoor had done their worst with us.

It was a great house really, a proper old boarding house, big rooms with high ceilings; I'd still been sharing a bunk bed in a small bedroom with my brother John at home, so I thought the place was cool once I got my head round being there. Two other apprentices were staying there at the time, both second-years. The first was a Scottish lad, Jimmy Smith, a good player but one of the most disgracefully unhygienic people I have ever had the misfortune to come across, let alone have to live with. He used to sleep in his shirt in the winter because it was a bit chilly, then get up, stay in the shirt that he'd slept in, put his jeans on, not brush his teeth and then go straight to training. Horrible.

The other lad was Gordon Murray, a centre-forward from Brighton, and we got on pretty well. We had some good laughs with Bill. We'd be sat there some nights, watching telly, Bill sitting on the floor, and Gordon and I would give each other a nod and a wink, then we'd both jump Bill and try to batter him. He'd humour us for a few seconds then he'd get hold of both of us, get us in a headlock or push our hands halfway up our backs, and we'd be half laughing, half screaming for mercy. Big Bad Bill: a real hard case.

The ground, Plainmoor, was only fifty yards or so from Irene's, but I was nervous as hell, stomach churning over, going up there for the first time. There was a bit of uncertainty, too, because the manager who'd offered me the apprenticeship, Stuart Morgan, had been sacked during the close season. Turned out the end of that 1986–87 season had been a real nailbiter: they were losing 2–1 at home to Crewe and would have become the first club ever automatically relegated to the Conference, then a police dog bit one of the players, the game was stopped and when they restarted Paul Dobson scored the equaliser in the third minute of injury time. They'd stayed up that freakishly, and Lincoln went down instead. Torquay had appointed a new manager, the legendary former Tottenham full-back Cyril Knowles, of 'Nice One Cyril' fame, who'd won Darlington promotion as their manager in 1985. A few of us awkward youngsters hopped from foot to foot in the reception at Plainmoor, not knowing if we'd be staying or sent on our way. Then Cyril Knowles said he would keep on all the youngsters signed up, and handed us over to the gentle, caring arms of the Dude, who'd played hundreds of games at full-back for Torquay and become youth development officer, one of the very few black guys on the management side of football, and Sean Haslegrave, an ex-Stoke City and Preston midfielder whom Cyril Knowles had brought down to add gristle on the field and off it, as his assistant manager.

It was quite pleasant at first. The senior players weren't due back for a week, so they set us off doing ground maintenance and odd jobs, weeding round the side of the pitch, cleaning and painting stands, tidying up, then a few bits of training. Quite tiring in a nice, physical sort of way, I thought, as I went back to the digs happy enough. A laid-back, enjoyable life, professional football.

Then the first team came back, and hell descended. The players themselves were a good bunch of blokes. They were all right with the young lads unless you were a poseur or fancied yourself too much, in which case they'd nail you. It was best to keep your head down at first, just show willing. There were a few characters. Mark Loram was a wonderful footballer, great left foot, magical skill, who could have gone a lot higher if he'd really wanted to. He was from Brixham, a local fishing village, and he liked a pint and to stay round with his mates in his close-knit community. Queens Park Rangers had signed him the season before I got there, but he just didn't take to London and came back to Torquay, where he stayed for a few seasons.

Paul Dobson, the striker who'd scored the equaliser against Crewe to keep Torquay in the League, was a prolific lower-league centre-forward, another good lad, while the captain was John Impey, a proper old pro who went on to be youth coach and the manager for a short spell after I'd left. Cyril Knowles brought a couple of players down with him, like Phil Lloyd, a centre-half who was a real fearsome hard case.

The keeper was funny, though. Kenny Allen. He could keep goal; he played the whole season, but he looked like a character out of *Scooby-Doo*, one of the grizzled villains who take their masks off at the end. He looked about sixty, had really long grey hair and a long moustache, and thin, long, really white legs, proper old man's legs. God knows how many fags he smoked, must have been forty a day; he used to sit in the dressing room with just his pants on at the end of training, no shirt on, really white body, sitting with his legs crossed, smoking a fag. I used to think: is this it, then, is this what the beautiful game is really all about? But he'd take absolutely no cheek; if any of the young lads chipped him in training or took liberties he'd chase them round the pitch trying to boot them up the arse. Mad.

We'd usually train with the first team, which was all right, then they'd be finished and go home, but we'd have a bit of lunch then come back in the afternoon and our real ordeal would start. The Dude and Sean Haslegrave seemed to believe in the physical and moral benefits of one activity: running. Torquay's a hilly place, and for starters we'd have to run from Plainmoor to the training ground, which was three or four miles up and down. When we got there, we'd start for real, some ridiculously excessive session – running, press-ups, sit-ups, shuttle sprints – we'd never see a football. Then we'd have to run back to the ground, another three or four miles, at pace, no letting up, and they'd be in our faces, ranting and shouting, calling us lazy bastards, saying if they saw anybody walking or going slowly we'd have to do more running when we got back.

They had a favourite torture trail down by the seafront. Even to get there was a half-mile steady run, then a steep, three-quarters-of-a-mile climb until we reached a sight to make our hearts sink: a massive flight of steps yawning up the banking from the beach. The Dude and Sean Haslegrave had us sprinting in pairs all the way up these steps, probably 140 of them. When we got to the top, the pairs would split and run round different ways, back to the bottom. Then they'd make us do it again, but split a different way at the top and run back the other way, and we'd do three or four of those, just to experience the first degree of misery. Then they'd send us straight up and down the steps, but alternate it, so that on one run we'd take every step, then the next one we'd take every alternate step, which was a killer, then down and up again, and again.

All accompanied by their charming, screaming idea of motivation: 'Come on, get it done, you lazy bastards!' In your face, ranting. 'Come on, you lazy little bastards! Get your fucking legs moving! Stop walking, stop being so fucking lazy, if you want to be a footballer you've got to get fit, shift your arse, you little fuckers!'

Really deepened your love of the game, that stuff. We'd go days without working with a ball. We'd do fitness with the first team, run to the training ground, run back, do some more running before lunch, then after lunch do circuits outside the dressing room with some poxy old weights, a skipping rope and some other dodgy equipment, six or eight goes around this circuit, then a load more running. I've never minded training, good hard physical training; you feel good when you're really lean and fit and swift, but this was excessive. I know that now but back then we all just felt it. At sixteen, seventeen, even eighteen, boys are still growing, and there's a basic fitness there anyway. The Dude and Sean Haslegrave had no doubt come through all this as apprentices and players themselves, and tearing a strip off people was how they had learned you tried to get people to improve, toughen up, but it got depressing, especially in the winter, when you're leaving in the dark with all that ahead of you, and by the time you've done it all, got not an ounce of joy out of any of it, then had to clean the dressing rooms, the boots, do the other odd jobs, it's dark again when you're trooping home. You're halfway up a hill some filthy Tuesday afternoon and you just want to go home and lie on the couch and be all warm and have your mum bring you cups of tea. Had Irene not filled that role herself, made her house so warm and welcoming for us, with proper nice dinners we'd all eat together with the family, a home from home, I'm sure I wouldn't have stuck it.

That was the main difference for my mate, Craig Whiston: he was in horrible digs. He'd spend all day struggling with the running, the Dude and Sean Haslegrave nailing him all the time – they used to bollock him a lot when we played matches if he made mistakes – then he had to go back to these digs where they didn't really care, where the footballers were just a bit of extra income to them. They'd give him dinner in the kitchen with washing hung out to dry right across his head, and the little boy doing a pooh in his potty right next to the table. Imagine what happened to his visions of football's glamour and glory when he had to watch the kid doing a number two right next to him as he ate his meagre dinner.

We played for the reserves, which was what you'd

politely call a learning curve. They played me at centre-forward, which was fine; I wasn't strong enough to hold it up so I used to come short or look for a ball over the top to run on to. I still went at it with plenty of appetite, but in these open-age leagues against sides from fishing villages, or towns like Dawlish, Taunton, Teignmouth, Exeter or Plymouth's reserves, there were plenty of hairy-arsed centre-halves, meatheads who were just dying to munch this stick-thin sixteen-year-old trying to lick them for pace. We used to drive for miles and hours in this little minibus down to face another war in some backwater with nobody watching, and the bollockings would flow thick afterwards if we'd got beat or not played well. I was never scared but I was thin, I had no body strength really and not much aggression, and these centre-halves used to go straight through you in the first tackle, just try to clean you out. I had to learn a few tricks, to protect myself.

Craig would make a few mistakes and they'd shout at him, in front of everyone – what the fuck was he doing, was he thick, couldn't he fucking play the game? – and in the end he told me he couldn't take it: 'I miss home, miss my mates, hate the digs, hate all the running and the abuse. I'm going home.'

I tried to talk him into staying, told him he'd never get another chance like this, tried to move him into my digs, but there was no room. He moved somewhere else briefly, but pretty soon he left, his football dream over in a couple of months. Despite Irene's nice digs, I had a think about doing the same; I was knackered all the time so just monged out in front of the telly every night. I was on £27.50 a week, went to college all day Thursday, which, with getting there and back and lunch used to eat up a few quid, so I was always skint. I'd sit on the couch wondering if this was worth it; I wasn't with my mum and dad, was missing my mates, Debbie – this grey drudgery wasn't quite what I was expecting out of life as a sixteen-year-old.

So I might have gone too, but then it all changed for me, and hope poured in, virtually overnight. In early October, when the nights were drawing in, Sean Haslegrave called me in and said: 'We think you're looking a bit homesick; we're going to send you home for a week.'

Credit to them that they could see it. They sent me home on the Tuesday, I remember, and it was brilliant: I saw my mum and dad, brother, sister, mates, slept in my old bunk bed, and I remember I popped back to my school to see Mr Shannon. I was going to talk it all over with him, tell him how difficult it was, when my mum called the school, saying there'd been a phone call from Torquay telling me I had to go back. What now? I'd only been home a day or two. Then, when I called the club, it was unexpectedly decent news for me. They had one left-sided player out injured, another had had to go up to Scotland for family reasons, so they wanted me in the first-team squad as cover for the local derby against Exeter in the league on the Saturday.

That was how I came to make my debut in the Football League, aged sixteen, on 3 October 1987, sitting on the Torquay United bench with a number 12 on my back. The crowd for the derby is listed in the records as 6,281, and Torquay won 1–0, with a goal from Jim McNichol, right-back and a Torquay favourite. With twenty-five minutes to go, they threw me on, a stick-thin lad, trotting out on gangly legs onto the tufty pitch at Plainmoor, my heart thumping hard and a great big smile inside me, hungry to get hold of the ball in a professional football club's first team.

If my early career, looking back, seems like a fairy tale, a brief moment at Torquay then straight to Man U and stardom, it wasn't quite like that. I didn't go on, slalom round three players, smash the ball into the back of the net, dance a jig with the corner flag in front the delighted fans and wait for the big clubs to come. That doesn't happen in reality – unless you're Wayne Rooney, and I think he's a freak, playing with total assurance at seventeen or eighteen. I went on eagerly, and did a few decent things: put a couple of tackles in, made one or two decent passes, had a couple of runs down the wing, sent some crosses over. There were some grunts and nods from Cyril Knowles and the players afterwards, which suggested I'd done all right.

They played me again four days later, a Wednesday night, again as sub, but this time there was some real glamour about it. It was a League Cup tie at White Hart Lane against Spurs, who had Ardiles and Hoddle, Clive Allen and Chris Waddle. Yes, me, Lee Sharpe, playing against all them. I remember rolling up outside the ground in our coach, and White Hart Lane was so huge you'd have been overawed going in as a fan, and thinking: what am I doing, walking into this official entrance like I'm going to play?

We young lads had been in awe of Tottenham when they'd played the first leg at our place two weeks earlier. It was the sheer quality of their operation, the way everything was laid out and prepared for them, their kit man coming down early, setting out the gleaming, silky kit just so, and in the right order. We nipped down when he'd gone and had a peek inside. It was immaculate, the glory game, all the kits spread out, clean and sparkling, numbered shirts on pegs, shorts and socks folded for them, all the boots polished, shining under the benches. Under Gary Mabbutt's peg were cans of Coke and other paraphernalia for his diabetes, and it really hit us then: oh my God, this really is Tottenham coming down here, to play us scruffs.

We still beat them that night at Plainmoor, tremendous, and who should score the goal but the veteran player–coach, Derek Dawkins, the Dude himself. It was a great night for Torquay, and the Dude made the most of it, having his picture taken for the local press kissing the ball, and we all took the piss.

I got to know the Dude better over time and understood he was a lovely guy underneath. He was firm but fair. A bit of a hard man, reckoned he was a kung-fu expert or something, bollocked us quite a bit and shouted, but you could tell he loved us as well and looked after us; he wanted us to do well. We were scared of him, but he had his soft side and we'd have a laugh with him too. He used to come in and have a go at everyone – tell us we hadn't cleaned the dressing rooms well enough and the place was disgusting – and when the mood was right, all twelve of us apprentices would jump him, slap his bald head, rough him up a bit and he'd laugh and take it. Underneath all the ranting, which seems to be the only way football management works, he was one of the good guys.

I remember ringing Mr Shannon when they picked me as sub for the return at White Hart Lane. He asked me who'd be marking me if I played on the left wing.

'Um, probably Gary Stevens.'

'Well,' he said, 'you've got nothing to worry about. You're better than him.'

'What?' I said. 'Nothing to worry about? I'm sixteen!

He's an experienced international who's been playing in the First Division for years!'

And my old schoolteacher said: 'Nah, you're better than him, you can skin him, no problem. I don't know what you're worried about.'

I remember that; it made a difference. He was a voice of authority, and instead of having a go at me, he always used to boost my confidence. Looking back on it, it was great man-management. Did he really think his sixteen-year-old ex-pupil could skin an experienced top professional footballer like Gary Stevens? I doubt it. But what was the best way to help me try? To be positive, tell me I was good, let me think I could do it, not fill me with fear and talk up the opponent, or talk me down. That always stuck in my mind when I went on to play for highly paid football managers who never seemed to have a positive word to say to anybody: if a teacher knew better, why didn't they? What were they missing?

That night at Tottenham, the crowd was 21,000, the lights were bright, the pitch was lush and I went on for the second half keen to have a go. The pace was lightning compared to anything I'd played before, but I did OK. I think I nutmegged somebody, I'm not sure who it was but I know I enjoyed it, then the ball went out for a throw, and as I went to pick it up, I was shoved in the back, and I turned round and Ossie Ardiles was in my face, wagging a finger, shaking his head, going 'tut, tut, tut'. I shrugged, like what the hell was that for, but I think he was saying you shouldn't go around nutmegging people when you're only sixteen, that it isn't respectful.

We lost 3–0, not unexpected, and afterwards, again, I had a few grunts from the direction of the gaffers which seemed to suggest they were pleased enough with me. Those two little tastes of the first team gave me a chink of light, a note of promise, a thrill, a carrot dangled in front of me as I went back to running up hills and the meaty battles in the reserves. I was sub for the first team again against Hereford in mid-November, in a game we won 1–0. The team Cyril Knowles had knocked together was doing pretty well, hard to beat, with Mark Loram joined up front by Dave Caldwell, an experienced Scottish striker with a bit of a temper, who'd signed a couple of weeks earlier. Then, in the reserves, some meathead did finally make contact with a serious clattering out on some godforsaken field. They scraped me up and carried me off, my ankle throbbing like in a cartoon, the ligaments done in, which kept me out for a few weeks. When I started back, they mixed my reserve football with some involvement with the first team, taking me along for the ride as a general dogsbody, fifteenth man, helping to collect the kit and carry the skips, so that I'd get used to the lads and they got used to having me around.

Around that time they introduced their sophisticated brainwave to toughen up the young lads. The name tells you straight away how deft and subtle it was: Murder Ball. The rules were – there weren't any. Well, just one: no punching. Kicking lumps out of each other was compulsory. We'd be playing five-a-side round the back of the social club in this hemmed-in little area I'd marked out with the groundsman's marker, then at a certain point they'd call: 'Murder Ball: anything goes.' And that was it. Madness. Fly in, go and get that ball, go over the top, snap people, ram them into the fence or the wall. Cyril Knowles and Sean Haslegrave used to throw the ball into the middle and watch us young lads batter each other, football's ragged-trousered hopefuls crossed with gladiators. Everybody piled in, volleying the back of people's legs, scraping trainers down their thighs, booting their calves; it was kill or be killed. There were fights occasionally. One time, the second-year goalkeeper went up for a header, one of the first-years bent down and tipped him over and the keeper landed on his arm and broke it. Not the ideal injury for a goalkeeper.

Murder Ball worked for me, though, I have to say. The games would go on for hours, all afternoon, and it did teach us to dig in, not be at all scared to put our foot in. It wasn't so much that it showed us how to be dirty, more that it provided the extra aggression in a tussle, a fifty-fifty, a chase down the line, to go and get that ball, not let the opponent beat us to it. After a while in those games we quite often settled down and stopped kicking lumps out of each other. Cyril Knowles might chuck the ball in and for fifteen minutes it would be carnage, but if the Dude was watching, we'd get the ball down at our feet, look up and start to play, enjoy ourselves, show what we could do. We all loved the game, that's why we were there; all the other stuff you just had to put up with. Ian Bastow was an excellent player, a midfielder with loads of skill, and he and I would try to get some real football going. I'd play up front and pin myself against their centre-half; our goalkeeper would roll it out hard and low to me. I'd have Ian running off me, another midfielder running the other way; I'd have options, pick one out, they'd start moving the ball around and playing one-twos, and suddenly there was an intense, skilful game of football going on.

I was getting stronger and doing quite well, so they

started taking me on the first team's coach journeys, making me feel part of it. Being Torquay United, the coach journeys were murder, and in late November I had the privilege of the most yawningly long trip in English football: Carlisle, away. Nine hours on a coach. They used to stop at a shop on the way and everybody used to buy crisps and sweets and sandwiches, then we'd rent a few videos from the shop next door and watch those on the coach. There was a drinks machine at the back, and because I was the youngest, it was my job to fetch tea, coffee and hot chocolate for everybody, so I was up and down like a yo-yo the whole way. It was good, though, because I got to know them all, the bossy ones, the loud ones, the bullies, the cheeky ones, the funny ones, and they got to know me too, as I gradually became part of the first-team furniture.

Looking back, Cyril Knowles was one of the best managers I ever had. He'd played at the highest level for Spurs and England, and he still had pure class. He was big, 6' 2" or something, and he'd put weight on, but in the five-a-sides he was the best player on the pitch, a different league. People would try to wrestle him or pull him down, and he'd hold them off with one hand while taking all the time in the world to choose his option. He could nutmeg these old pros whenever he liked. He'd show us free-kicks, just take one step, talking all the while, telling us where it was going, then clip it right in the top corner with his left foot. He was hard, brutal at times. He had this strong, powerful voice which could intimidate you a mile away. He dished out his share of abuse and bollockings, to some more than others; he used to rip into Dave Cole, the centre-half, because he thought he was underachieving and could have done more in the game, telling him he was a lazy bastard, fucking rubbish, and they hated each other, used to kick each other when they got a chance in the five-a-sides. Mostly, though, I think he commanded respect; he had authority, he'd been there and done it, and you could tell he knew the game.

He liked me anyway. I was a bit of a favourite because I was doing well, and at the end of February, after another couple of months travelling with the first team, helping out round the dressing rooms, the Dude's training, Murder Ball and playing for the reserves, Cyril Knowles finally gave me another first-team chance. It was the derby against Exeter, at home. The crowd was nearly 4,000, big for us. Our pitch was hardening by then and was really bobbly, the game was quick and fierce, we drew 1–1, and that's about all I can remember of it. In midweek he made me sub in another long-haul away fixture, Scarborough, where Paul Dobson and Mark Loram scored in a 2–1 win for us. The following Saturday he left me out, then on the Tuesday, 8 March, we were playing Wolves, away at Molyneux, in the Sherpa Van Trophy, the lower divisions' League Cup, and he put me on the bench.

That was good from the off, pulling up in the coach outside the scuffed gold of Wolves, on my own patch where I'd turned down a trial, walking through the players' entrance into the dressing room. The old ground was crumbling, but was grand and impressive to me from the inside, and down through the tunnel and under the brilliant floodlights, the pitch was deep green, gorgeous, lush, like a carpet, stretching away, fantastically wide.

Wolves had declined, nearly gone bankrupt, but they had bottomed out by then and were heading for promotion from our division as champions. They'd drawn o–o at our place in the league, and here at Molyneux there were 11,000 fans, making a good noise, mostly for their warrior-hero, Stevie Bull. At half time, Cyril Knowles was absolutely nailing one of the players, Russell Musker, accusing him of bottling out of a fifty-fifty, calling him a fucking shithouse, the usual helpful stuff.

'Get yourself off!' he spat at him. Then he turned to me: 'Sharpey, you're on.'

I think I was ready for it by then. I'd done my running, my Murder Ball, I was stronger, faster, hungry. I'd played my few games coming off the bench, been with the first team a lot. The manager said: 'You go out there and enjoy yourself.' And I thought: OK, that's just what I'll do then. I jogged out onto that lovely, wide green pitch just wanting to get that ball and have a good time, use my pace, create some havoc, take them all on, and I felt no fear. I wasn't even nervous, just a few butterflies in my stomach letting me know they were there.

Within three or four minutes, wouldn't you know it, the ball broke into the most even fifty-fifty you ever saw, and of course it was with a 6' 4" giant of a Wolves centre-half, thundering towards me as if he could mow me down and pick my remains from between his studs. I was like: oh no, the manager's just ripped into someone for not going into a tackle; I've got to do it. I kept going, right into it – I might even have closed my eyes at the last minute and put my studs up a little to protect myself – then I slid in and we both crunched each other. The ball ricocheted out, neither of us were hurt and I peeled myself up off the pitch, still alive. Congratulations, you've just survived your first fifty-fifty.

Then our lads started throwing the ball over to me. Sean

Haslegrave was playing, a little scrapping dog in midfield, upsetting people, digging the ball out, then every time he got it he floated it out to me. I just hogged the line, stretching Wolves out wide, controlled it when it arrived, then set off to attack the full-back, go round him, outpace him in a sprint for the line, then send a nice cross over. We were losing 1–0, our lads were crowding the box, and Cyril Knowles was on his feet on the touchline, screaming: 'Get it to Sharpey! Give it Sharpey!' I was still only sixteen, and absolutely loving it. The pitch was great, the arena, the floodlights; I found my feet and started to play like I'd always done in my own age group, just freely, running with the ball, getting past people, really getting in behind them. I didn't want the game to end, but eventually it did. We never quite managed to score, and we lost 1–0. Wolves went on to win the trophy.

We showered and changed and the lads were good with me, telling me I'd played well. The Dude, Sean Haslegrave and even Cyril Knowles had the odd word for me too. On the coach on the way back, I sat next to the Dude as usual; and, in the seats in front, the manager was talking to Sean Haslegrave about how I'd played.

'The lad's only sixteen,' he was saying, with a note of wonder. 'He's just gone out there so natural – I've never told him to do all that on the pitch, take people on like that, have you?'

And Sean Haslegrave, to be fair, was saying: 'No, not me. He looks a natural.'

'He really looks the part, doesn't he?' Cyril Knowles was murmuring, and the Dude sort of nudged me, nodded over to them and said: 'Can you hear them? They're talking about you.'

I just shrugged, a proper teenager: 'Oh, right.' Grinning inside though, as wide as the Molyneux pitch.

Still, Cyril Knowles didn't play me for a few more games. That's what I mean, he was a good manager, he took his time with me. They eased up, did me a few favours, let me have the odd day off college if we'd been away midweek, little breaks which kept me sane. I'd have the odd afternoon to potter around town, go and get a McDonald's, look in the record shops, whatever you do at that age. I slowly realised I was actually enjoying it, because I was part of it. It may have been the Fourth Division, but it was tremendous going away to the grounds of these great, big-name clubs, Carlisle, Swansea, Wrexham, Bolton, a massive buzz being a player at a club doing well and heading for the play-offs. They gave me a first-team tracksuit, and my own seat on the bus every week, little things which made me feel I belonged in there rather than a kid being taken for a special treat. My cousin and his mates used to come to Torquay quite regularly for weekends, so I would meet them in the pub after a match. My mum and dad came down for nearly every game, sometimes my sister and brother too, so I wasn't too lonely. And I was beginning to become a little famous around Torquay, which never hurts.

It was already April before Cyril Knowles picked me again, this time Stockport at home. He told the lads just to get the ball to me; I was a big part of the tactics, such as they were. Cyril Knowles had brought the pitch in, made it narrow, and short. We had three big, strong centre-halves, two wing-backs getting up and down the line, three in midfield and two up front, so we used to pack the defence then get the ball forward early, not play it through midfield. We used to train on the pitch in the winter as well as play on it, so it churned up into a real mudheap, and by this stage in the season it was hard and bobbly. The wings were about the only part of the pitch with any green on them. I used to stand right out there, like a foal looking to graze, and Cyril Knowles would tell me he wanted dust on my heels like a proper old-fashioned winger, wanting me to skin the full-back and get crosses into the box, so that's what I did. He was giving me a lot of responsibility, which filled me with confidence, and I went out and really loved it. The lads were great and looked after me; when a full-back started to give me a kicking I'd just get up and smile, but I knew one of our lads would find himself over my way sometime soon and deliver a kicking, with interest, back to the full-back. We hammered Stockport 3–0, and Cyril Knowles kept me in the starting XI for the next game, away at Hereford, a tough 0–0 which wouldn't feature in any Brazilian coaching manuals.

The day before the next game, Cardiff City at home, a big one, we had a penalty tournament in training. I buried all mine and won the competition, and the deal was that the winner would get to take them in a match.

The lads were sneering: 'No way will you take one if it's a game.'

We were in the top five, looking to maintain our play-off spot, while Cardiff were second, going for automatic promotion. George Wood, the ex-Everton keeper, was in goal, and what do you know, one of our lads gets floored in the box and it's a penalty. George Wood was mad, booted the ball away, and it landed by the dugouts, where Cyril Knowles caught it. I jogged over to get it: 'Here you are, boss, give me the ball.'

He grabbed my arm. 'Are you all right about this?'

I was like: 'Yeah, just give me the ball. I want it, come on.'

I didn't feel nerves; I just wanted to put the ball down and bang it in the corner like I'd done in training and put us in the lead. My mum was in the stand nearly dying. I wasn't; I was a kid, I didn't feel the weight of needing promotion and the money and all the creaking effort which goes into keeping a lower-division club like Torquay in existence. I just wanted to score my first league goal. I put the ball down, chose my corner, walked back, ran up, struck it and, shit, George Wood dived the right way and got a hand on it. But I'd hit it just too hard for him and it went in, and before I knew what I'd done, the rest of the lads, some of them twice my age, were jumping all over me.

I was a bit of a local hero after that, and life round Torquay was turning out nice. With £30 first-team appearance money and a few bonuses added to my £27.50 apprentice's wage, I felt rich, too, and started going out, on the night of a match. There was a nightclub, Monroe's, just down the road from my digs, which I used to end up in sometimes with a couple of other apprentices. Legally we weren't allowed in because we were only sixteen, but we used to take our players' passes down and get waved in. It was a nice, friendly scene down there, no trouble, and everywhere shut at one o'clock, so we weren't out at stupid times. It was a good place to start out, really.

Debbie and I were still together on and off, but there were always a few girls around Torquay to keep the young lads' spirits up. There was a school right opposite the ground with some nice-looking fifth-years and sixth-formers – our age, remember – and we used to chat a few of them up. If there were any errands to run or jobs to do, like picking up the wages from reception, we'd all be desperate to volunteer for them because it'd take you on a long walk opposite the school and we'd see some of the girls. There were also a couple of language schools with Swedish students over to learn English, which is always a handy thing to have around when you're a young footballer starting to have a bit of time to play with.

I can't remember much at all about the next game, Colchester United at home on a Friday night, 15 April 1988. Just another crunching night in the Fourth Division, I think. I got clouted a couple of times, the full-back elbowed me in the head when he went up for a header, and I took two or three meaty whacks round the shins. I had a few runs at him, I think, but we couldn't get the breakthrough, however hard we tried; it was a war which finished stalemate, no prisoners taken.

From memory, my mum and dad met me after the game and drove me back to the digs. We sat around, had a bite to eat, maybe a cup of tea, then they dragged themselves out and into the car around 10.30, for the long haul back to Birmingham. Dave Caldwell was round at the digs that night, because he was seeing a woman who was a friend of Irene's. I might have chatted to him for a while, then gone up to bed, not late. I remember I couldn't sleep. I never could after a game, at any stage of my career. I'd always brood on it, run everything through my mind; things I'd done well or badly. I used to dwell on mistakes, passes or shots which could have been improved, replay them in my mind, again and again, all night. All of it, churning round in my head. When players are older, that's another reason why they go out drinking on the night of a game; not just to unwind, but to get their heads away from constantly going over it all. I was too young to be getting drunk as a routine, and I definitely remember being up in my room, in bed but wide awake with it all clanging about in my brain, when there was a knock at the front door.

I heard some talking, then there was a knock on my own door. It was Irene's friend.

'I don't know what you've been doing,' she said, 'but the manager and club secretary are both here to see you. You'd better get your arse downstairs.'

I leapt out of bed, got some clothes on, took myself downstairs, and there, true enough and larger than life, was the weathered, grizzled figure of Cyril Knowles, taking up the hallway. He beckoned me down, and we went into the dining room, where there was a little pool table for the lodgers to play on. My heart was pounding – what had the manager come to see me for, at one o'clock in the morning, the night after we'd just played a game? What the hell had I done wrong? We pulled out a chair each, sat down slowly, then Cyril Knowles said, in a matter-of-fact, seen-it-all-before tone:

'Alex Ferguson's been to see me. He wants you at Man United.'

CHAPTER 3

United wonderland

When I think about everything that followed, in my career, in my life, I often come back to that night, that knock on the door, Cyril Knowles's deadpan delivery, so calm and steady, as if this sort of thing happens all the time. But does it happen – ever? Has it ever happened before? Because I'm sure it'll never happen again, given what's happened to football now, with the big clubs existing on another planet from the likes of Torquay. Let's be clear about it: I was only sixteen, and I was plucked straight from Torquay United in the bottom division to go to Man U, one of the country's and the world's biggest clubs, and when I got there I went straight into the first team, playing Liverpool, Arsenal, Tottenham, in the top flight. Sorry, but I'm struggling to think of a precedent. I know Kevin Keegan went to Liverpool from Scunthorpe in the seventies, but he was twenty by then and he'd done his time: three full seasons at Scunthorpe, played more than 100 games, learned the ropes, cut his teeth. I'd been sweeping terraces, running up hills identified by the Dude and Sean Haslegrave for their ability to cause maximum distress, been a tea and coffee waiter on the first-team coach and played six – yes, just six – full games in the Fourth Division, plus five as sub, yet here was my manager, who'd done everything in football, turning up in the middle of the night rumbling on about Alex Ferguson and how I had to be down at the ground all smart at ten the next morning to sign as a player for Manchester United. Unheard of.

There hadn't been anything to prepare me for it: no speculation, no paper talk, nobody even knew Alex Ferguson was in the area that night. Some of the older first-team lads had given me a bit of a nod after recent games, saying: 'You won't be here long, son, don't you worry about that,' and there had been some talk about Norwich being interested, even that Cyril Knowles had been telling Tottenham about me, but none of it seemed real.

Alex Ferguson had been tipped off, Cyril Knowles told me, by an old Man U scout who had retired to Torquay and still went along to games out of habit. He'd seen me play, maybe in the Cardiff game when I'd scored my penalty, and let Ferguson know I was a prospect. I think Ferguson and his assistant, Archie Knox, had been at Wembley for some reason, so they travelled across on that Friday to watch me play in the grim 0–0 against Colchester. Cyril Knowles said he had been leaving the ground late, ages after the match had finished. The lights were off and nobody was about as he walked out the front. A Jaguar was parked there, on its own with no lights on, and as he came alongside it, the door swung open and a voice said: 'Get in, we'd like to have a chat with you.'

He said he crapped himself at first, thought it was gangsters, then he peered inside and saw Alex Ferguson in the driver's seat.

'Let's have a little spin,' Ferguson said, so Cyril Knowles got in the back, and they had a drive round Torquay in the dead of night. 'We'd like Lee Sharpe to come to Man U,' Alex Ferguson said, and Cyril Knowles, being a man who knew his way round football, played a poker face, showed no surprise, went straight into talking business, and by the time they'd finished cruising, they'd agreed that £180,000 was a fair price for this sixteen-year-old prospect, plus a friendly and other payments which would eventually take the fee up to £300,000. They shook hands, agreed to tie it all up in the morning, then Cyril Knowles came straight round to my digs to put me in the picture.

'They're staying overnight,' he was telling me. 'They want to see you at ten in the morning, and they're not leaving Torquay till you've signed.'

What do you say? Do you kiss Cyril Knowles smack on the cheeks, dance up the banisters of your boarding house, do cartwheels across the ceiling, somersault back to the worn carpet and give thanks for the miracle, or, if you're sixteen, do you sort of mumble into your hands: 'Right then, thanks, gaffer. I'll have to have a word with me dad'?

Cyril Knowles sat there for a while, telling me what a great move it was, not just for the obvious reasons – that Man U is one of the biggest, greatest clubs in the world, playing in the First Division – but that I had to get out of the Fourth Division because full-backs had already marked me out as a tricky little danger man and were looking to kick lumps out of me. It was raw professional football in the bottom division with small, hardcore crowds who wanted to see their teams give everything, and there were assassins lurking about, people who would go over the top, two-footed, studs up, really trying to hurt players, and one day, he said, they'd hack the talent out of me.

'You want to go to a quality club, with great facilities and top players. They'll have you in the reserves for a couple of years, teaching you good habits, turn you into a real footballer, and you'll play in a standard where your ability is respected and you have some space to play. It'll be a great move for you.'

He let himself out, leaving me standing on the landing. Mum and Dad would still be on their way back to Birmingham. There were no mobiles then, so I had to wait an hour or so before I could phone them. I drifted, stunned, into the living room, wandered over to an armchair. Dave Caldwell was sitting in there with his girlfriend, Irene was there too, and straight out Dave Caldwell said: 'Aye aye then, who's in for you?'

I said: 'How do you know someone's in for me?'

'Well, you're not in any trouble, are you?'

I shook my head.

'Well,' he said, the experienced journeyman footballer, 'managers don't come knocking on players' doors at this time of the morning unless there's some serious trouble or a club's come in for you, so come on, who is it?'

I sat down, looked at the floor, took a deep breath, then smirked just a little. 'Man United.'

Irene sort of yelped, I think, then ran off to make a cup of tea. Dave Caldwell was brilliant, sound; he was known as a rough player, he used to smack people on the field and get sent off, but like all the senior players, he was great with me, and he was happy for me, too, not jealous, not a bit. He started trying to give me advice – what to ask for when I went to meet Alex Ferguson, how much to try for, what to say if they came back with a different figure, what to demand for bonuses and appearance money, ask for this, ask for that, don't settle for any less than the other – then he just stopped.

'What am I going on about? Forget everything I've just told you. Just sign. Whatever they offer you, just fucking sign.'

The third or fourth time I tried my parents, my mum finally answered. She was worried; they'd only just left me and it was 2.30 in the morning. Was I in some sort of trouble, what was I phoning for?

'I'm fine, fine,' I told her. 'Will you put Dad on?'

She shuffled my dad on and I told him straight out: the manager's just been round and, er, he's had a meeting with Alex Ferguson in the back of his Jag, and Alex Ferguson wants me to sign for Man U.

Silence. Total and utter.

'Are you there?'

'Yeah, yeah,' he said.

'So what do you think, then?'

It was interesting really, looking back. My dad wasn't bowled over, starstruck, lost in his boy's great fortune. Actually, he was quite apprehensive.

'Man U?' Really quiet. 'It's a big place. I don't know whether you'd be better staying another year where you are before you go somewhere as big as that.'

My dad, as I say, is a steady sort of person; he thought I was doing well at Torquay and could do with growing up a bit more there. My mum would probably have told me to grab it.

I said: 'I know what you mean, but I've got to go, haven't I? The opportunity might not come again. The manager thinks I'm getting kicked now, and I need to go up there and learn how to play properly.'

'Yeah. Yeah, I know.' He was getting his head round it. 'It's just so early. But 'course it's a great club; you've got to go.'

Next morning, after no sleep, I was up putting on my one shirt and tie and this jacket thing I had, going down to Plainmoor like Charlie wobbling up to Willie Wonka clutching his golden ticket. The secretary was in reception and he told me, yes, Cyril Knowles was in the boardroom with Alex Ferguson and Archie Knox, and he'd come and get me. I paced outside for a bit, mind blank, then Cyril Knowles came out, told me they'd had a little chat between them, sorted out the deal, and now I should come in and they'd tell me all about it.

I walked into the boardroom with Cyril Knowles. My tie was done up so tight round my top button it was affecting my breathing. I was in a fairy story, the ragged orphan summoned to meet the man from the big house, who'd chosen me as the one he'd transport to a life of privilege and breeding. There, at the end of the table, relaxed and perfectly in control, a benevolent, fatherly smile across his face, his blue eyes peering carefully at me, was, in the flesh, really, definitely there, Alex Ferguson. Archie Knox was sitting by him, more recognisably human. It was unreal: Alex Ferguson was someone you saw on telly, wrestling with the fortunes of his massive club and its footballing superheroes, Bryan Robson and Norman Whiteside; he wasn't someone you'd see in the boardroom in Torquay. But here he was, in glorious Technicolor, cup of tea on the table, asking me, in a kindly sort of way, how I thought I'd played the night before.

'Not great,' I found myself saying. 'I took a couple of elbows; I've got a lump on my head and a few bruises – I didn't really get the chance to do much.'

No, no, Alex Ferguson said, he thought I'd done OK, because even after I'd taken the knocks, I picked myself up and kept going, kept looking for the ball. It showed I wanted it, that I had a good attitude, and they were going to get me out of this league and into a proper standard, where I'd be able to play football and they'd coach me properly, turn me into a really good player.

It's very significant, considering all the rubbish written about me at Old Trafford – how I threw it away and my career flopped afterwards, with some people saying I didn't work hard enough or have the appetite for the game – to remember that Alex Ferguson's initial impression, his reason for signing me in the first place, was my toughness. It wasn't my pace and ability to fly down the touchline, or at least not that alone. It was the fact that I dug in and kept going, that I was obviously a hard worker with real determination, and I wasn't intimidated by meathead Fourth Division full-backs twice my age. That was true throughout; I played with a smile on my face, but he could see from the beginning how much effort I put in, how hard I always worked.

In an interview for the video *Life at the Sharpe End*, which Manchester United made about me several years later to sell in the superstore, Alex Ferguson also said that he'd seen my potential as an athlete that night. He said I had 'good lines' – which perhaps makes him sound a little like a racehorse owner, casting his professional eye on some bloodstock galloping about in a paddock.

He started to talk about money, I remember; saying they

wanted to give me a four-year contract, pay me £170 a week, with a £5,000 signing-on fee; that my wages would go up to £320 as I'd get £150 for an appearance for the first team; there was money for this and money for that, bonuses in the reserves and bonuses in the first team ... He said I'd probably spend a year or two in the reserves, then they'd look to edge me into the first team. I just sat there, saying nothing, mumbling, shrugging, nodding, being ever so polite, while inside I was screaming: give me a piece of paper, anything! I'll sign anything!

There was no negotiation but it was, it would be fair to say, more than satisfactory to me at the time. I wasn't seventeen yet, so I couldn't actually sign, and we shook on it. The deal was that I would see out the season at Torquay, but go up for a couple of days to Old Trafford at the end of the following week, meet the lads and see the set-up, then sign a professional contract in the summer and become a United player.

Alex Ferguson was gentle, softly spoken, and he made me feel as relaxed as I could be, the perfect gentleman. The business concluded, off he went with Archie Knox, while Cyril Knowles and I stood at the front door at Plainmoor waving off the two fairy godfathers in their Jaguar chariot. 'Let's keep this quiet for a while, shall we?' Cyril Knowles said, and I went back to the digs in a daze, to ring Mum and Dad, tell them what had happened – yeah, your son's a Man U player now; yeah, I've just said ta-ra to Alex Ferguson; yeah, nice guy – then take my shirt and tie off and get back to the ground to start sweeping terraces with the other apprentices.

At noon, we all met up at the ground, and I had this absolutely massive grin on my face. Cyril Knowles came bustling up: 'Have you told anyone?'

No, I told him, and he said, 'Well, let's tell them.'

So Cyril Knowles gathered all the apprentices together, waited for a bit of quiet.

'Right, lads, I've got some good news. Sharpey's off to Man U.'

They all practically fell over their broomsticks.

'Yep, Sharpey's off to Man U. Alex Ferguson's been down and it's all agreed. He's going up there for a couple of days, then he's signing for them for next season.'

They thought it was a piss-take, but Cyril Knowles didn't really do fun. No, it was actually true. All the lads were stunned. They came and shook my hand, and then we went up to sweep the stands. I was with Ian Bastow, and we were there, sweeping up the Bovril cups, tin foil off the steak pies, crisp packets, and he just kept looking at me, as if he was one of the chimney sweeps in *Mary Poppins* and all wasn't as it seemed.

'How good is that?' he kept saying, shaking his head. 'Man U. Unbelievable. Man U!'

At one point we just stopped and stood, up on the empty terrace of Plainmoor, sweeping up the litter of a 3,500 crowd from the previous night's 0–0 draw. We had our hands on the top of our brooms, elbows out, leaning on them like a couple of old men. Man U in for one of us. That doesn't happen.

The local papers came down and ran a huge story with pictures of me; I did some local TV interviews, one of which made it into *Life at the Sharpe End*, this sixteen-year-old youth with a real Brummie accent who can't stop smiling.

We had a game on the Tuesday, against Newport. After

that I was going straight up to Manchester for my couple of days' training and getting to know United, then on the Friday we were playing away at Tranmere, so Archie Knox was going to drop me back there to meet up with our squad. I went out against Newport full of confidence, soaring, euphoric, young master goldenboots. There was a camera there that day and there is film of me going on some mad dribble from the left side of the halfway line diagonally across the pitch, past everyone, right up to their box, this stick-thin, gangly kid, finally getting nudged off it and ending up in the dried-up mud. I scored two in the game; the best was a half-volley. The keeper punched it out from a corner and it arrived perfectly at the edge of the box; I cushioned it on my chest, let it drop and blasted it into the roof of their net.

The hard-working young man whose good lines Alex Ferguson had so admired set off on one of the early exuberant goal celebrations of his football career. I always loved scoring, and I always loved celebrating with the fans too; it wasn't for me to wander back to the halfway line, head down, like some of the players do these days, as if they've just had news that a great-auntie has an abscess in her bum. I'd got to know a couple of guys, Torquay fans, round the town, and I knew where they were in the stand, so after I scored that half-volley, I set off running round the track, laughing my head off, all the lads chasing after me, and started high-fiving these blokes. Funny to wonder, would Alex Ferguson have been as keen to sign me if he'd seen that? If he'd watched me in that game against Newport, when I played really well, danced round the opposition and we won 6–1, but I'd run round the pitch after my two goals with a huge smile, showing the joy I felt in my football? Would he have approved of that, as much as he did of the way I picked myself up after a couple of elbows to the head in the 0–0 against Colchester? Don't know, but perhaps he was never prepared for the fact that I loved my game, and that when I scored, I did like to show how ecstatic I was, not jog back as if world famine was uppermost in my mind.

The morning after, I woke up really nervous, pulled a few things into a bag, put on a tracksuit that I wore to knock about in, went down to Plainmoor to pick up my train fare and a few expenses, then set off to the station for the long haul up to Manchester. Anyone who'd looked at me sitting in the train carriage would have seen just another sixteen-year-old kid, with a magazine and bottle of Coke, whiling away a long journey, but inside I was fit to burst. Madly excited too, of course, still struggling to take it all in.

I'd thought United might send a taxi for me, or a minor member of the coaching staff, but when the train finally pulled into Manchester six hours later, I hopped off, walked through the gate, and there he was, tall and lean, shirt and tie, in the forecourt of shabby old Piccadilly Station. Alex Ferguson himself. I was nervous in his presence, but very impressed, too, that he should have come personally to pick me up. He smiled – did I have a decent journey, was I all right? – and he was soon doing all he could to put me at my ease.

'We could have done with you last night, son,' he said, nice and chatty. Oh really? 'The youth team got beat, but we'd have probably won if you were playing.'

'Dunno if I could have made that much difference,' I

said with a shrug, but it made me feel good to hear it.

We snuggled into his Jag and he drove straight to Old Trafford. We parked, went inside and he took me all the way round, guided tour, showing me everything in the huge, great ground: the dressing rooms, the pitch, the stands, the executive suites, boxes, the seven restaurants – introducing me to everybody as wc went as 'the new player', as if I was a million-pound signing, and they all smiled, shook hands and wished me luck, wave after wave of staff. It was a totally different world, vast, compared to the battered old reception where I'd picked up my few quid that same morning, the doughty Fourth Division club with its sussed old manager and wiry players, the 3,000 crowds and games of Murder Ball at the back of the social club. Alex Ferguson devoted so much time to me, made me feel so special, and he was paternal with it, radiating pride in his new young boy, keen to show me off. He impressed me as a man and made me feel that he liked me, cared about me as a player and a person. The fact he'd met me at the station and ushered me everywhere with an arm around me made me want, from the beginning, to do the best I possibly could for him.

I was going to train with the first team the following day, Thursday, so Alex Ferguson drove me to some digs, a way out of town, a nice big house owned by an older couple, with just one other player in there. I said goodbye to Alex Ferguson, and thanks for everything; I'd see him tomorrow. The lad in the digs was Wayne Heseltine, a full-back, bit older than me, Yorkshire lad. He didn't make it in the first team and was sold to Oldham the year after. He was a bit flash, I seem to remember – he had a white XR3i and nice gear. I'm not sure we talked much but, after a night lying awake in a strange bed wondering what on earth it was going to be like trotting out with the Manchester United legends, I think he drove me down to training in the morning, ramming it in his flash motor, the old hand with the new recruit.

The first thing that hit me at the training ground, the Cliff, wasn't the saloons in the car park, the lawn-like pitch or even the superstars wandering in; it was the kit. It was like one of those adverts for washing powder you see, in which a housewife buries her face in ecstasy in the impossibly soft, fluffy linens. In the dressing room, the training gear was all laid out on the benches, T-shirt, shorts and socks with the player's own number on them, clean, crisp and rolled up in a spotless towel. On the pegs were sweatshirts and tracksuit bottoms, a dream to slip on. At Torquay you were given a bit of kit at the beginning of the season, but by the winter you were having to buy your own wet top and trackie bottoms. You washed it all yourself, but with training twice daily and all the jobs we had to do and making tea for the first team, we didn't have that much time to wash our kit, so we just used to hang it up in the boiler room to dry, and it used to go all crispy; by Thursday or Friday it'd practically be getting down itself and walking on over to us.

I trotted out for the first time ever in my gleaming Manchester United training gear, and a couple of reserve-team players, Paul Dalton and Wayne Bullimore, left-sided midfielders whom United had high hopes for at the time, were knocking a ball around to each other, waiting for training to start. But they weren't knocking it in the way I understood knocking a ball around; they were drilling it, striking it, pinging it forty yards across to each other, and it was arrowing over and landing right at each other's feet, then they were killing it dead with just a cushioning touch, then drilling it all the way back without thinking. I was like: oh my God, what planet have I landed on here?

Then the first team started to emerge. Steve Bruce, Viv Anderson, Bryan Robson, running out. In Real Life. Just knocking a ball about waiting for training to start, and their touch was incredible. They killed the ball dead first time without thinking, sometimes without seeming to look. Gordon Strachan was out there just stretching and limbering up, chatting to someone. People were pinging balls to him at full pace and he controlled them without even looking or just laid them off perfectly first time and didn't even break his flow of chat. I thought: no way can I control a ball like that. We started on a warm-up, in a square with five or six players round the outside and two in the middle who had to get the ball, one-touch, and I was having to concentrate really hard on my control, to make sure I didn't cock it all up and let the ball fly off my foot. I can remember Gordon Strachan, again, rapping away while doing the most beautiful things with the football, laying it off exactly where he wanted without the slightest hint of effort, and I knew I was out of my depth.

I was thrilled to be there, privileged, flattered, but it was unreal. I felt like somebody who'd won a raffle: first prize, spend two days training with Manchester United. Or that Mum and Dad had contacted *Jim'll Fix It*. In the end, it was like diving in; I took a huge psychological breath, tried to do my best for two days and hoped I'd come out gasping fresh air on the other side of it.

I didn't think any of the senior first-team players would really want to know me, a sixteen-year-old who wasn't going to be anywhere near their dressing room for a couple of years. I thought they might introduce me to the reserves and youth team, but the first team were friendly, approachable; Steve Bruce and a couple of the others even came over to introduce themselves. He had a bit of a joke with Alex Ferguson, telling him he was rude for not doing it himself: 'Don't worry, gaffer, don't you bother introducing us to the new player; we'll get on with it ourselves.'

To me this was, simply, Manchester United: enormous, a legendary name, a dream unfurling itself, but in the club's history, it was a nervous, transitional time. Alex Ferguson had arrived only eighteen months earlier, in November 1986. United hadn't won the League for nineteen years by then and although he inherited great players like Bryan Robson, Norman Whiteside and Paul McGrath, United considered themselves to have been underachieving for years, having the players, quite often, but without the discipline to succeed. Alex Ferguson had won trophies in Scotland with Aberdeen; they thought he was the man to replace Ron Atkinson and instil the winning spirit, but he hadn't turned it round yet, he hadn't found it at all easy, and the fans were not convinced. It is well known now that he believed the club wasn't disciplined enough and that some of the big-name players were underachieving, although I think this has been too easily summed up as a 'drinking culture'. He'd signed some players of his own: hard-working, great professionals – Brian McClair, Viv Anderson, Steve Bruce – for big money at the time, and also implemented his other big plan, to develop young players of his own. He'd overhauled the youth system, tightened up the scouting and also the way they went and talked to parents, so that United would try to recruit all the best young players and not lose them to Man City. He was just beginning to give one or two of United's current youngsters a chance. Russell Beardsmore, the little right-winger, was starting to poke into contention and Lee Martin – 'Schnozz' as everybody called him for his unfeasibly tremendous nose – would be given his debut at full-back at the end of the season, just a few weeks after my couple of days up there.

The turnaround of United was, however, taking time, and seen in that context, I suppose I was an important signing for Alex Ferguson. To go to Torquay and pay £180,000, rising to £300,000, for a sixteen-year-old was to make a big statement. I think it was more than just that I was a good young prospect; I was part of his hopes for a whole new generation at Old Trafford, who would eventually replace most of what he saw as the old lags he'd inherited from Ron Atkinson, youngsters he could mould in his ways: clean-cut, dedicated, athletic, disciplined, their heads full of United and the United way, focused on titles. None of that, of course, occurred to me at the time; I just worked as hard as I could not to make any howling mistakes. There wasn't much physical training going on because it was so late in the season; we did one-touch, a bit of keep-ball, some crossing and finishing and a bit of five-a-side to finish. All the lads were really encouraging and accepting. Gordon Strachan can be quite cutting and tear people to shreds, and I think he tutted a bit if I made a mistake, but everybody else was fine. The following day I trained with the reserves, but that was quite light, too, and again I just wanted to hold my end up. It was all exhausting, being on edge every minute of the day, not really knowing anybody, worrying – and then it was over.

Archie Knox took me back to my digs, I got my stuff and he ran me in his car over to Birkenhead, where the Torquay lads had arrived to play Tranmere. It was great to see them all, a relief to be where I was known, and they were crowding round me: Charlie's schoolmates, asking him what Willie Wonka's chocolate factory had really been like. Funny, but it was the kit which got them, too. I tried to tell them what Alex Ferguson was like, Bryan Robson, Gordon Strachan, the ground, the training, who I met. I was saying: yeah, quality, everyone was quality. Then I told them you got your kit with your own number on it, and someone else washed it and it was all spotless and hung up for you, you even got a nice fluffy towel – and it absolutely slew them, tears in the eyes of old peasants, learning of the riches of faraway lands.

The dream was over. I stepped back into myself. I was glad to. I could chat to the lads and have a laugh with them and they took the mickey, in a nice way, about me being a superstar now. In training after that, if I ever made a mistake they were always saying: oh no, the price has dropped now, oops, it's gone down again. Cyril Knowles dropped me to sub for that first game back, we drew 1–1, another long, coach journey and Monday morning I was back with my crusty training kit on and a broom in my hands.

It was a bit of an anticlimax in a way, having to see out the last few weeks with Torquay, even though we were having such a good season and made it to the play-offs.

Cyril Knowles played me only in the home games after that. He was protecting me from away crowds; at Torquay there were never many away fans. He used to tell me to be careful who I was taking on; he didn't want me kicked out of sight before I could get up to United – Torquay wanted their money. We finished fifth in the league, beat Scunthorpe in the play-off semis, then had Swansea to play in the final. It was before play-off finals were played at Wembley; instead they were decided with a home and away battle, and we played away first. Cyril Knowles left me out for the away leg because the Vetch Field could be a really hostile ground and there were over 10,000 fans in it for the game; we lost 2–1. I was sub for the return, and we had 5,000 at our place, the highest crowd of the season. We gave it everything; Dave Caldwell scored and Jim McNichol scored two, but we drew 3–3 and Swansea went up.

Still, it had been a great season, not just for me but for the club. I don't remember any big send-off for me; the players used to go to a pub round the corner from the ground for a few drinks after matches and I was never allowed in because I was sixteen, but they had a bit of an end-of-season do, let me in and bought me a few beers, which felt like acceptance from the older lads. They'd been great with me, and all seemed pleased; it was a touch of glory for everyone that Alex Ferguson had been down to watch them, and one of their young lads was going to Man U. Cyril Knowles and Sean Haslegrave told me it had been a pleasure to work with me – I just grinned, because I couldn't honestly say that working with Sean had been pure pleasure all the way along. In fact, whatever the warm glow around the place, and inside me, at the incredible way it had all turned out, it's still true that had it not been for Irene's dinners, cups of tea and her family's human warmth in those brutal early weeks, I'd have been long gone. I might have been on a building site somewhere, or turning metal with my dad, not looking ahead to a few weeks on Mum and Dad's sofa, then taking to the stage at the biggest football club in the world.

CHAPTER 4

The original Boy Wonder

What happened when I got to Old Trafford was the next unheard-of development in my unbelievable journey. The manager's plan, as he told me, was that I would spend two years in the reserves, learning good habits, being coached, schooled in the Manchester United ways, groomed to be part of taking the club back to where it belonged. As it turned out, that did not happen at all. It was 100 years since the Football League had been established, and they held a Centenary Trophy competition between a few of the top clubs, a series which didn't exactly over-excite the fans but did give me a start in the first team – at left-back, against Newcastle, at home, on 21 September 1988. Only 15,000 fans turned up, but Alex Ferguson put out a strong side, which included Steve Bruce, Bryan Robson, Brian McClair and Mark Hughes, the superhero in human form whom the manager had brought back from Barcelona that summer. We beat Newcastle 2–0, after extra time – two hours on the huge, wide, loamy Old Trafford pitch. I was getting cramp towards the end, but I played pretty steadily at left-back, took care to track back and not make too many mistakes or give the ball away; I got through it.

Afterwards, Alex Ferguson was chuffed with me, singing my praises, saying how well I'd done, asking me how my legs were, whether I was tired or stiff, and I told him, no, I was fine. Then he dropped a little question:

'If I was to play you in the first team on Saturday, would you be ready?'

What do you say? 'Er … yeah,' is what I came up with.

'OK,' he said, 'get a couple of good days' rest, because you might be involved on Saturday.'

On the Saturday, 24 September 1988, not even a month into my first season at the club, Alex Ferguson put my name, Lee Sharpe, into Manchester United's first-team sheet, not on the bench as I'd expected, but in the starting XI, to make my full debut, at left-back. I was just seventeen, thin and leggy, kitted out in a gleaming red shirt with a number 3 on the back, on a gorgeous autumn afternoon, playing West Ham United, who, I seem to remember, wore all white for the occasion.

Again, thinking about my career and everything that followed, you have to wonder at how quickly it all happened. I'd arrived as a professional, on a four-year contract, even though I was the same age as the lads in the second year of their apprenticeships, who were sweeping up, doing odd jobs, getting up to all kinds of mischief and pressing for just the hint of a chance in the game. I was still barely a year out of school and the little senior football I had played was in the Fourth Division with Torquay. I completely bypassed the two years' coaching planned for me, the time to be served and experience gained in the reserves, the work to be done on technique, teamwork and tactics. Here I was, thrown in, a member of Manchester United's first team, being hailed as a future player of promise at the great club, walking out of the Old Trafford tunnel to hit the sunshine and the throaty roars of 40,000 fans, in a line of senior players headed by the awesome figure of Bryan Robson himself.

It was all still unreal, a dream, maybe a bumper fly-on-the-wall *Jim'll Fix It* special. I'd had a few weeks of reality at home over the summer once my mum and dad had been down to Torquay and picked me up with my stuff. It had been all over the local papers at home; my mates couldn't believe it. I pottered about, did bits of work for Dad. Debbie and I got back together properly and we went on holiday to Spain, so life was sweet.

I passed my driving test, and with the first instalment of my United signing-on fee, £1500, triumphantly bought my first car, a Ford Escort 1.6L, a pretty standard trundler – or so I thought until its bonnet flipped up at eighty miles an hour on the motorway and we found out it was two cars welded together. That's a pretty standard scam with a second-hand car. Isn't it?

I went up to Manchester in that car, and my mum and dad came too, because there was a load of gear, a telly for the room and stuff. Scary, again. New digs, new lads, a whole new experience ahead. Heart pounding, nerves scraping. We pulled off the M62 and down Bury New Road and there we were: Lower Broughton, Salford. It was a dark, dingy area, rough as anything really, but the training ground, the Cliff, was there, and United used as landladies some people owning the big old terraced houses in the streets opposite. My first digs were with a woman called Brenda, a nice lady on her own, in her forties, who had a house in a cul-de-sac across from the Cliff, near the Priory pub, which United players and bored United apprentices had kicked around in for generations. Either she or the club itself had bought the one next door and knocked through, so she used to live on one side of this big yawning place, and all the lads, ten of us, used to live in the other, truly an animal house.

She gave me the room at the front, with a big bay window, a gas fire struggling to make any impact, and two single beds, one for me and one for my first room-mate, Shaun Goater, the young striker from Bermuda, a great lad. I remember going in there for the first time, dumping all my stuff, my mum and dad fussing around, then finally leaving, and I had a lump in my throat standing in this big, high room, a similar emptiness to when they'd dropped me at Irene's a year before. I'd been through it now though, and I was more steeled, stronger for having made a success of myself at Torquay, so I gave myself a talking-to: this might be a bigger, grander challenge, but it's the same thing, the same emotions to go through. Your stomach will be churning round like a washing machine for weeks, it'll be really uncomfortable, all the players are going to be better than you and you'll have to raise your standards. But you get your head down, do the work, play the football, and soon you'll know people, be a regular face in the digs and in the dressing room and it'll be no big deal. You'll get through it. I kind of talked myself round, into being ready for it all.

I remember sitting back in the first few days and weeks, getting changed in the reserve-team dressing room at the Cliff, smiling and being obliging enough but watching closely, feeling my way into who was who, the leaders and the quiet ones, the general atmosphere of the place, the different personalities. We all trained together round at Littleton Road, where there were four pitches, in a mass group at first, twenty or twenty-five first-teamers, Bryan Robson invariably at the front in all the running, sixteen to twenty reserve-team players and probably the same number of apprentices: fifty or sixty footballers in a clump with their Man U training sweatshirts on, jogging two laps of the field for a warm-up.

The first few days were nice and easy – get the stiffness out of our muscles, some jogging and a Jane Fonda-ish workout – up to the weekend, when we'd have Saturday afternoon and Sunday off, then come back to hit the fitness training hard on the Monday. There was a screaming silence where the Dude and Sean Haslegrave might have been. At United, we very rarely did anything long distance; we did some more laps of Littleton Road at the end, and two more to start afternoon sessions, but it was just a general fat burner – some players would go off and do more running or do it faster to lose a couple of extra pounds if they needed to. There were a couple of tough runs, but actually I found it easy compared to the horrors of Torquay, then once we were into speed fitness work, the furthest we ran was 300m, round a track Archie Knox had marked out in the grass.

Instead, most of the work was with a ball: passing, crossing, finishing, maybe a bit of shadow play, one team up against another, players tracking each other. Archie Knox had a friendly, light-hearted way with the lads; he'd wander around, talk to a few of the first team, crack a couple of jokes about their weight if some of them had a bit to lose. I remember Alex Ferguson coming over: how was I, were my digs all right, how were my mum and dad? He told me if I worked hard I'd get on really well at United, wished me luck. Warm, friendly, paternal.

I was in dreamland. I kept thinking I'd turn up one day and find it was all some awful mistake, the show was over, they had to send me back to Torquay, or make me re-sit some O-levels. But I just kept turning up at the Cliff every day and there it all was, Manchester United Football Club, saying good morning. I'd wander in and there my lovely spotless kit would be with my number on it, training sweatshirt up on the hook, a bag full of twenty new, clean, pumped-up Tango footballs, to be picked up, run off with and stroked about with Bryan Robson. Is this what everyone does when they leave school?

When I started playing in the reserves, I was baffled that some of the players were moaning and bitching. Graeme Hogg was one; he was a centre-half who'd played quite a few games but wasn't in the first team any more, always having a good moan about it, saying his agent was going to get him out of there. I used to think: what the hell can there possibly be here to complain about? Lee Martin, too, was unsure and dissatisfied at this time; he was three years older than me, twenty, and he'd been at United as a youngster, so had had a few years in the reserves. As I'd find out myself years later, the reserves are fine when you're on your way up, if you are. If not, if you get stuck there, they're not called the stiffs for nothing. They're a stagnant netherworld, the land of the walking dead. But not to me then, a kid still pinching himself that he's there at all; it was unbelievable.

The hardest thing for me was finding a rhythm in the touch-and-passing game which United played. At Torquay there was more lumping the ball forward into channels, fighting to win it, or to win the second ball if it came back. Here, the ball was played to feet, players controlled it perfectly first time. It was mostly two-touch or even one-touch, laying it off and making yourself available, keeping the ball for long periods, the players off the ball always looking to make themselves available, so that the player receiving it has several options for an early pass in turn. There is a whole other skill to be worked at, nothing to do with your feet, but awareness, being able to look up, see behind you, in front, take the time to assess the options before the ball arrives, then make the right choice when it comes, all very quickly.

None of it is rocket science, but I found it difficult at first because I'd always been the best player in the youth teams I'd played in, and at Torquay we were playing on awful, bobbly pitches where you couldn't have a hope of playing two-touch. I had to concentrate on my touch, then in practice matches I'd take three or four touches when the other lads were pinging it around first time. I just had to put my head down and work. Archie Knox and some of the senior players would drill the basics into us: play it simple most of the time, pass and move, control, pass and move, just find a man on your own side – and very often, choose the first option you have, because that is usually the best. Don't overcomplicate it and try to do something difficult, particularly in an area of the pitch where it makes very little difference: find your own man, keep the ball, it's a team game.

As pre-season went on, the first team and reserves started to play friendlies and the training quite often split up; the different squads training at different times or on different pitches. I was in the reserve team's dressing room, which was a good thing, because as I got to know them and the scene cleared in my mind, I learned that the second-year apprentices, who were the same age as me, could be most accurately summed up as a bunch of dog-eat-dog lunatics and it was a true result not to be with them.

They were as bad back in the digs, ten testosterone-charged lads, there to play football, without much money and not a lot to fill the time in the afternoons. Starving too, with all the training and physical work; meals were like feeding time at the zoo. Brenda would plonk the food down on the table, decent meals; we'd pile in for a free-for-all, and it was gone, in seconds flat. Then, refuelled, we'd have long evenings to fill, desperate hunts for anything, however ridiculous, we might have a laugh doing, which might eat up a bit of the time. The maddest apprentice I ever came across in football was a Sheffield lad my age; he was a tough, decent full-back actually, with a name to strike fear into the heart of anyone in Man United digs in 1988–89: Sean McAuley.

He didn't make it at United; he lacked a bit of pace, which was often the deciding factor, and eventually went to St Johnstone, then carved out a career at Scunthorpe, Rochdale and Hartlepool. More recently, he did all his coaching badges and is now put forward as a case study of the responsible footballer, but back then he was the ringleader for all the teenage madness. I suppose it was inevitable, because there was nothing to do. We used to go up to the Priory pub, perhaps three times a week, and have a little drink, or mooch up to the snooker club, but mostly we'd have our tea in five seconds flat at 5.30, then look to Sean McAuley to dream up some ridiculous games to occupy the time. One of these was called 'Darkness' and here were the ingenious rules. The curtains would be shut, the lights all turned off, so it was pitch black in the living room, and we'd all be sitting round on the couches. Then people would throw things round the room, anything and everything – ornaments, shoes, pictures – but you weren't to make a sound; if you did you had to let everybody give you a dig, a thump on the arm or the leg. No, you don't need me to run that past you again, that was it, just one of the ways in which the gilded youth at the world's most glamorous football club used to pass the time in the evenings of their apprenticeship. Some of it went a bit beyond the mark, and I really did pity the schoolboys who'd come to chase their football dreams in the holidays. During the day they'd train with their heroes, then in the evening they'd be lined up in the living room of these digs, a porno film would be put on, and these poor unfortunate young lads would be made to watch it. If one of them got a hard-on, he'd get a dig off all the lads. What a game.

I was a step apart from it all because I wasn't an apprentice but a professional. Some of the stuff in the apprentices' dressing room was just sheer, uncomplicated brutality, like getting a ball in a sock and whacking people full on the head with it – they called that the bong, getting a bong on the head. I think they finally stopped when one lad had one bong too many, six of the best I think, nearly fainted and they all thought he'd suffered serious damage to his neck. Wouldn't be the career-ending injury of choice for most aspiring players: cut short by a ball in a sock. I can't say it wasn't funny, I was only seventeen, you're still in hysterics most of the time at that age anyway, and most of the lads wanted to show they could have a bit of a laugh behind teacher's back without getting into any serious trouble.

There was a teacher figure trying to bring all these young animals to heel, a famous figure now at United, Eric Harrison, who a few years later would bring through the Nevilles, Nicky Butt, Paul Scholes, David Beckham, the generation of home-grown lads who would be the backbone for Alex Ferguson's second wave of success. Eric Harrison was a nice bloke, who wanted the best for his young players, but he was really strict, stood for no nonsense, demanded respect and discipline. They were all scared stiff of him; they used to call him 'the shadow', because they would never hear him coming. They'd be up to the usual tricks, absolute carnage in the apprentices' dressing room, then suddenly Eric Harrison was right there, on top of them, with a huge frown on his head. He'd dish out the bollockings, but they did seem to have a constructive point to them, and he'd get his message across. Nobody who ever played for him has a bad word to say about him. When I look back, I feel I was unfortunate that I missed out on an apprenticeship there with him, because he was a proper coach, drilling good habits into the lads. I bypassed any of that coaching, and went straight into the reserves pre-season.

I did OK. My fitness was fine, the running was pretty easy for me, I was always trying to raise the standards of my game. I had a few reasonable friendlies, but only one stands out for me, and not for anything to do with how I played. It was up in Hartlepool, on Wednesday, 24 August 1988, just three days before the start of the season, so Alex Ferguson was probably nervous and tense anyway, but then a particularly appalling performance and result –

Hartlepool 6, Manchester United o – did nothing for his mood.

We had a good side out, when you think, with a few first-teamers playing, Norman Whiteside, Paul McGrath, Viv Anderson and Mike Duxbury, along with me, Russell Beardsmore, Mark Robins and some of the other young lads, but I suppose we were just finding our feet and Norman and one or two others were coming back from injuries. Hartlepool were a better-organised team, really wanted it against Manchester United and we got absolutely stuffed. Chris Turner was the unfortunate in goal.

Alex Ferguson was always going to be angry, so he came in ranting and raving as we sat deflated on the benches in the dressing room. 'You're not fit to wear the red shirt of Manchester United; you're a disgrace, you shouldn't be picking up your wage packet this week; no team of mine ever goes out there and doesn't work hard,' all that sort of thing, for five minutes or so, laying into the team. Fair enough. It wasn't that shocking and nobody said anything. Then he said that the only player who could hold his head up and say he'd performed properly that day was big Paul McGrath, who stopped the score from being eight or nine.

Fine. No problem with that. We all sat and took it – it was probably true. But, for some reason, Chris Turner decided he didn't agree. He was a senior player, coming up to thirty, and he'd been at United three years, having played for nearly ten at Sheffield Wednesday and Sunderland, so he probably felt he had the seniority to speak up in a dressing room. That was his first mistake, just to think it. The second was to go and tell Alex Ferguson he was out of order. That was really quite a serious misjudgement of the situation.

'You can't single out one person,' Chris Turner said, all reason and sense. 'It was a bad team performance. You can't single one person out and say he's done well – you know, big Paul did well, but we win as a team and we lose as a team.'

I'd actually thought Alex Ferguson had gone mad before, thought that was the famous temper, which was pretty bad and you didn't want to see it overheating too often. But it turned out that had been nothing at all, not a twitch of the temper glands. It took twenty seconds or so for him to take in what had been said. He went silent, just looking at Chris Turner, and I thought for a misguided instant he was going to agree with Chris, say sorry and leave it. But then his face started to turn the colour of a tomato, ripe enough to burst. I think he booted some kit bags out of the way to get at Chris Turner. He walked over to him and put his face just three or four inches from Chris's face – this, I was to be initiated, was what they meant by the Alex Ferguson 'hairdryer'. Then he released it all and started tearing in, the air turning blue.

'You little fucker,' he said, 'who the fucking hell do you think you are, telling me how to run this football club? When you've been a manager you can tell me what I can and can't say. I'll say what I want to my players – these lot weren't good enough, they were all shit and they're not fit to wear the shirt...' And then he was off, absolutely laying into him for what seemed like five or ten minutes.

Third mistake, Chris Turner tried to reason again: 'Hang on a minute, all I'm saying is...' and we all just rolled our eyes, thinking: Chris, just leave it, let the manager erupt, get it out of his system, then we can all have a shower and go home, but he had to try, so Alex Ferguson absolutely launched himself back into him, and I had my first experience of that nice, caring father figure when his boys weren't following the rules.

It's worth noting that the main issue wasn't the 6–0 defeat, or even the content of what Chris Turner had said, whether big Paul McGrath should indeed have been singled out as a saving grace. It was that Chris Turner had dared to say something about Alex Ferguson's management, that he was seen to have disregarded the hierarchy and, as Ferguson saw it, trespassed on his authority. That was the unforgivable crime, to presume, as a thirty-year-old professional, to offer an opinion.

Alex Ferguson growled a bit, saw Chris Turner wasn't coming back, then told us all to have a shower and stomped out. When he'd gone, we all just looked at each other, stunned for a little while, then slowly we relaxed and started having a laugh.

'Fucking hell, Chris,' somebody said, 'why don't you just shut up, man? We could have been out of here twenty minutes ago.'

I remember talking to some of the young lads, saying: 'Jesus Christ, he lost it there, didn't he?' and they were going: oh that's what he's like, that's normal for him, how he doesn't have a heart attack they'd never know. I thought: Christ, I hope I never play badly and lose another game because I don't fancy that. Everybody was scared of him and now I realised why: it wasn't just respect for his qualities as a manager, or the natural fact he was our boss; it was genuine fear, of these awful bollockings, of being ripped to shreds in front of the others. I think everybody at the club was in fear of him, from the apprentices to the senior players. I think even Bryan Robson had a hint of fear in him. For all his undoubted qualities as a football manager, that was the way Alex Ferguson ultimately, underneath it all, ruled the roost: by fear. It is this added element that often makes the difference for many successful managers and one aspect they feel they have to have.

My chance in his team came about just a few weeks later. I'd played in a few more reserve games and been told I'd done OK, then we played a practice match, in which, for some reason, there was no left-back available, and as a left-footed player, the reserve-team coach, Brian Whitehouse, asked me to play there. It was a surprise, because I'd never played in that position since I was about eight in the Cubs team, but I actually did really well: I made a few strong tackles, some runs forward, got some crosses in.

Brian Whitehouse didn't say a great deal, but he must have logged it, because shortly after that, we were having another practice match with me playing left-wing and Alex Ferguson was drifting across, so Whitehouse called out to me:

'Sharpey, come back and play left-back; come and show the manager how good you are playing left-back.'

I didn't think I was particularly good there, and never felt it was my natural position because I loved attacking, but I went back there, and again I was pretty steady, could do everything necessary to defend but still got up the line, and when I came off they both said well done. Next thing, I was in the first team for that Centenary Trophy match against Newcastle, then Alex Ferguson was asking me if I was going to be ready to play in the first team on the Saturday against West Ham.

I remember speaking to my dad on the phone and him saying I was bound to be sub, because I'd been on the bench a couple of times already; this time, he said, they might give me the last twenty minutes, ease me into it. In the digs the night before, I couldn't sleep. How was it all happening so quickly? How was I picked out to be goldenballs?

In eight years there, the nerves of matchday Saturday mornings never left me. Stomach beginning to churn around eleven o'clock when I put my suit on, get in the car, start driving with that sinking dread feeling, then, on the way into Old Trafford, this sickly, sweetish smell, like hops; I'm not sure if it was a brewery, but I always associated it with suffocating nerves.

We'd arrive at twelve o'clock to have a pre-match meal in the grill room in the Main Stand; by the time we were finishing, punters on corporate packages were turning up to eat their lunch in the same restaurant. I could never eat a lot because of nerves and it was always high-fuel stuff like chicken, beans and pasta, all quite bland and it never went down very well; it seemed to make the nerves worse. Then we'd go down and while away a bit of time in the players' lounge, reading the papers or watching the football preview programmes on the telly, and it would all be building up until around 1.30, when the kit man or physio comes in and says: 'Team meeting!' Then we'd all go into the dressing room and the manager would say: 'OK, this is the team.'

He used to take people aside in advance if they were being dropped or were playing for the first time; he was good for that. This time, he hadn't prepared me, I presume because he didn't want to completely slay me with nerves. We went in and he did it quite casually, just said: 'Right, same team as Wednesday,' which, it crashed into me, meant I was in the team. He ran through it: 'Jim Leighton,

Clayton Blackmore right-back, Sharpey left-back, Stevey Bruce and Paul McGrath in the middle…'

Slowly, the banter started up and the characters began asserting themselves. People had their own routines for getting changed and ready for the game. It's true that players develop their own way of dealing with the nerves and many have superstitions, routines they believe give them luck – but I was never one for that stuff. Steve Bruce always put his shorts on last, so he used to walk around for twenty minutes in his warm-up T-shirt, his underpants and his shoes and socks – he looked like someone's dad walking round the house calling the wife to ask where she's put his trousers. Paul Ince and Gary Pallister, when they got to United, used to have miniature bottles of brandy and take a little swig just before we went out.

I was just this young teenager who couldn't believe what was happening. I didn't need any treatment or special massage, I had no changing superstitions or routines; I just walked into the dressing room, saw that there was a red shirt with a number 3 on the back, shorts, socks, boots all polished and ready for me, and I whipped my suit off, rolled my kit on and I was ready, with half an hour still to wait before we could even go out on the pitch and warm up. I sat back on the bench and watched some of the giants go through their routines, a certain shin-pad on first, pacing the place, some talking, some silent. Finally we went out onto the pitch to warm up and then the nerves eased off just a little because there was something to do, get on the ball, control one or two nicely, ping a few, get a feel for the ball, and I did relax a bit, regained some control, remembered who I was and why I was there.

Then, back in for the final preparations, the nerves

building up again. The manager didn't say too much to me. I was playing left-back, I'd be marking their right-winger, Mark Ward, and I just remember Alex Ferguson telling me to make sure I looked after myself in the tackle. That was one of his real strengths, knowing the game of all your opponents inside out. He'd give you plenty of advice about how to play someone, but in this case I think he was quite confident I could deal with Mark Ward's pace; he just wanted me to watch out for any rough stuff from him.

Then he gave the final few words, the last bits of wisdom, and we were about to go into battle: 'Come on, lads, let's get stuck in about them, defend from the front – Sparky [Mark Hughes], you set us off right in the first tackle; Robbo, you set the pace of the game...' and then we were going out to the tunnel and I was getting seriously scared, hitting that wall of noise when the fans get their first glimpse of the red shirts coming out; 40,000 fans erupting and the hairs on the back of your neck stand up and your stomach's churning and you're so nervous and excited that your vision can go blurry. Then you're out, running onto the pitch, just wanting to get hold of a football and control it and spray it out to someone else because it's familiar and it's something you know you can do.

When a game starts, it does settle down, especially if you're doing OK. You get into the zone, really concentrate on the match, and you don't hear 40,000 different people; just general background noise. It has to be that way, or you couldn't play. Particularly on my debut, probably for the whole of that first season, I was just concentrating really hard on not making a mistake or letting anybody down. At seventeen I couldn't allow myself to take in the enormity of the atmosphere and what I was doing, playing in Man U's first team. As you get older and more relaxed, you aren't quite as nervous and can appreciate it more, but I couldn't let myself do that, otherwise I could have gone under. The ball would go out of play and suddenly I'd find myself right next to this huge crowd and could see them all and hear everything, but I had to block it out to play my football, make myself play the game, not the occasion.

I can't actually remember too much about the debut. There are a few clips on *Life at the Sharpe End*, and any memories I had seem to have merged with those. I have a decent run up the left wing and square a pass to Bryan Robson, who has a shot, and the commentator mentions me, that I was only seventeen and had only just joined the club. There are a few interesting details, one of which is easy to miss: there are fans standing, behind fences, all round the pitch. My time at United is associated in a lot of people's minds with the new success of United and general boom in English football, but I started back in 1988, when we still had fences, people paying at the turnstiles, before Hillsborough when it all changed, the grounds became all-seater and football within a couple of years was suddenly sexy. The pressure on me was massive then, and so was the opportunity, but it was still football, a passionately supported game, not the all-consuming global media monster it is today. Imagine the fuss and attention now if a seventeen-year-old kid was picked for Man U after playing six games for Torquay United and went straight in the first team. Billy Elliot, meet Wayne Rooney.

I think I did OK, played steadily again, concentrated mostly on not making mistakes. I don't think I got into any fifty-fifty challenges with Mark Ward. I closed him down and I was quicker than him, so he couldn't push it past me.

It was actually quite an easy game for me, and we won, 2–0. Peter Davenport and Mark Hughes scored them. It was more a relief than a total thrill, but it was still completely unbelievable that I had just played a full Football League match in the First Division for Manchester United, in a team containing Mark Hughes, Bryan Robson, Gordon Strachan and Brian McClair.

Later in the week, I found out from one of the apprentices that Archie Knox had taken them all to one side on the Saturday before the match and told them to watch me. He was pointing me out, apparently, as an example to the lads, who were still the same age as me. He told them that obviously at seventeen I wasn't the best player they had in the team, but to watch my work rate, saying that I'd concentrate completely throughout the game and give my best. He was holding me up as an example, showing them I was doing what they all needed to do: give 100 per cent and keep running all day. It was good to hear that, made me feel big inside. It's good even to think about it now, but funny too, in a sad sort of way, to realise how much I was, back then when I arrived at United, Fergie's model fledgling.

CHAPTER 5

The drinking culture

I found out what people meant by the drinking culture one afternoon off during those early months when I was new in the first team. If we'd played a match on a Tuesday night we'd have Wednesdays off, and that day I'd driven my welded-together orange Escort into town and had a nosy round, been shopping, wandering about, doing what you do in a new city when you're seventeen. It was the end of the afternoon, five o'clock-ish, I was on my way back, walking along a side street past a restaurant the senior players used to use, Harpers. There was a knock on the window from inside, tap tap, I looked over and they were beckoning me in, so I went inside with my shopping bags and they ordered me a glass of Coke.

Mal Donaghy was in there and a few of the senior pros, including Norman Whiteside. They'd been drinking a while; sometimes they would get there for pre-lunch drinks, have lunch, bottles of wine and turn it into an all-dayer, drinking and talking football; they'd been doing it for years on days off – it was team bonding, team spirit, United style. None of them was in any state to drive and they'd been trying to work out how to get Norman home safely and away from the eyes of the manager's spies, when along comes me, a fresh-faced young lad, trotting past with his few new clothes. So they asked me to drive Norman home in his car – leave mine in town, drop Norman off at his house, then get a taxi back into town to get my car. I was like, OK, no problem, but I haven't got a clue where Norman lives and I don't even know Manchester that well. That's OK, they said, he could direct me, which was the first good joke of the afternoon.

So they give me Norman's car keys and I go and get his car, a lovely, brand-new Jaguar XJS, with all-leather seats and sublime gadgetry, and drive it back to Harpers. They dump Norman in the passenger seat and wish us well on our way. I look at Norman. His head's dropping onto his chest, his eyes are closing, he's mumbling every now and then. And I haven't a clue where we're supposed to be going.

I'm shouting at Norman: 'Where do you live, Norman? Whereabouts is it?' and he says Altrincham, so I start driving out of town. He gives me a few directions, all slurred speech, mostly without opening his eyes: left here, straight on, right here. I'm not convinced but I don't know any better, so I follow them and after half an hour of the mystery tour, we find ourselves in Stockport. 'Norman!' I'm shouting. 'Norman! You don't live in Stockport, do you?' And he shakes his head on his chest. 'No, turn back, go back.' So I start driving back into the centre of Manchester, then we're passing some pub and Norman suddenly shouts at me to stop, and he gets out and goes in for another drink. He's got no cash on him, I've only got about a fiver, so I tell him I can't buy him a drink, but he says it's all right, the landlord here knows him and won't charge him. So in we go and the barman gives Norman another pint or a glass of wine or whatever it was, he necks that and then we get back in his car and I start driving around in circles again with Norman not able to tell me where his house is.

My mobile rings; it's Mal Donaghy. 'Have you got Norman home yet?'

'No, I haven't; we're still driving round. We've been to Stockport and back, we've been to a pub on the edge of town and back; he keeps directing me round and round in circles.'

So Mal Donaghy tells me to drive back into town and bring Norman to the Midland Hotel, because Mal's staying there and Norman's wife will come and pick him up. Back I go, pull up at the front of the Midland, Mal's there to meet us and we practically pour Norman out of his car.

'Good lad, we'll sort him out from here,' Mal Donaghy says.

Which is fine, but, er, what do I do with Norman's car? Oh, Mal Donaghy says, you'd better keep it, bring it to training tomorrow, then they could drive me into town after training to get mine. Well, I say, no problem, and I'm already back in the XJS, gunning the ignition, straight back to the digs. Look, lads, look what I've got – and they're straight into Norman's car and off we go, joyriding round Manchester all night, racing cars, up on the M62 in the pouring rain: class.

A few things to make clear about the drinking culture before we go on: it was made an issue at Old Trafford, that Alex Ferguson cleared it up, so there's the impression it was out of control and particular to United, but it wasn't. Drinking was a part of English football like liniment or terraces. That was how players socialised, brewed team spirit, bonded as friends not just colleagues, and always had; when they were young lads, they'd come into clubs where the senior players drank and they became part of it themselves.

It's also wrong to say that Alex Ferguson completely disapproved. I suppose he did, in an ideal world; he'd have preferred it if players didn't drink at all, spent their days off playing golf and were always tucked up in bed at 9.45 having watched a few training videos. (Which does, come to think of it, pretty much describe the Neville brothers' lifestyle.) Alex Ferguson did try to steer the young players away from it, didn't want them growing up into it. But at this point everybody drank, not just Norman or big Paul McGrath, at United and probably at every club in English football at every level, although some more than others. It was the game – football and beer – and many of the strongest characters on the field have been the biggest drinkers off it. Alex Ferguson himself had been a pub landlord for a while when he finished playing, so it's not as if he was horrified by drink. Eventually, he did want the drinking culture to finish, and I think it did through the 1990s, as the game became more serious, a business, and foreign players came in from cultures where the game was all sobriety and athletic discipline. At that time, though, it was a predominantly English game, the players drank, and Alex Ferguson's problem was not with the drink itself so much as what he believed to be a slack attitude. He might have tolerated all Norman and Paul McGrath's benders if he didn't think that they were underachieving, wasting their

With my mother, Gail, as a little baby.

Sitting on the lap of Bill, 'the Duke', and Lil, my grandparents with whom I spent so much time as a young lad.

Top left: The Sharpe family: me, Dad Leo, John, Mum and Nicola.

Top right: Aged three and already with a ball. Alarmingly, the hairstyle isn't that different to today's!

Left: Lining up for my Cubs team in Blackheath. I've brought my own ball just in case we lose the smart one.

Me aged eleven showing my skills to brother John in the street.

Top: It's 1987, and that's how we all looked then! Cousin Sally, Nicola, my girlfriend Debbie, me and Dad.

Above: Another celebration: Nicola's marriage to Gary, with me, John and my parents happy to look on.

In action for Torquay reserves in August 1987, just a few weeks before I made my League debut. I'm the stick insect in yellow battling for the ball.

Just three and a half years later, in March 1991, and still not twenty years old, I came on to make my debut for England, against Ireland and my United team-mate Denis Irwin. (*Colorsport*)

Relaxing with Gary Lineker, who was my room-mate ahead of my debut and helped ensure that that I stayed as calm as possible. (*Popperfoto*)

Always a highlight for anyone: taking on Brazil, here during a summer friendly in 1993. (*Colorsport*)

August 1996: signing for Leeds, while chairman Bill Fotherby and manager Howard Wilkinson look on. Sadly, Howard Wilkinson was soon out of a job and I faced a period of injuries and uncertainty. (*Empics*)

Taking on former team-mate Gary Neville. I was never to end up on the winning side at Old Trafford after I left. (*Colorsport*)

My last game in the first team for Leeds, against Roma in the UEFA Cup in November 1998. I'd been out for ages and hadn't a chance. After that, I just wanted to move on. (*Empics*)

Celebrating promotion to the Premier League in May 1999. (*Getty Images*)

A 1–0 win over Liverpool in May 2000 kept Bradford up in the top flight. Now Geoffrey Richmond had his chance to put his stamp on the club. (*Empics*)

Every picture tells its own story: on loan at Portsmouth, where Graham Rix was one of the very best managers I ever played for. (*Colorsport*) magnificent football talents. The reason you can see that this was Alex Ferguson's attitude is because one of the biggest drinkers at that time, an awesome drinker not under any circumstances to be kept pace with, was the manager's great warrior and standard bearer: Bryan Robson.

Robbo was king of everything at United at that time. There were occasions when he'd start drinking in an afternoon or evening, then drink all night. I've seen him carry on through, have a champagne breakfast, then go on into the next day drinking, even up to the evening, and have another night out on the piss. Throughout, he mostly just chats away, doesn't look like it's touched him. He might get a bit glassy-eyed, slur his words, but that was usually all.

Then, the next day, Bryan Robson would be in training, in his kit, right at the front of the group running round Littleton Road, sprinting as fast as anyone, usually the best player on the pitch in a five-a-side, covering every blade of grass, Captain Marvel.

He used to organise nights out for everyone, team bonding sessions that he'd clear with the manager. He'd book somewhere and get everyone out, young lads included. Or in those early days I'd sometimes find myself out with them because I was in the first team, and the real old-schoolers would be there, Robbo, Norman Whiteside, having lunch at two o'clock, drinking all day, ending up in some pub or club. Some of us would be chatting up women and taking phone numbers.

When I started going out a lot myself three or four years later, Alex Ferguson called me in. In eight years under him, for all that passed between the manager and me, that was the only time I can remember a proper, calm, sit-down chat, a few moments for some fatherly advice. The advice was this: I must never think I could be like Bryan Robson. I told him not to worry, I never would. Alex Ferguson said: 'Robbo's a freak. Nobody could be like him; nobody could go out like him, drink like him, and still be able to perform as a player as he does. You can't live like that.'

On the field, Robbo was awesome. He used to run the whole show. The pace of a game depended on how quick or slow Bryan Robson wanted to play. He controlled their fans, our fans, the referee, both sides. That first season, we played Tottenham at home in early February. I was playing left-back, and I'd just nicked the ball away from Paul Stewart, the Tottenham striker, back to our keeper, Jim Leighton, then as I turned away Stewart's studs caught my Achilles, which put me down on the floor in agony. Bryan Robson thought he'd done it deliberately and was straight in, saying that it was out of order, I was only a kid, it was uncalled for, all the rest of it. As I got up, Robbo was asking me if I was all right.

Twenty minutes later, one of their centre-halves played the ball to Paul Stewart just inside the centre circle. Stewart was on the half-turn, he was going to let the ball run on then come at us with it, and as he turned Bryan Robson just came steaming in from the side. He got the ball all right, but he wasn't worried if his boot also caught Stewart's shin. His fists clenched in determination, Robbo caught him in the stomach as he was falling to the deck, which practically lifted him up in the air. Then Stewart fell to earth, not knowing what was hurting him the most, his leg or his stomach.

Mark Hughes was another: so good it was scary. He was only 5' 11", a quiet, unassuming family man off the pitch – although he liked a drink with the lads too – but when he got out onto a football pitch he was like a Marvel comic hero, Popeye on a tin of spinach, suddenly all rippling muscles and elemental aggression, wrestling 6' 4" centre-halves, perhaps two at a time, holding them off, controlling any pass, however poor and wherever it arrived, on his ankle, his Adam's apple, anything, then, without looking, volleying it forty yards right to the feet of our winger on the other side of the pitch. His legs were probably three times as thick as mine. I saw Terry Fenwick break his own leg booting Sparky on the shin; it was just scary.

For me and his team-mates he was a dream; you could give him the worst ball in the world and know that he'd turn it into quality. Half the time that first season at left-back, I'd have a quick look up, see Sparky coming across in his red shirt and know I could just knock it up the line and he'd make it look like a good ball. Awesome, and a very important signing for Alex Ferguson, bringing presence and aggression to the team, which was still in transition, still under a lot of pressure.

Lee Martin got into the side at left-back in the first game of the season, then I replaced him, then he was in and out a bit, playing right-back sometimes, or left-back if I was moved up to left-wing. Russell Beardsmore, the little right-winger, got his debut in the same game as me, against West Ham, coming off the bench in place of Billy Garton, the centre-half. One or two other young players, like Mark Robins and Giuliano Maiorana, were given a few games that season, and that flush of youth in the United side earned for Alex Ferguson some favourable press talk, a bit of a buzz about 'Fergie's Fledglings', which was quite important to him. It gave him something positive to show, that he was bringing on a new generation, particularly as we now know he was planning to clear Norman Whiteside and Paul McGrath out of the club that summer, which was a dramatic decision. It gave Alex Ferguson that play on 'Busby's Babes', a link made in the public's mind, and the fans', with United's great days, even if this side was far from what he wanted yet. The fledglings were a statement, even if few ever really flew.

It was magical for me, all of this, but also a bit weird, once I found my feet a little. I was in the first team right through until March, when I got a hernia. So I played against Liverpool, who we beat 3–1 on New Year's Day at Old Trafford in front of a massive crowd, and away at Arsenal – rolling up at the great old ground, stepping off the coach and into the players' entrance, into the grand dressing rooms with under-floor heating, the kit all laid out, number 3 for me, to play my steady left-back game. I went to Villa Park as a player, making runs down the left wing. How unbelievable is all this? I used to think. Am I living the dream or what? I couldn't get my head round it, it was so utterly fantastic to be there.

Then I'd have to come back to a shared room in digs in Salford, where there were nine apprentices nowhere near the first team, whiling away their youths with pranks, mayhem and carnage. There was no privacy whatsoever. It didn't matter that Shaun Goater was a great guy and I liked sharing a room with him. I'd come back from away matches really late at night or early in the morning. The coach would drop most of the senior lads off in south Manchester, where they lived in Hale Barns or Wilmslow or further out, then by the time we got to Old Trafford, there'd be just me and a couple of other young lads who still lived with their mum and dad, the kit man and the physio. They'd drop us off and we might do something silly, like race our cars from Old Trafford back to Salford or wherever, and finally I'd pull into my digs in Brenda's house at one or two in the morning.

The big, sagging house was dark and usually quiet. I used to let myself in, then I'd open the door into our room and find Shaun Goater sitting right in front of the gas fire, with two pairs of jogging bottoms on, three pairs of socks, four jumpers, gloves, a woolly hat – poor guy, he'd come over from Bermuda, was living in deepest, darkest Salford in the middle of a Manchester winter and he couldn't get warm. I'd ask him what he was doing.

'Man, it's absolutely freezing; it's hell.'

Then we'd sit up chatting away for hours, till three, four in the morning, eating biscuits and chocolates. He was really funny too. He used to do brilliant impressions, whole routines in fact. He'd come into the dining room where we all were and would act out a sports scene, maybe Muhammad Ali boxing, and he'd jab and punch and commentate on himself, act out hitting the ropes and bouncing back, or he'd be Michael Jordan with thirty seconds to go in a match, bouncing the basketball, passing to Scotty Pippin, getting it back, shooting the basket. The lads would all sit, mesmerised, and at the end give him a huge round of applause. He was great, barmy. He came home with me a few times and stayed with my mum and dad in Birmingham; I think he liked a bit of home comfort because he was so far away from home himself in our freezing hellhole of a country.

The digs did my head in after a while because when I was away so much with the first team, the lads used to rifle all my stuff. My dad had a card for Makro, the cash-and-carry, so we used to go and buy big job lots of sweets and jellies,

Maltesers and biscuits, mainly for me to have when I was getting in from matches at midnight or one in the morning and there was no food in the kitchen. But I'd get in and find the lads had just been through everything, scoffed the lot. It started to get me down. I'd find they'd been wearing my clothes to go out on a Saturday night; my jumpers and coats would be gone or thrown down on the bed or the floor. Nothing was private.

Down at the Cliff their dressing room was still a barrack-room free-for-all. They used to hold mock court cases, in which players would be 'tried' for something that had happened in training. Someone would speak for him and someone against, then a jury would decide if he was guilty or innocent. There was a nice range of sadistic punishments lying in wait for the guilty: in the winter, in the snow, one seventeen-year-old lad had to do a lap of the pitch with nothing on apart from his boots, and everyone stood in the middle snowballing him. They had all sorts of games; there was one where a player had to put his face in front of the space between the legs of the treatment table and people had to volley a ball just right, through the space and into the guy's face. Kids used to be put in kit bags and skips and tied up, or stripped off and shoe polish put all over them when it was their birthday, then sent out to run round the pitch.

Sean McAuley used to get lads on the medical bench in the middle of the dressing room, simulating sex with their girlfriend, how they'd done it. There was a classic one with a young lad, Jimmy Shields from Salford, a chunky, cheeky kid always ready with the backchat. He was up on the bench; he had his shorts on but he was really getting into it, moaning and screaming and oohs and aahs, and by the end he really was having full-on sex in his mind, slapping the bench and all sorts. When he finished, there was complete silence, because Archie Knox had walked into the dressing room and been standing there for two minutes watching the climax.

So Archie Knox said to Jimmy Shields: 'Wait there, lad, don't move a muscle.' He went straight to the first-team dressing room, rounded up all the first-team players into the apprentices' room and said to Jimmy: 'Right, lad, do it again. Show the lads what you've been doing.'

Jimmy had no choice; he was deep in trouble as it was. So he had to do it again in front of twenty apprentices and twenty-five first-teamers, plus the reserve team could see something was going on and were starting to arrive to have a look. So Jimmy got to do the whole show again in front of forty, fifty people, screaming and moaning and shouting and going aah, aah, aah at the end and slapping the bench until finally he collapsed on the bench and got a massive cheer and huge round of applause from everybody.

It was another thing which went around in circles; generations of young boys had come into football clubs and been messed about. Some of it was a good laugh, larks, pranks, passing the time, but underneath it was very competitive too. All the young lads are in competition for places, for jobs. None of the lads I was with, not one, came through to a decent career at United. And that is always there underneath, that it's dog eat dog, on the pitch, in the dressing room, in banter, so you never really relax. I laughed with everyone and enjoyed what there was to enjoy, but some of it was bullying, especially of the schoolboys who came in, and I think they had to stamp some of it out in the end.

At first, I didn't stay around at the weekend. I used to go home, straight after the game sometimes, and go out with my mates, potter about at home, or see Debbie, because we were back on again. It was probably around Christmas that I first started staying up for the weekend, edging into Manchester, and my mates from Birmingham used to come up sometimes and stay over in a hotel somewhere. I had a few bob from being in the first team, £150 appearance money, which knocked my basic wage up to £320 a week, plus bonuses, and another £150 if we played twice in the week, so fantastic money, really, at seventeen.

The first place we started to go was called Saturdays, a little nightclub under the Britannia Hotel in Piccadilly. It was one of those places where you could take your player's pass and get in for nothing, so quite a few of the reserves used to go on a Saturday night, and I tagged along, all unsure of myself. It was an awful place really – small, dark, cheesy, tacky. We used to have a few beers, maybe try to chat girls up. It was all quite tentative and innocent; I'd never really been out in a city before. My mum and dad's house is ten miles outside Birmingham and when I'd lived at home I never looked old enough to get into pubs or clubs anyway, so never really went out. In Torquay we did get in under-age, but it was a homely little place, very placid and manageable. This was my first taste of living in a big city and having a certain amount of freedom – within the limits of Alex Ferguson's prying eyes. Manchester's obviously a big place for going out; there's an edge too, plenty going on, and I felt my way shakily but eagerly into sampling its delights.

Coming back from the hernia towards the end of the season, I was playing with the reserves to get fit, and a few of us used to venture out on Saturdays after the game. Giuliano Maiorana, who'd come from non-league, so he'd lived a 'normal' life for a couple of years before joining United, Deiniol Graham, a Welsh lad, Andy Rammel, who joined Barnsley later – we'd go to Saturdays, or up to a couple of bars near the top entrance of the Arndale, a Yates's Wine Lodge, and another place whose name escapes me, which served hot wine.

I didn't drink much at all. I didn't drink beer because I didn't like the taste; but I found I could take a few bottles of cider, which would give me a bit of Dutch courage eventually to talk to girls. We used to have some lads' nights out, find a nightclub we could get into, get back at two, three in the morning, and slowly, five, six months later, I found I was comfortable enough going out in Manchester to start enjoying myself.

Debbie and I got back together properly, now I had a car and we could see more of each other when I went down to Birmingham. I'd been seeing her for so long, on and off – she was my childhood sweetheart; my mum was still utterly convinced we were going to get married – and we talked about whether we should make a real go of it and move in together. Towards the end of that first season I was desperate to get out of the digs, to escape Sean McAuley's regime, the games of Darkness, the non-stop pranks and not enough to eat and everybody pilfering my gear.

I had a long chat with Debbie; I had to talk her into it really. We'd been out and split up and been out again and split up again so many times, so this was me really saying that if she left her mum and came up to Manchester we'd give it a real go. I told her everything would be fine, she'd make new friends eventually, find a new job and I'd look after her, and in the end we decided that, yes, she was going to give up her job and come and live with me. So I then had the small matter of asking my nice father figure of a manager for his blessing. It wasn't normal for a young lad to move out of digs; it was football club practice to have the young lads looked after by landladies who they thought would keep an eye on them and where the temptations were fewer – which was true, as there was nothing to do. But I'd been in the first team for the whole season until I had the hernia and thought he should let me move out.

I went to see him, said I was sick of the digs, that my girlfriend would move up and live with me if he let me get my own place. Alex Ferguson wasn't at all sure, and he took his time over it. 'Do you love this girl?' he asked me, and I was like: 'Yeah, I've been with her steadily since I was fourteen; I wouldn't be moving her up if I didn't.'

He said: 'Well, I'm not keen really. I think you're a bit young to live on your own, but OK. But if it affects your performances, you're straight back in digs, right?'

That was a great deal, believe me. You could tell he liked me, then. It was a relief and a coup, to get his permission, so at eighteen I bought my first house, a little new-build in Whitefield, five miles north of Manchester near the M62 roundabout. In the summer, Debbie moved up to be with me. How perfect: a Manchester United starlet and his adorable young missus, school-time lovers, cosy, with our own house and a couple of cars, a bit of money and a lovely future stretching away ahead of us.

CHAPTER 6

Moving out the house

While Debbie and I were buying a bed and kitchen gear, and making sure the telly was at exactly the right angle to be viewed from cuddling position on the sofa, Alex Ferguson was making his era-stamping moves at United. At the time, clearing out Norman Whiteside and big Paul McGrath was seen as almost reckless, but he wanted fewer drinking sessions at Harpers and more shuttle sprints at Littleton Road, I think. Gordon Strachan had gone to Leeds in the March, and Ferguson was given big money to spend to create his own side: Neil Webb, one of the country's most authoritative central midfielders, came from Forest for £1.5m; Gary Pallister, just twenty-four, arrived from Middlesbrough for a £2.3m fee which made him a nervous wreck for months. Paul Ince was the self-styled 'guv'nor' in midfield, all over the pitch, and there eventually to take over from Bryan Robson, a good lad and a great player at the time, although the guv'nor thing did make him ripe for a bit of piss-take, especially as the longer you spent with him, the more you realised his wife was the real guv'nor in their house. Mike Phelan, who is still involved at United as a coach, arrived that summer from Norwich, another major signing at £750,000. And people forget that Danny Wallace, a major star at the time, a left-winger, so a challenge for me, came to United for £1.2m in the September.

Beneath the headlines, there was a constant letting-go of the young lads I'd lived with: Wayne Heseltine, to Oldham for £40,000; Shaun Goater, sent to Rotherham, who paid £30,000. One of the fledglings, Tony Gill, one of the nicest lads you could ever meet, had been clattered in a match against Nottingham Forest the previous season and had to give up the game through injury. One by one they were falling. I was there, straight in the first team again, moved up to left-wing in my second season because Clayton Blackmore was playing left-back at first, Russell Beardsmore was pushing for a place, and so was Lee Martin, who would finally get a good run in the team and have a fantastic season.

The first game of that season, against QPR in the August sunshine, is best remembered not for any of the new big-name arrivals, but for someone none of the players had ever heard of, a guy with a moustache and kit which was tight round his considerable frame, jogging out onto the pitch and scoring a hat-trick in the goal at the Stretford End when there was no keeper in it – Michael Knighton. His juggling act was as bizarre to the players as it was to everybody else; as a player you don't have too much to do with the directors, except every few years when it is time to renew a contract. I was never the kind of player who took much of an interest in what was happening in the boardroom, certainly not at eighteen, and even now, with United being taken over by the American, Malcolm Glazer, for a lot more than Michael Knighton was ever committed to, you can see the players keeping out of it, mostly concerned with their own positions, their own game, their own contracts. Obviously we thought he didn't belong on the pitch, and not long after that his deal with Martin Edwards was called off. Generally it is seen as the moment when United recognised the commercial opportunities for the club in the game's future, leading to their float on the Stock Market two years later and the start of the commercial revolution at Old Trafford.

Backed with so many millions by United's board in the summer of 1989, Alex Ferguson, the players and the club were under tremendous pressure to deliver success in return. We used to see it in him, the nerves, eating him up, making his fingers twitch, his face mottled. He used to talk too much before matches, although he always tried to hide it from the players. The first game of the season could hardly have gone better, a 4–1 win against Arsenal, who'd won the League the previous season, and I played in the first six games, although after that start we had a bit of a nightmare, drawing at Crystal Palace then losing three on the trot, including 2–0 at home to Norwich on 30 August. Gary Pallister had come in for that game so right from the beginning he was having to prove that United had bought more than some lanky lump who froze under pressure. We beat Millwall 5–1 a fortnight later, when Mark Hughes scored a hat-trick, Robbo got one, and the last one came from me – my first goal for United. That was Incey's United debut, so things looked reasonable the week before we were due to play the derby at Maine Road against Manchester City, who'd only just come up from the Second Division, with a team of youngsters, the previous season.

It was all so exciting for me. I wasn't wrapped up in the soap-opera history of the great football club. It was a dream to be playing for them and, at home, life was sweet. Debbie and I had our nice two-bedroom little mews house; I'd drive into training and to matches, then come back to domestic bliss. We didn't go out much; we'd cook tea, then sit around the house, watch telly, cuddle up and go to bed. I spent all my time with her, especially at first, because she was away from her mum and all her friends and didn't know anyone. She used to watch me play, sitting with the other players' wives and girlfriends, not every match, but quite a few, then on Saturday nights we'd usually go out, meet up with a couple of the other young reserve-team players, some with girlfriends, some not. We'd have a night out in Manchester, go to dingy old Saturdays where people knew us, or Piccadilly 21, which was a big club at that time. We'd have a few drinks, a dance and a laugh; she got to meet some people, girlfriends, gradually. Quite a few weekends, we'd go back to Birmingham, where everyone was more than happy with our situation. I was too, it was all perfect and I'm sure I thought we were heading for getting married and that'd be nice.

Alex Ferguson made me sub for the City match, I think because he thought it might be too hostile for me at eighteen, away at Maine Road, and I'm not going to argue with his decision now. It was the most famous defeat of Ferguson's early years, shell-shock, our team of expensive new signings losing 5–1 to City's mostly local lads, Ian Brightwell, Paul Lake, Steve Redmond, David White, who were totally up for it, desperate to give United a hammering. No United player performed really well, the City fans chanted 'waste of money' at everyone, and Pally, particularly, had a nightmare. The manager sent me on with about twenty minutes to go – I think he wanted me to experience what it was like to lose like that – but I didn't get any of the vitriol afterwards because it was all over by the time I got on. Actually, I think he was fairly quiet, just stunned afterwards; it was obviously his worst day at United, possibly ever in football management, and it really piled the pressure on his head. We could all see it, the whole club could feel it, as we went into an awful run during which all the papers were saying he was going to get fired.

He put me back in two weeks later; we beat Coventry 4–1 away, then Southampton at home. Pally managed to get one to beat Forest 1–0 at home in November. The crowd was down to 34,000 and the fans were calling for the manager to go. He earned a lot of respect from the players because he tried to shield us from the worst of it and never criticised us in public, something players always appreciate him for, but then December was the cruellest month: we didn't win for weeks, losing to Arsenal, Palace, Spurs and Villa.

That was when my honeymoon with Alex Ferguson ended. My memory has played tricks on me because what happened is mixed in my mind with a fearsome bollocking he lashed out on Ryan Giggs and me at half time in a match at Anfield against Liverpool, but Giggsy was still an apprentice at this time, didn't even get his full debut until the end of the following season, 1990–91, so this first bollocking must have been during one of the grim December defeats in 1989. Nobody was particularly playing well, me certainly included. I couldn't find my feet, I'd given the ball away a few times, I wasn't getting past people or causing enough of a threat. But the team was on an awful losing streak; it can't have all been down to me.

The manager came in at half time and he was absolutely fuming, losing it, going red. He had a go at everyone, at a few individuals, at the team, then he turned to me. It was as if he wasn't the same person who asked how your mum and dad were, did they have tickets, was everything all right.

'And Sharpe,' he roared, 'I don't know what the fuck you're doing out there; you might as well be sat next to me, you're fucking rubbish! I don't know what's going on in your head.'

He didn't come right over to me and do it in my face, not this time. He kept the hairdryer in reserve and did it from the middle of the room.

'Sharpe, you're fucking rubbish. You're playing like a fucking schoolboy.'

All that sort of stuff, which I took. It's pretty unpleasant and personal, and I'm not saying it didn't get to me, because I think it affected me very badly, but you deal with it by thinking he's getting stuff off his chest because he's under pressure, so you try not to take it to heart. But then he said:

'I've fucking had enough of this. You've been playing shit lately. Your girlfriend's down the road and you're moving back in digs where I can keep an eye on you. I told you if your performances dip then you'll be back in digs and you've been shit ever since, so that's it, I've had enough, she's going back to Birmingham and I'm going to sort some digs out and you'll be in digs on Monday. Now go out there and perform.'

Pretty easy to concentrate after that. If my head hadn't

been on it in the first half, I'm sure it was nowhere in the second. Of course, after the game, there were a couple of mickey-takers on the coach; you don't look to a group of footballers for tea and sympathy. I remember Steve Bruce having a joke at me, asking me how much I wanted for my house, saying he'd give me a good price.

The manager might just have been releasing his own pent-up frustration, because he was under pressure for his own job. But I had to move out of my house; and my girlfriend, who had moved up just a few months earlier, had to go home to Birmingham. So I had to troop back to our little love nest and tell Debbie she had to leave. How pathetic must I have looked to her? She'd jacked her job in and left her mum and all her friends, to come up to Manchester where she knew nobody, just to be with me so we could really make a go of it, and now, a few months later, I'm crawling back from a defeat, moping and sulky, mumbling something about Alex Ferguson telling me I had to go back to digs and sell the house, and that she had to go home.

She was like: 'What? He can't say nowt, it's not up to him.'

I started to explain, uselessly, my arms dangling limp at my sides, that, well, he could, and it was a sort of unwritten rule that players stay in digs until they're nineteen, twenty. Before that they're usually apprentices so they either live in digs or at home with their parents. I said that the manager had said I could move out but if my performances dipped I'd have to go back in digs, and now I was going to have to do what he said.

Debbie didn't stomp around or scream, she was just silent. I don't think she could believe what I was saying.

Then she got quite upset, started crying. It was horrible. She said: 'I hope you realise, if I've got to go home, that's us finished.'

She didn't mean definitely; she just meant that we'd moved forward, gone from childhood sweethearts to living together, and if she went home it would be a step backwards, change everything again. We'd see each other only at weekends and it could split us up in the end. And she was right, that's pretty much what happened – she went back and we struggled to keep it together, living in different cities, me back in dismal digs with nothing to do.

Because it was the first time I'd taken it from Alex Ferguson, that total, unmitigated bollocking, not much humanity seeping out at the corners, I thought I must be finished. I thought it must mean he was fed up with me and couldn't stand me any more. I'd never experienced people talking to me that way before, and I'd never had it from anybody in authority. I always respected my granddad, my dad, my teachers, football managers, and everybody had mostly been positive, pats on the back, words of encouragement. I was brought up to believe what authority figures said, and to act on their words, so when my manager started nailing me, I thought he must really think I'm rubbish, he hates me, he's going to get rid of me like he is most of the other young lads. I talked it over with my mum and dad, but they said, no, it wasn't like that, he was telling me off because he cared about me, otherwise he wouldn't have bothered. So I thought: OK, maybe that's true. And I did work hard to get my form back.

The digs they moved me into were, guess where? Back in Lower Broughton, opposite the Cliff. Hello Darkness, my old friend. I refused to go back to Brenda's because there were too many in there and it was carnage, so they put me round the corner where there were fewer United lodgers but the family were real Salford scallies. There were a mum and dad, a son of about fifteen and a daughter of perhaps twenty or so who used to look down on us all for being kids, have a go at us and tell us to shut up all the time.

Wayne Bullimore was one of the players in there, so we knocked about together quite a bit. Good lad, Bully, and I loved him as a player; he had unbelievable feet. I went on holiday with him a few times; we used to stand on opposite sides of the swimming pool and play keepy-uppy, knocking the ball across – you weren't allowed to drop it or let it land in the pool – and the things he could do were phenomenal. He just lacked that natural pace which I was blessed with, but his feet, ability, the things he could do were out of this world, scary. There were a couple of Irish lads in there too, and Mark Bosnich, the young Australian goalkeeper, who was just discovering his unique ability to get himself in loads of bother.

The food in these digs was abysmal. I remember in the pre-season we'd done two sessions and we were absolutely starving. It was roast night, and the family were all tucking in; lovely juicy beef, thick gravy, loads of potatoes and steaming dumplings. And we young footballers, on a separate table, were all given one cold slice of ham, and a bit of salad.

We were like Oliver Twist: 'Er, have you got any more ham, like?'

I had to pay £60 for this privilege, on top of the mortgage on my house, which I had to put up for sale but wasn't allowed to live in. I went from living and sleeping with Debbie to a tiny box room up at the top of this house, where it was freezing cold because the heating wasn't very good. I had a single bed, a chest of drawers with my telly on top of it, and a wardrobe, which left barely enough space to walk through to get to my bed. I can't say I ever worked out why that was meant to be better for me than living a decent life like a grown-up. Perhaps the manager had something, in his old-fashioned idea that I'd gone soft living with Debbie, too comfortable. Down in digs in Salford there is nothing to think about but the football; you get treated as a kid and the club is your only existence. The landlady is supposed to keep an eye on you; she knows what time you're coming in, what you're eating, and they can keep you on a Spartan regime. Perhaps, though, there ought to be other ways of motivating a young player than doing this to him.

I'd now seen a different side to Alex Ferguson, and I would never lose that impression. Looking back, whatever his reasoning, it seems heartless to me, doing it like that at half time. The end result was that a year or two later, when it was all happening for me, my career had taken off, I was famous, a young superstar and women were practically queuing up for a chance to get their hands on me, Alex Ferguson was concerned that I was seeing too many girls, and wanting me to settle down. He used to ask, 'Are you not married yet?' Occasionally, in a jokey way but with a bit of steel behind it, I used to say: 'Well, I could have been, but you made my girlfriend go home and kicked me out of my house.' He just used to laugh at that, as if I were ribbing him; as if it were just banter.

Debbie and I never got back to where it was, although we tried. We drifted apart because it was difficult long distance. I used to go out a bit more in Manchester on

Saturdays after matches and in the week. On my travels, I met a girl from Oldham, Georgina, and saw her for about three months, but I still had strong feelings for Debbie and we used to talk on the phone. One time there was a call for me on the payphone we had downstairs in the digs. I was on the top floor, so Mark Bosnich answered it and this girl asked for Lee, and he said: 'Oh yeah, is that Georgina?' I came down the stairs and it was Debbie on the phone, wanting to know who the hell Georgina was, so I had a hole to dig myself out of. Cheers, Bozzy. But that brought us together again, because we got talking, and one time we arranged to meet up at Keele service station, which was about halfway between Manchester and Birmingham on the M6. It was tearful, emotional; I was madly in love with her, besotted by her, and I had wanted to spend the rest of my life with her. She was telling me she still loved me too, and what the hell should we do about it, so we did get together again after that, and tried to keep it going.

Meanwhile United had continued their losing streak, with Alex Ferguson scurrying about, red-faced, under tremendous pressure, and you could feel the club almost struggling for its breathing. It's widely accepted now that with United going into 1990 fifteenth in the league, despite all the millions he'd been given to spend, Ferguson was facing the sack when we went down to the City Ground to play Forest in the FA Cup third round. I didn't play, because I was injured by then – after a 0–0 draw against QPR on New Year's Day, I was out for the rest of the season with a double hernia. Lee Martin had made the left-back spot his own – another right-footed left-back for United. Russell Beardsmore played on the right wing, and in the end, in a really grim battle, it was another fledgling, Mark Robins, who scored one of his poacher's goals, won the game for United, saved Alex Ferguson his job and began to take United back up again.

I watched most of that FA Cup run as a fan. My cousin's a Man U supporter and I used to go to the games with him and stand up with United's fans. I loved it, went mad, jumped around and sang all the songs. It was a great way to follow United – I was still only eighteen, younger than most of the fans – and I got to know what it was like for them, to follow us. I felt as if I bonded with them and understood them, became one of them as a result of it. United played away at Hereford in the next round and I went to that with my cousin, standing with all the hardcore away fans, and when we scored I was jumping up and down, I was on someone's back, like a proper supporter, chanting all the songs. A few months later I was at a home match in the stands at Old Trafford with my mum and dad, still injured. I was coming through with a cup of coffee or something for my mum, and spilt it all over the back of the leather jacket of this big, burly, hard-looking guy in front.

He turned round. I thought I was in big trouble, then he went: 'Oh it's you.'

So I started saying: 'Listen, I'm really sorry, mate…'

And he said: 'Forget it. I was at Hereford a while back and when that goal went in you jumped higher than any of us, so I know you're one of us. Don't worry about it.'

Every week leading up to matches at this time, you could feel the tension building in the club again, then if we won or got a decent draw, there would be a massive release, then it would all start to build up again till the following

Saturday. League form was never great; there was a decent patch at the end of March and into April when we won four matches on the trot and Mark Robins was knocking them in, but that only took us up to fourteenth in the league, not what the board had been looking for. The manager was still under pressure.

What saved him, and ultimately created a platform for all the success we'd have, was the FA Cup run. We beat Newcastle 3–2, Mark Robins scoring again, along with Brian McClair and Danny Wallace, then Sheffield United, 1–0, in the quarter-final. The semi-final saw those legendary, brilliant games at Maine Road against Joe Royle's excellent Oldham side – whose full-back, Denis Irwin, impressed Alex Ferguson so much he signed him to play eleven unbelievably consistent years for Man U. Eventually, in extra time in the replay, who else but Mark Robins, the little local lad with a Vauxhall Nova 1.2 which he kept painfully clean, came on as sub and scored the winner to take United to Wembley to play Crystal Palace.

I still couldn't play but I got measured up for a suit with all the lads, we made a record which went to number one, we stayed together for two or three days at a hotel before the match, did lots of bonding and team-building activities, in fact, really made the most of the whole experience of being in a Cup final. It was a big thing to Man United then; not like later when we used to turn up and it was just another game.

The first game was 3–3, the entertaining one when Ian Wright came off the bench to score two, make his name and get himself a nice move to Arsenal, so we went back in midweek for a horrible game when Crystal Palace kicked our lads all over the pitch, then, late on, Neil Webb stroked the ball across to Lee Martin, who was arriving from absolutely nowhere to cut inside and lash the ball into the roof of the net to win Manchester United the FA Cup. Great moment for Schnozz: you can see him in the film of it lying on the ground with all the lads on top of him; it was because he had cramp, he always got cramp, so he couldn't get up.

So, after a grim season, United's worst for years, we somehow won the Cup, Alex Ferguson's first success, the one everybody says kept him his job, earned him another chance. A sigh of relief settled over Old Trafford, not complacency, but at least the club had won something, had a platform to build on for next season, more time for some of the new lads to find their feet. Of those I came through with none lasted very much longer. Wayne Bullimore, Nicky Wood, Paul Dalton, skilful players who were the big hopes when I got there, Shaun Goater, Deiniol Graham and others were gone to the lower divisions after barely a sniff of a chance. Tony Gill was crocked out of the game. Lee Martin had back problems and other injuries, maybe struggled a little for pace although he was a very good full-back. Eventually he went to Celtic, but couldn't keep a career going for many more years. Mark Robins was another who lacked just a bit of pace as the game quickened up in the early 1990s and was sold to Norwich in August 1992. Russell Beardsmore struggled too in the Premier League era and went to Bournemouth in June 1993. People say I chucked it all away later on, but there's another way of looking at it: I did phenomenally well. I was the only one to come through, and I never got any of the coaching they'd said I'd have. I came from Torquay after six games and was just thrown straight in, sink or swim. I played left-back with barely a word of advice about what to do there: just stay goalside of your man; that was about it. But I did it, I put my head down and worked, and kept my place, when I wasn't injured. I was still regarded as a great prospect. I had golden days ahead. Some of the lads weren't ever going to make it, especially when the game began to speed up, but some feel they might have done, feel they were thrown in early, to make a statement that United, Alex Ferguson, believed in youth, then they were moved on without much ceremony once they weren't needed. United have a reputation as a club which nurtures young men, but a hell of a lot came, stocked up those high, damp terraced houses down in darkest Salford, and were shipped right out again. We'll never know if some of them might have made it, given more time and a more stable club, a manager not always one defeat from the sack. What we can say is that in the end the young lads kept him his job. It was the fledglings wot won it.

CHAPTER 7

Highbury hat-trick

It was 28 November 1990, a Tuesday night, a League Cup fourth-round tie under floodlights, United wearing that blue and white away kit which didn't last long, the night it all came together for me, when I hit the big time and found myself dancing round Highbury scoring a hat-trick for Manchester United in a 6–2 win over Arsenal. When you're a boy, tucked up under your duvet with your football and new boots for the coming season, your little head full of thoughts of one day being a footballer, do you dare dream of it being that good? Not just that you might one day play for a big club and score a goal, but score three – a twenty-five-yard curler, a nice little header and a crisp right-foot finish – on telly, for Manchester United, against the England goalkeeper and League Champions? Can it get that good?

That's the night everybody remembers about my career. Football wasn't all over the TV at that time and still not on satellite. It wasn't long after Hillsborough, before the Premier League started, football was only beginning to be thought of as sexy and acceptable and there seems to have been something memorable about my enormous smile, beaming through the gloom on the ITV highlights. It was the culmination of everything I'd dreamed of since being a small boy, and worked hard to achieve as a young man, from breaking through at Torquay, to training and playing at United. It was a fabulous night, unbelievable, that it could actually happen, to me.

We always did well against Arsenal, even when they were winning Leagues under George Graham with their dreary defending and breakaways for 1–0 wins. As I was to discover when the great man became my own manager at Leeds, he used to make his teams defend by trying to push wingers inside all the time. He was paranoid about the opposition getting down the line and crossing it. At United, we countered this by passing the ball across, playing possession, across and back, across and back, probing for when the defence would crack and leave an opening, then hit them really hard. That night, we didn't do anything very different, but Clayton Blackmore scored from a free-kick after just eighty seconds and I suppose that rocked them back. I played a part in the second goal, which Mark Hughes scored. The ball came to me, I controlled it, passed it on to Danny Wallace, he touched it across to Sparky, who put it away – and that was typical of how we played, two-touch. People see highlights of my time at Man U and think I must have been getting crosses in all the time or scoring spectacular goals, but in a good side it isn't like that; most of the time I was playing my part in the team, two-touch, possession, running off the ball, so that whoever was on it had options. In some ways, that night my goals were a freak.

The first one, Danny Wallace had a run at them and was blocked on the edge of the box. Nigel Winterburn knocked it forward to Lee Dixon, who was about twenty-five yards out over towards our left-hand side. He couldn't control it; it spun off his foot and I ran in on the diagonal and nicked it away from him. The ball was stuck a little under my feet, so I had another couple of touches to get it in front of me, then they were closing me down. I actually slid and, as I did, side-footed it with my right foot. It left the floor beautifully, soared up, curled, dipped just a little over David Seaman as he dived, hit the underside of the bar and went in. In! A twenty-five-yard side-footed curler, with my right foot, had just beaten David Seaman. You can see on the highlights that I celebrate, but I also run around in a circle. I'm delighted, but I can't believe it. Then I'm down on my knees with my arms outstretched – just look at what I've done! – and the lads are coming up, Brian McClair, Sparky, Danny Wallace, Gary Pallister, all over me, and none of them can believe it either.

So, 3–0 at half time, but then Arsenal came out, scored two and for a while it didn't feel so easy. Then I got my second. A header. I don't score headers; I might have scored three in my career. This one was actually quite a textbook finish. Mark Hughes, inevitably, rode some horrible challenge in the box, knocked it wide right to Denis Irwin. He crossed it high and inviting into the middle. I was running in from midfield with nobody near me, leapt high off the ground, met the ball on the edge of the six-yard box and headed it down, glanced but firm, into the opposite left-hand corner. David Seaman got absolutely nowhere near it. This time it was where our fans were, behind that goal, so I went running over to them, down on my knees, my arms at my sides, and you can see the fans, who'd gone down to London on a

Tuesday night, absolutely beside themselves.

Then I got another. Danny Wallace had the ball between the centre circle and their box, surrounded. I sprinted past him with nobody coming with me, and he laid it into my path. I was perhaps fifteen yards out, just to the right-hand side. David Seaman was narrowing the angle, and I hit it, right foot again, low to his right. He got a hand to it but it was too hard and it went straight in the corner. This time I hardly knew what to do with myself. It was the absolute peak of everything you could ever imagine happening: we'd got the League Champions, at their ground, and they were so totally beaten, they didn't know what day it was. We were playing great football, on the deck, just slicing through them. I was fast and strong and everything I was doing was flying in, so I ran over to our fans and actually did a somersault this time, getting up with this enormous smile, as wide as the Highbury goal, as bright as the floodlights. Our fans were going mad, already thinking this is one of the matches they're going to be boasting proudly of having been at. On the ITV commentary, Clive Tyldesley said: 'A boy has become a man tonight. Lee Sharpe has grown up, with a dramatic hat-trick.'

Danny Wallace ran in the last one: 6–2. Shall we have a look at that again: 6–2? This was more than a win, it was the beginning of a new era in English football, when Man U were going to be back as a major, successful force. Arsenal had been to Anfield in 1989, just a couple of weeks after Hillsborough, and taken the Championship off Liverpool, which was symbolic, almost as if they had gone there to take away Liverpool's domination of the game, and we, going to Highbury, winning that well, dancing joyously all over their dour style of play, made a major statement that we were coming to take the top spot away from the suffocating grip of George Graham's Arsenal. In our dressing room afterwards, everybody was laughing, smiling, joking, couldn't stop talking, bantering. A few of them had a bit of a piss-take, talking about right-footed curlers and headers and where on earth they came from, which I took as expressions of love from the lads. The manager had his delighted face on, all pats on the back and well played, Sharpey, and chuffed with himself and life in general. He was good in these moments, showing he was happy with us, and he organised getting the match ball for me and having all the lads sign it – sweet. Lawrie McMenemy, who was Graham Taylor's assistant as England manager at the time, was there telling me well done; soon I'd get a call to play for England. It was just superb. I was still only nineteen, the Boy Wonder, bringing a smile to football.

We had a few beers on the bus on the way home. Everybody was drinking, laughing, chuffed – what a result, what a night; run that past me again, Sharpey, two right-footers and a header, what's that all about? – and I was laughing too, ringing my mum and dad: can you believe what has just happened? I was high as a kite; I floated back to Manchester on adrenaline. I didn't sleep a wink for going over it in my mind. You have to think, as I did when I lay in that cold single bed at the top of the boarding house in Salford: I've achieved my life's ambition. In some ways it was never going to be this good again, because people would expect it of me, so it could never again be this fresh and sensational and exciting. This was it, this was the moment, the night; I am one of the lucky few in this world who got to experience the thrill of fulfilling their dreams.

Press coverage of football, even as recently as 1990, was quite innocent compared to today's voracious media. Imagine now, if Wayne Rooney scored three for United in a 6–2 victory at Highbury, the attention he would get from all over the world for the rest of the week. In my case, a couple of pressmen got in touch on the Wednesday, asking if I'd pose for a few pictures and do an interview. That was it. Everybody remembers the hat-trick, my smile, but they must have the image stored from seeing it on the ITV highlights, because there were no thumping sports sections to be filled with follow-ups for days, no Sky TV with twenty-four hours to fill showing it over and over again. No, I ended up doing a nice, straight, positive piece in one of the red-tops, next to a picture of me with a big grin on my face and three top hats on my head – for the hat-trick, gettit? Class. In the interview I was all humble and nice, nothing big-headed, saying it was a team effort, it was very pleasing to beat Arsenal, I hoped we'd go on and do well that season, that sort of thing.

The following day, Thursday, the first time we'd trained since I'd scored my goals on the Tuesday, as I was coming into the Cliff, feeling pleased enough with life, somebody came up and said the manager wanted to see me. Alex Ferguson had an office upstairs, down a corridor where nobody ever wanted to go because he might see you and nail you for something. His office overlooked the pitch, so he could see what was going on; he had his desk, phone, all his videos lining the shelves, where he'd spend hours watching replays of how we played, accumulating information on all our opponents. I knocked, walked in, and he just looked up and launched straight in at me:

'What's all this rubbish I'm seeing in the papers?'

I was too shocked to say anything – not that it would have been advisable.

'I don't know who the fucking hell you think you are! Get your feet back on the floor! I didn't tell you you could do these interviews. Who gave you fucking permission?' He had a copy of the paper on his desk. 'You're getting carried away with yourself. You need to keep your feet on the ground, get yourself back down to earth and concentrate on your game. It's a big game on Saturday and we need to win – and I don't want you all over the fucking papers again, understand?'

His approach to this issue surprised me. There was no preamble, nothing to say that I'd done well and could go on even further, but, a little word, we don't want you all over the papers, do your talking on the pitch, or whatever, if that's what he thought. He was just straight into a bollocking, telling me that doing a little interview in a newspaper after a groundbreaking win at Highbury and a hat-trick people remember to this day was an unforgivable show of arrogance that overshadowed the achievement itself, what I'd done for the club. I'm not saying he didn't have a point. If he believed that it wasn't a good idea to be in the press, and if, more importantly, he was concerned that it was a sign I might let success go to my head, and he wanted to make sure it wasn't going to, then I'm not saying he shouldn't have told me that very firmly. Keep your feet on the ground, concentrate on your game. I'm the kind of lad who would have accepted it – perhaps I might even have been able to reassure him of that. I felt he could have got it across in a very different way, sat me down, talked man to man, done it gently, with a bit of an acknowledgement that I was a young lad who'd worked very hard and had just hit the greatest week of my life. Instead, I felt crushed, like a naughty boy. I wished he could have found a little space to say something encouraging, well done for the hat-trick, telling me how to keep improving; perhaps some professional managerial talk: what he was looking for from me, how tactically I might work down the left side with Denis Irwin, anything which might actually be useful. But on this occasion there was none.

We were playing Everton in the league on the Saturday. We'd been doing better from the beginning of the season, winning most matches, staying steady around sixth place. Alex Ferguson's United was taking shape; we were more disciplined, strong, playing a flowing, attacking game which he loved and encouraged. Denis Irwin was the only major transfer, and he settled into a groove straight away, which meant few chances for Lee Martin. I had a niggling ankle injury pre-season, but soon came back on the left wing, and there was a sense in which I'd served some time now, two seasons under my belt, and was stronger, fit, had filled out; I was ready to do more for the team, take people on. I began to play with some confidence at this highest level, enjoy myself, break free from the tension I'd felt when I'd started, when it was all safety first, head down, desperate not to make a mistake. The Arsenal game was a flowering of all that work, and already it was making me start to believe I could actually go on to do well in the First Division.

The week before the Everton game, we'd lost 3–2 at home to Chelsea, so we went to Goodison needing to win. Although it was 1 December, the pitch was bone dry, really hard. In the warm-up, I was messing about and chatting to Paul Ince.

'Hey, if I score today, Incey, I'll have to think of

something different to do to celebrate. It's too dry; I won't be able to slide on my knees like I did at Arsenal.'

I remember him chuckling, saying, yeah, he'd have to work something out himself, if he scored.

Everton was always a battle, a big old ground, with plenty of needle between the fans as with any match against one of the Liverpool sides. Everton had had a terrible start to the season and sacked the manager, Colin Harvey, and brought Howard Kendall back to get them scrapping. They still had Dave Watson, Martin Keown, Stuart McCall, Kevin Ratcliffe, Graeme Sharp and Neville Southall in goal, so they were going to stand and fight.

It was a horrible game, I remember. Neither team played well; it was scrappy and dour, the pitch was too bobbly, our passing was poor compared to the parade we'd had on the Tuesday. We were quite listless and lethargic, probably coming down from that 6–2 and finding it difficult to fly again. Then, right at the end of the game, Mark Hughes, again, was winning yet another impossible battle against their defenders on the edge of the box and it broke nicely for me, coming in from the left. Neville Southall had no time to narrow the angle and I just side-footed it past him towards the far corner. One of their defenders was desperately thundering back, but he could only slide it into the net with his studs.

Our fans were behind that goal. They'd waited a whole cold afternoon for that winning goal and they were jumping up and down, going mad. I ran over to them and it just happened, I hadn't really planned it. I'd done something similar ten-pin bowling with my mates when I scored a strike, and here I was in front of the Man U fans stuffed into the away end at Goodison: a little shimmy forward with one leg, with one hand twirling, a shimmy with the other leg, the other hand twirling, twirl, shimmy, shimmy, twirl, give it loads, massive smile, thank you, we have scored! They were loving it, I was loving it. I was on a high again: hat-trick in midweek, and now I'd gone and scored the winner at Goodison. What a time, fantastic.

We came off pretty pleased with ourselves again; a great, hard win, which, in fact, set us up. We didn't lose for ten matches and went up to fifth in the league. The manager was chuffed, happy with life, handing out the well-dones, one specially for Sharpey for a good finish. His team was on the up, on its way, where he'd urged them to be, so everything was cool. For the moment.

After showers and a bit of a laugh and banter, we were all on the coach waiting to go. The older lads, Bryan Robson, Steve Bruce and Brian McClair, used to sit round the table at the back, where they usually had a card game going. Gary Pallister used to play cards too; the manager as well sometimes. I'd sit round the table in front with the younger lads; I think Lee Martin was next to me that day because he'd been sub, and a couple of others who'd come along to be part of the squad. Perhaps even the young Ryan Giggs was there by then, getting a taste of life on the first-team coach. We were full of the joys; two wins in two games in the last few days, and I'd scored four goals, which was unheard of. I was grinning, laughing, clowning about, looking forward to getting back to Manchester and having a rip-roaring night out with my mates. I couldn't be happier with my game or with life; it was everything I'd ever wanted.

We had to wait a few minutes for the manager because he'd gone into Howard Kendall's office for a drink after the game, as they do. We were all chatting, messing about, jackets off, waiting to get going, then finally he came out of the ground and climbed onto the bus. But for a man whose team had just come away with a 1–0 win, his face had the look of thunder. I swear there was smoke rising above his head. He came on the bus, not a word, stormed right up to where I was sitting, then leaned over, right in my face, and roared:

'Who the fucking hell do you think you are?'

I knew what he was like by now but I was honestly shocked this time. What was he on about, what could I have done wrong? I'd just scored the winner in a 1–0 victory at Everton.

'What's all that carry-on after you've scored? Fucking stupid dancing, what the fuck do you think you're doing? If I see you doing that again you'll be out of this club. I'm not having any of that carry-on.'

There was no point saying anything at all. I just looked down at the table, naughty boy. Bollocked again in front of all my classmates. I kept my head down and muttered: 'Yeah, yeah, right,' just wanting him to stop, then he turned round and stormed back down to the front, and silence descended on the coach.

Most of the lads couldn't believe it; even Steve Bruce had nothing to say. Even the experienced ones, Robbo, Brian McClair, were looking at each other: no way has he just bollocked Sharpey, for what? Finally, Brucey chuckled, trying to break the ice: 'What the hell was that all about?'

I turned round, all miserable: 'I dunno; it just came out of nowhere. I haven't got a clue. Yeah, I did a bit of a dance when I scored the winner. Is that not allowed? Is that so terrible?'

What had happened, it turned out, was that the manager hadn't seen it at the time because when I scored everybody jumped up in front of him and he was up celebrating himself. When he went into Howard Kendall's office, to have a whisky or glass of wine, he'd watched a video replay of my goal, seen me doing my daft little dance afterwards, and he'd not liked it.

The older lads told me to forget it, ignore it, the manager was just off on one. In hindsight, again, I'm not saying he didn't have a point. Very probably he did – he was, is, a great football manager. You couldn't argue with the huge success he was bringing to United. I was part of this lovely period where we were finally beginning to blossom, and he believed it was really important to keep working and not let any of it go to our heads. But I feel there are two things wrong with what he did. First of all, he didn't talk to me. If we could have talked it through, I could have told him it wasn't going to my head; I was just incredibly happy for that one moment, and did a little shimmy lasting five seconds. He could have said, no, it's part of something bigger, I'm worried about it; and I would have accepted that. Then, secondly, even if he believed I needed a talking-to, did he have to do it there and then? Did he have to do it on the coach, just after the game, when I was on the crest of a wave, so happy in the middle of it all? Could he not have let me have my moment, enjoy it, have a good night out, a great weekend, following this crazy, wonderful week, then pulled me in on Monday, sat me down in his office and talked to me?

No, instead he came up to me when I was in the glow of success and total well-being, when I was achieving my ambition, when I'd won gold, broken a world record, had a record at number one, whatever the equivalent would be in another sphere, and he just had to crush it all, stick a big size-nine on it, tell me I was getting above myself, try to knock me back into shape. Perhaps it was because this came so soon after he'd told me off about the article in the paper and he felt I was disobeying him. It seemed to me that he did things on the spur of the moment, he didn't count to ten and think things through, but still I felt he was out of order.

Something cracked between me and the manager that day, on that coach. He certainly wasn't my father figure any more, and I wasn't his blue-eyed boy. Ridiculous, over such petty things, when I was delivering him phenomenal performances. I didn't feel he was with me any more; I didn't feel he was looking out for me, or that he particularly even wanted me to do well. It seemed that he wanted me to be something I wasn't: a football robot. Score a hat-trick, wander back to the halfway line, head down, don't speak to the press, don't smile. Score the winner at Goodison, trot back like you've just heard your car suspension's gone, don't celebrate, go home, watch *Match of the Day*, bed by eleven. I felt that he wanted me to do it for him as a player, but he didn't want me to have a personality, my individuality, my joy in it all. He left me sitting on the coach with that nasty humiliated feeling in my stomach again, embarrassed in front of the senior players, self-esteem and confidence draining out of me. There was a contradiction in it, too. He was giving me the adult responsibility to go out, a nineteen-year-old in a man's game, and be grown up, have bottle, aggression, beat people, but at the same time he wanted me to be the little kid who'd come from Torquay on the train and hung on his every word, had only him for guidance. They'd thrown me in at the deep end to sink or swim, and I'd swum better than anybody had the right to think I would, and now that I was out there, surging into the big ocean, it was as if he wanted to pull me back, put me back in my place.

So those are my own memories of the greatest week of my life, the one everyone remembers, the hat-trick at Highbury, the winner at Everton, the big smile and the start of the Sharpey shuffle. Funny, when you look at the film of it, you can see the fans squashed into that little terrace at Everton when I'm doing my little dance, and they're loving it, their faces are pure delight. We've won, and they've got a young player showing he's just as delighted about it as they are. Well, now they know. An hour and a half later, their club's manager, the most renowned in English football, the man for whom I'd done it all, left me feeling no bigger than the muck on his shoes.

CHAPTER 8

Lovelorn in Rotterdam

It wasn't as if there was no proper management for him to do. I'd come in from Torquay and gone straight into the first team and there were all sorts of things I'm sure I needed telling. Nowadays the clubs have sports psychologists spending time with the players, because so much of performance depends on what's going on in your head, but then there was nothing like that; you got on with it, certain things were expected of you, and if you didn't measure up, you were told so in no uncertain terms.

In my case I don't think the work I needed was to bring me down to earth, in fact it was the opposite. Underneath the smile I had a gnawing lack of confidence, because it had all happened so quickly. I did have a problem for a short while when I was getting arrogant and carried away off the pitch. So much had happened, you get such a huge adrenaline boost with thousands of people chanting your name and roaring when you score and, well, my mum and dad would say there was a short period where I was a bit horrible, but that was more coming to terms with how you go out and express yourself, be arrogant on the pitch, but still be humble, your normal self, off it. I was only nineteen. I think I managed that after a brief time, and most people have always said that I come across as a likeable, down-to-earth sort of lad, even if I like having a laugh and a good time and being the life and soul of a party when I'm in the mood. Maybe the manager saw some of that and was trying to knock it out of me.

I was starting to enjoy myself around Manchester. I was better known, older and so more confident in myself. Debbie and I were still off and on, struggling to keep it going. She saw other people, I saw other people, and, as time went by, lots of them. I suppose I'd grown up from the shy, leggy seventeen-year-old, sheepishly clutching a bottle of cider in Saturdays, and was beginning to realise that I was young, women found me good-looking, I had the glamour of playing for Man U, I liked a good time and it was actually quite easy to pull women. I did, it would be fair to say, take full advantage of my happy situation.

That winter Alex Ferguson recognised I was doing well and wanted me to sign a new contract. This would be a proper, well-paid, professional footballer's contract, and I said I'd sign it, but I was sick to the back teeth of those horrible digs and wanted my own house. My dad did the contract for me, £40,000 a year, and we came out of there with Dad looking like he'd won the Lottery for me but me having a dig at him, saying we could have got more. So we went back in and came out eventually with £50,000 a year, which shook him, I think. Plus, it was agreed I could move out of those digs, and I bought a house in Timperley, on the south side of Manchester, which did become a bit of a madhouse. My mates from Birmingham used to come up and because I was pretty much famous by then, we'd get into bars and clubs for free. We had great nights out; Manchester was on the up because of the music scene, Madchester and all that, new places opening all the time, and the girls were lining up. My mates used to say there should be a red light outside my house because it was like a brothel. Every Sunday morning there'd be girls draped everywhere, asleep in our beds, on the floor downstairs, the settee, everywhere.

My mates went from coming up every few weeks to being up in Manchester three weeks out of four. They'd come to the game, watch me play, we'd have a couple of beers in the players' lounge at Old Trafford afterwards, then go into town, maybe to a carvery or somewhere for a nice meal, go to a couple of bars. We didn't get paralytically drunk; we weren't into that. We were into girls, so we used to drink quite slowly, head on to a nightclub and dance and chat girls up, not get falling-down drunk. We used to go to a club called Discotheque Royale. At the back behind the DJ box was a big long bar, where we used to stand; it became Lee Sharpe's corner, and there were always flocks of gorgeous girls there with us. My brother John and my mate Greg came up to play for Man City at that time, and they always used to say how awful it was that the best-looking girls were in our corner, while the stragglers who couldn't talk to us ended up over with the Man City lads. That's when I began to get a name as a party animal, because people used to see me out in nightclubs with a great big smile on my face, bottle of beer in hand, surrounded by mates and girls – what could be better than that?

There were some mad nights, but it was more about staying up late, having some laughs and sleeping with lovely girls than alcohol and drugs till all hours. We'd be quite compos mentis when we came out of the nightclub, then go back to my place and carry on the party. We might have a couple of drinks when we got back, then make a load of tea and coffee, gravitate around late-night telly or some music, then all go to bed.

Alex Ferguson had his spies out, obviously, and didn't like all the going out – this is when he started to tell me I should be married. In that year, after Debbie had gone, I chased women voraciously, and I don't know if that was a reaction, a release, or just being a young lad who could. Whatever, I started to get lots of minor tickings-off along with the big hairdryer set pieces. My clothes were too fashionable, my hair wasn't sober enough, my car was too flash, I was going out too much, I should be married; a dig here, a nail there. He phoned my mum once.

'Mrs Sharpe,' he said, 'Lee seems to have developed a taste for young ladies.'

She said: 'Well, what do you want me to do about it?'

I felt he was trying to suppress it all, and could have done more to deal with me as I was, iron out any concerns, work together to make me a better player, rather than just trying to get me back into the grey box, telling me what a footballer should look like, dress like, act like. As I say, it's not as if there was no work to do. I think I was wrestling with my confidence all the time really; most players probably do, but for me it was because I had come from Torquay, and not had that foundation of coaching, the work on technique which can sustain you when things aren't going too well. People saw me out and thought I was out all the time, but in fact it was just Saturday night after a game, or midweek after a game. The rule at United, at all clubs, is no going out to a place serving alcohol from forty-eight hours before a game, and I don't believe I ever broke that rule.

The rest of the time I'd be at home. And when I was at home, I used to internalise, brood, question how good I was, all the time. I've always been like that, love being out with my mates, but I'm quiet too. I sit and think perhaps too deeply, dwell on things; psychologically I probably tend to be too negative. I've always been quite deep, keeping things to myself. At United, I was never fully confident that I was that good. I'd been playing by the seat of my pants since they first threw me in for my debut against West Ham, and I always had plenty of doubts about my ability, even at that stage, when it was all coming together. Even the hat-trick at Highbury. I loved it, loved the moment, the acclaim, the joy, loved replaying the goals in my mind, but I couldn't avoid the feeling that it was all a bit of a fluke, that on another day I wouldn't have scored any at all.

Let's go over them: the first was a twenty-five-yard right-foot curler against the England keeper – if I tried that in training, how many times would it come off: two out of ten? None? The second was a header, which I miss seven times out of ten because, let's face it, I'm not the best header of a ball. The third was a right-foot shot across David Seaman, pretty much hit and hope really, just drilled it as hard as I could, and he got a hand to it, so seven times out of ten you'd expect him to save it. So really, I'd think to myself, it was all luck. It could have gone completely the other way, I could have not scored at all and it would have looked like I'd had a poor game, because I had hardly touched the ball otherwise.

In January 1991, the wink which Lawrie McMenemy had tipped me at Highbury opened up into an England call-up, with Graham Taylor picking me for his squad to play the Republic of Ireland at Wembley in a European Championship qualifier. Meeting up with the squad, I felt the same conflict: delighted, living the dream, but, underneath, nervous, nagging at myself that I wasn't really good enough to be in this company. John Barnes and Chris Waddle were two of my favourite ever players. I'd grown up inspired by watching them on telly. They were awesome, brilliantly skilful left wingers, and here was awkward little me supposedly belonging in a squad, in a team, possibly even replacing them – no way. They were all good, the senior pros, encouraging and welcoming me. Someone made sure my first England room-mate was Gary Lineker. But I was nervous all the time, whether in training or even coming down for breakfast in the morning, feeling sure they'd all be there looking at me. Then, same routine as at Old Trafford, I just put my head down and tried to do my best, get through it.

Graham Taylor wasn't, it would be fair to say, dazzling these older players with his management skills. Perhaps they were too experienced: they'd reached the World Cup semi-final in Italy with Bobby Robson just a few months earlier, and they weren't keen to change their own ideas. I liked Graham Taylor a lot; I thought he was a genuine, really nice bloke, like somebody's dad or your uncle. He was passionately, almost unnaturally, in love with his football – rare, human qualities which would ultimately lead to his hideous, public crushing.

I suppose he had a strange way of communicating, so different from the firestorm of an Alex Ferguson team talk; Graham Taylor was calm and earnest, but he spoke in a monotone which some senior players didn't respond to. For me, it was the next level on my ridiculous fairytale career. Pulling on the England shirt, I felt the emotions generations of England players talk about: pride, fear, disbelief, amazement. I'm nineteen, two years ago I was playing for Torquay, just three years ago I was playing Sunday league football in Birmingham, now I'm in a dressing room at Wembley with Lineker, Barnes and Waddle, three lions on the chest: that doesn't happen.

Half time in the game, we weren't doing too well, playing a 5–3–2 formation the players didn't like, and Graham Taylor came in: 'We're going to change it round.' Tony Adams came off, and who came on to try to make a difference? Only me. The drama of the moment was eased by a strange homeliness to the occasion, not so much that it was Wembley, but playing Ireland; Denis Irwin was up against me, and running the midfield inside me was the familiar, massive presence of Bryan Robson. Lining up on the halfway line ready to kick off, Robbo jogged over to me, shook my hand, wished me luck, told me to relax. The man is a legend, a true leader. They showed it on TV, a Man U family moment, one generation handing fatherly encouragement to the next.

It helped. I did all right in the game, which we drew 1–1. I didn't singe the turf, but I didn't make a fool of myself. I got through it. Although it was another landmark for me, I never really felt I was good enough to be there.

Looking back, I do see missing out on those two years with Eric Harrison, not even finishing my apprenticeship, as very important. Even though my career was flying, I didn't have that learning, that earning of spurs I could fall back on. I still felt a lot of the time I was playing off the cuff, that I knocked the ball down the line and ran after it, and got to it just because I had natural pace. In a way, that meant I didn't develop enough of another dimension to my game, and being in the first team, there was never any time to really work on technique; there are too many matches, then you're recovering, a brief training session, then you're playing again. You work hard on the basics of technique in apprenticeships, in reserves, but I'd missed out on that. When I got to Bradford later in my career, there was a midfielder at the club called Gareth Whalley. He wasn't blessed with great pace, which is probably why he didn't become a top-level player consistently, but he'd been at Crewe since he was a kid, under Dario Gradi's regime, a more scientific coaching system where they work on the players' skills and technique from an early age. He told me Dario would have him out for hours, just working with him in the middle of the pitch. He'd pass it to Gareth, who would have to control it with one touch, then spray his pass out wherever was the best option. His touch was absolutely superb, awesome; it could make you weep, and fans should perhaps understand that that's not just natural talent, it's the result of hard work over a long period of time. Because I missed out on that sort of work, which the kids coming along after me were going to get from Eric Harrison, I always had doubts about how good I was, whether I really belonged at United, whether I really was a top player or one just living on his pace and luck. There is a job for a manager, to tell you you are good enough, that he believes in you, that you're there because he has confidence in you, but that rarely came from Alex Ferguson. He'd show you he was pleased if you'd played well, but when I probably needed it most, I started to get bollockings for seeming to enjoy life too much.

Around this time, when I first became involved with the England squad, I was delighted, but felt the same way. People would write that I was so hot on the left wing I should be playing instead of John Barnes and Chris Waddle, and I'd think: no way, they are brilliantly skilful wingers I've looked up to through my youth. John Barnes is one of the best wingers I have ever seen in my life; no way am I as good as him.

What I'm saying is that it was a high-pressure, very high-profile and also very challenging level at which to be playing sport while growing up and living your life in public. What I was doing on a Saturday night was what nineteen-year-old lads do, and it was probably a lot more tame than people think, because I was a footballer, and I was by and large very responsible. It was a sideshow, a distraction, to the business of playing football for Manchester United, but I don't feel that any account was taken of me as an individual – not even from the perspective that if they dealt with me in the right way, they might have got more out of me. Instead, they tried to squash the bits of personality I was expressing and I think it was then, pushed hard by authority, that I began to push back for the first time in my life. I'd never been a rebel at home or at school, but I think I was probably becoming one. It was the only way to maintain my self-respect at Manchester United.

There was more success to come, and I was a big part of the side, playing so well. I played on the left wing throughout that season. I was rested for the odd game against weaker sides – Sheffield United, Wimbledon,

Southampton – but was always picked against the likes of Liverpool, Chelsea and Tottenham. I played well, in the improving team, with Gary Pallister and Incey really having found their form by now, but I didn't score again until nearly the end of the season, against Villa. We were losing 1–0, then I popped up and stuck one in for the equaliser – so I had my chance, to be delighted, to grin, to smile, to go across to our fans, to do a little dance, swivel my hips and totally love it. They loved it too – how can there be something so wrong with a little dance? I felt I was showing the fans that I was as ecstatic as they were, that I was one of them, that I was celebrating as they probably imagined they would if they were on the pitch scoring for Man U. People still come up to me now and say I brought a smile to their face the way I played in that period. But the lads told me later that Alex Ferguson was halfway down the pitch to have a go at me, until Archie Knox stopped him. Maybe they were just winding me up.

He still played me in the big games, though, and he showed confidence in me by making me important to the team, although I was always on edge with him; I think I was becoming the official naughty boy. He rested me for the final few games of the season, and I got myself fully fit, all niggles ironed out, for the great occasion coming up on 15 May, the European Cup Winners' Cup final against Barcelona in Rotterdam.

Rotterdam lives in the memory for me as the ultimate high and low at the same time. It was a massive occasion for us; winning the Cup the previous year had won Alex Ferguson and this team some time, but it wasn't enough for United's board or their fans, or the manager. Winning through to the European Cup Winners' Cup final, with

English clubs just back in Europe after the Heysel ban, was a step way above that; it really felt as if Man U were coming back as a big force. I played in all those great European games, too: both quarter-finals against Montpellier, and both semis against Legia Warsaw, when we won 3–1 away and I scored our only goal in a 1–1 draw at home to put us through. Yes, I have to admit, I celebrated that one. No, I did not keep my feet firmly on the ground, jog back to the halfway line with my head down as if someone had died.

The week after that, Ryan Giggs made his full debut against Man City and scored the only goal in a 1–0 win. How good is that, and how much of a star was he going to be? Giggsy and I were close in age although obviously he'd had longer at Man U, having come through the ranks with Eric Harrison after they pinched him away from City as a kid. We'd got pretty friendly, knocked about together quite a bit. He lived at home and was a Salford lad, so he knew his way around probably more than I did. His mates liked to use my house in Timperley as a dosshouse, which was OK with me.

Rotterdam was all about a great football night, and my tattered love life. I'd had myself an interesting time with girls for a few months, and Debbie had been seeing somebody else, but we were still off and on, talking to each other about getting back together, and she'd said she was coming over to Rotterdam for the final with the other wives and girlfriends. They were due to arrive the day before the final, but for a couple of days leading up to that I couldn't get hold of her. Then I started to hear from home that she had got back with her ex-boyfriend, so I was quite heartbroken, thinking it really was finally over this time, and I was trying to speak to her. We were in Rotterdam preparing for the biggest game in my life and in the club's history for many years, and all I could think of was, 'Where's Debbie?'

I was friendly with Darren Ferguson, who was at the club at that time. He was a really good lad; it didn't matter to me that his dad was the manager. He was doing what lads' mates do, telling me to forget about her, that there was a big game coming up. I was doing the teenage thing, saying I wasn't bothered about the game, forget the game, I wanted my girlfriend. Finally, on the Wednesday, Debbie did arrive, but something was obviously not right. It was quite cold and strange; she was distant, and it was all worrying and unsettling.

When it came to the match, I was ready, though. I was incredibly nervous, more tense in the dressing room than I'd ever been before a game. Brian McClair came up to me afterwards, I remember, and said: 'You were nervous today, weren't you? I could see it in you.'

And I just smiled, looked down. 'Yeah, I was shitting myself.'

I don't have any football memorabilia round my house; I never have had. My three Premier League medals, two FA Cup winner's medals and the one I took away from that night in Rotterdam were just given straight to my dad and he's got them in the loft somewhere. I think it's to do with me wanting not to live, eat and sleep football, but to have a life outside, so I've never wanted my house decked out in football stuff. But I've never been able to put away a great big rolled-up picture I have of the two teams lining up before that European final. It's tatty now, but it's there in the living room all the time. I love it; it tells you everything about that night, the smoke, the flares being let off, scarves being swung round the fans' heads. There was so much noise, it was a tremendous atmosphere, but tense too, and different, exotic, because it was on foreign soil against one of the great names of European football.

In the dressing room, everybody was quiet, and you could see everyone was focused – it was the biggest game not just for me but for most of the players: Paul Ince, Pally, Mike Phelan was in the team, Denis Irwin, Clayton Blackmore. Steve Bruce and Brian McClair hadn't done anything like this with United up to that point, and even for Robbo and Mark Hughes it was a massive night. You can see the nerves and tension in the folded arms and taut expressions in that team picture.

Barcelona had some of the big names playing for them, including Michael Laudrup and Ronald Koeman, and I remember thinking: let's just get out there, get this game on and get it over with. I was totally outside my comfort zone. We walked into the stadium before the game and we had loads of fans there. Two-thirds of the crowd were ours, and they were singing, making so much noise it made the hairs on the back of your neck stand up. Flares and fireworks were going off; it had an intensity you don't experience in purely English football. It was a real European event, like something on the telly, with us right in the middle of it, about to step off at the deep end.

It turned into a great night. I don't remember all the details, just that we had to work really hard at our jobs. They kept the ball very well, as you'd expect them to, probing for a chance, quickening up in the last third and knocking it about all day at the back. I remember having a much more defensive role than usual, doing loads of running up and down the line tracking their full-back, helping Clayton Blackmore out at left-back.

Mark Hughes scored to make it 1–0, before he scored the one everybody remembers. Bryan Robson clipped it over to Sparky – I think they shouted for offside because he was clean through – then his first touch wasn't particularly great, so he went really wide round the keeper. I was pegging it into the box, making one of those runs, and got myself onto the penalty spot, a perfect position for a cross, and I was shouting. I was just waiting to side-foot it into the net. Then, with his back practically to goal and almost running the wrong way, Sparky, the bastard, absolutely smashed it without thinking, and I thought: oh no, he's not even given it to me. But the ball just rocketed through the air, it never got above knee height, straight into the back of the net, pinged into the bottom corner, and I could not believe he'd scored. I just changed direction and ran off chasing him; I got to him first and jumped all over him; awesome, unbelievable. That was Sparky, a big-game player, who came up with the goods when it mattered. In that position, in that game against those opponents, he had no fear whatsoever, just banged it straight in: sheer quality. Still think he should have squared it, but there you go.

At 2–0 we just had to defend; it was a lot of hard work, keeping with our men. Ronald Koeman scored a free-kick to make it 2–1, so we were holding on, working hard, and then the final whistle went and all our subs came running onto the pitch going mad, and we were jumping all over each other. All the staff came on and we wandered around the pitch for ages before getting our medals, celebrating and hugging each other, waving to the fans and taking it all in. Darren Ferguson was along for the ride, really; – he wasn't on the subs' bench – but he just came running up and gave me a big hug. We were jumping up and down: can you believe this, we've won the European Cup Winners' Cup, we just beat Barcelona. Our fans had taken a real liking to the James song 'Sit Down' for some reason, so virtually the whole 50,000 crowd seemed to be singing it, and there we were in the middle of the pitch, giggling like a couple of schoolkids.

The best part for me was the party afterwards; I did really enjoy that, it was an incredible relief after having been so nervous. I remember talking to Bryan Robson about the game, saying I hadn't had much of a chance to show any quality, and him telling me he thought I'd played really well, done a very important job staying with people on different runs, shown a lot of experience for my age, still only nineteen, the youngest in the team. It had taken huge concentration, so at the party we were just letting our hair down. It was mad; we had the hotel to ourselves, the reserves came down, I got too drunk to remember much about it, except that Mick Hucknall was there knocking around. It was a huge release, a massive celebration, to have come and won in the first year back in Europe, when nobody had given us a chance against Barcelona. I don't think anybody went to bed before 6 a.m., although I'm hazy on the details.

Debbie enjoyed it too, had a drink and forgot about everything, but the next day when we got home we had to talk. In the end she told me, yes, she'd been seeing her ex-boyfriend and we were finished. I'd been seeing other girls, but none of them was as special to me as she was, and I was devastated. We did see each other for a little while after that, but really that was it. She was the love of my life, and

I don't think I've ever truly trusted a woman since. Too many women who came afterwards have paid the price for her. Last time I saw her, she said it was the other way round, that I broke her heart – so she must have felt let down that I went out with other girls in Manchester. Whichever way round it was, my heart was broken.

Sounds very teenage, doesn't it? But that's the point. We were still only nineteen. As a footballer, you have to grow up, you're not a robot. Splitting up, seeing other people, finishing, getting back together, talking and loving, falling out and having your heart broken, they're all normal growing pains, aren't they? Except for me I had to do it all while living life in the public eye, and it came to a sad end at the European Cup Winners' Cup final in Rotterdam. I was a European champion and a gutted, lovelorn teenager at the same time.

I haven't really thought about what might have been with Debbie; not so much. I've just pressed on with my love life, seen many, many girls, and lived for several years with two in particular, Lisa and Joanne. When it came to it, though, I didn't settle down and make it permanent with either of them, and I do find it hard to commit, to trust women. Yet there I had been, committing, moving in with Debbie, at eighteen. If we'd stayed in our house, who knows? Would we have stayed together for ever? Was that it? Maybe, maybe not. I did really chase girls at nineteen, twenty. I was the worst for it then, so maybe I needed to do it, get it out of my system, and it was too early for me to be married to Debbie. On the other hand, maybe I did it as a reaction to losing her, to being on my own again, and if we'd stayed together we'd have been happy and I'd never have felt the need to go out with women as if it was an Olympic endurance event. We might have lived happily ever after, the two of us, or we might not have done. It is one of those things I will never, ever know.

CHAPTER 9

Coming round the house

The European Cup Winners' Cup win set up United. The club was buzzing, stirring, we'd had a fantastic win and also made a huge statement that the inconsistent, underachieving years were being left behind, and we were going to reach the top with this group of players. However, this would be a time when Alex Ferguson's style would begin to undermine my confidence; but I recognised his qualities, all the players did. In his calmer moments, he did genuinely care about his players, or at least did within the limits of the ruthless job of football manager: a buyer and seller of young talent, rejecting ten for every one retained. He took an interest, knew players' names right through the junior ranks, and most of their parents, which sounds as if it should go without saying, but many managers don't even bother with players below the first team.

As a football man, a coach, he was forensic, a workaholic. He would get back from a night game, take the video home and watch it, then have a few hours' sleep and be in his office at the Cliff at 7 a.m. watching it again. Tactically, he knew down to the fine detail how all our opponents played as a team, and the strengths and weaknesses of every member of their side. We were absolutely prepared, in that way, for every game, although his philosophy was that Manchester United were going to play good football, attack, take a risk to win – one of my bollockings was for taking the ball into a corner when we were drawing with Queens Park Rangers. He was saying: 'Manchester United don't go for a fucking draw against QPR!' and I considered myself told. One of the vital reasons for the loyalty players showed to him was that he showed the same to his players in public. Whatever he said to us in the dressing room, which was severe and abusive at times, he would never give a chink of that to the press; he created a strong feeling that we were a club, together, it was us against the world, which bonded the lads together even more.

He is a creature of his time, though. He grew up in a very poor, desperately hard-working environment in Glasgow, and I'm sure all he ever knew, in work and football, was shouting and bollocking. There was no sitting down to talk things through; he was king, his word was law, the worst crime was to question it, let alone disobey. He'd pat you on the back if you played well, but I could have done with more detailed analysis of my game from him – after all, I knew he could work out the opposition so well. If you were a young lad like me, loving it, but beset, in private, by doubts, his method wasn't what you needed. There was, though, something in his fury, his relentless, obsessive desire to win, to be better, never to be satisfied, to rant when standards fell, which did push everybody on. I just feel you can have that, but be positive and treat people like grown-ups too.

Which isn't to say I didn't play well. Looking back, watching the video, I surprise myself by how good I actually was: quick, strong, making it look effortless. I was to have another golden period at United – but unfortunately, this season wasn't to be it. I was raring to go after Rotterdam and having been picked for England, ready to take my career on another stage, on and off the pitch, because I was getting some commercial endorsements alongside the fame, acclaim and female attention, all of which I made the most of. Then, right at the beginning of pre-season, I had a nasty groin problem which nobody seemed able to diagnose properly; another injury at the wrong time. Giggsy was arriving to make a first-team name for himself, and Andrei Kanchelskis had signed as a winger too. I was still first choice on the left wing, but couldn't play because the top of my leg was seizing up, and it took a long time for anybody to find out what was causing it.

I don't know if I would have made the England squad for the European Championships, but there was no question of it now because of the injury – a disguised blessing, surely, because England bombed out after that awful defeat to Sweden when Graham Taylor substituted Gary Lineker and the *Sun* gave the manager the infamous turnip treatment. Poor guy, they really did slaughter him, and he didn't deserve it.

I made just three appearances on the bench for United all season until March, except for playing one game, that awful televised New Year's Day battering at home to QPR, when we lost 4–1. I missed almost the whole season having injections, an operation, different forms of treatment; they didn't know what it was, until they finally fixed it and I was able to return to training and get back in the team for the Championship run-in. It was the final year of the First Division before the top clubs split off and formed the Premier League, when the massive money poured in. The team had started really well, were unbeaten for thirteen matches, always top of the league or second throughout the season, with Leeds our main rivals, managed at the time by Howard Wilkinson. I came back on the left wing when I played, and Giggsy played on the right with Andrei Kanchelskis dropped to sub, but I was working my way back to fitness. Alex Ferguson used to show some understanding there too, knowing that it would take you a while to get back to fitness, that you might do well for two or three games on adrenaline, but then the underlying lack of fitness would tell and you'd need a break or some patience. I did play a few decent games towards the end of the season, but it was difficult to get any real stride or rhythm going. In the end, what made my name that season was nothing to do with football at all, but an episode which came to define that era at Manchester United.

It was a tale that grew on the wind, with every telling, about the manager storming into a house to pull young, innocent Ryan Giggs out of a wild party organised by the Svengali-like Lee Sharpe, snakehips himself, who was leading winsome Giggsy astray. The poor old manager, the father figure with his wayward charges, had to come out of a dinner in his bow tie and tails, burst into the place and bring some order to a den of corruption.

In real life, it was all a bit more, er, mundane than that. The context, as ever, was the football, the tension of our position in the league, the pressure Alex Ferguson was under, this time to finally get United their first Championship since 1967. We had just four games left, and were top of the league, when we played Forest on Easter Monday, 20 April 1992, so we were edging the manager into potential heart-attack territory. Especially when we lost 2–1. We were due in London on the Wednesday to play West Ham, so the manager told Giggsy and me that even though it was a match night, when usually we'd be free, we weren't to go out, and we should both go home and stay there.

I went home after the Forest match and was sitting round my house with my mum and dad; we'd had something to eat. Then Giggsy rang up and said he was going to Blackpool with his mates and a couple of girls. My mum and dad were off back to Birmingham anyway, so I told Giggsy I'd pop round and go with him. I'm not saying this was the most responsible and tame thing we could have done that night; thinking about nothing but football, watching videos of our own performances, reading statistics on the West Ham right-back, then going to bed with liniment on may well have been how Phil Neville would have coped with the situation, but I'm not him. Perhaps it was a bit out of order, as the manager had told us to stay in and it was two days before the West Ham game, but it wasn't a breach of club rules, which said that from forty-eight hours before a game, players cannot go onto licensed premises. You can't just make the rules up as you go along, and we were young, free, single footballers who liked to have a good time, so we went to Blackpool. Nothing scandalous happened. We drove over there, which doesn't take long, went to the Pleasure Beach for a couple of hours, then came home, and, yes, we had a couple of girls with us whom Giggsy had met. We all had a nice time but, two nights before a game, there was no drinking or debauchery.

I don't suppose the manager's mood improved much when we lost to West Ham 1–0, leaving us second to Leeds, for whom Gordon Strachan had been outstanding all season. The next game, the second-to-last of the season, was a massive one, Liverpool away on the Sunday. Alex Ferguson was really on edge, you could feel it; the lads used to joke about it. He had this nervous cough, he'd twitch his hands behind his back, snap even more easily than usual. Archie Knox used to crack jokes to try to lighten the atmosphere, but the nervousness wormed its way into the players and made us tense before matches, which affected the way we played and, I think, was the reason we lost it right at the end that season.

On the Thursday night, the day after the West Ham defeat, at 9 p.m., the doorbell rang at my house. I opened the door, and there he was, Alex Ferguson himself, all dressed for dinner. His face was red, a serious mood brewing up. I've always assumed, thinking about it, that he thought I'd be in on my own watching telly, and he was going to tear a strip off me for going to Blackpool on the Monday, and supposedly leading poor, innocent Giggsy astray. He'd been at some dinner, where, I've been told, one of his lookouts told him that Giggsy and I had gone to Blackpool the night of the Forest game, instead of staying at home. Apparently he'd exploded there and then, just ripped his napkin out of his neck, stormed out of the dinner, driven straight round to my house in his black tie and tails. It tells you a lot that he came to my house, not Giggsy's, even though Giggsy's was nearer to where he was that night. I was obviously the evil influence, leading clean-living Ryan astray, and I was the one who needed putting right, not Ryan.

When he arrived – well, you do have to laugh, really. A few of Giggsy's mates were round the house, one or two of the younger Man U apprentices, a few girls some of them knew, and we were getting ready to go out. We weren't playing until the Sunday and this was Thursday night, so we were allowed. There was no wild party going on. In fact there were just two beer bottles left in the whole house – but Giggsy's mate opened the door with both of them in his hand. Just one of those things.

So look at this scene through the eyes of Alex Ferguson, imagine all the no-good he thought we were always up to, this crowd of young people partying away their precious athletic youth. There were three nice-looking girls, sitting on the settee, all dolled up, ready to go out. One young lad was walking through the kitchen with no shirt on – he was only looking for the ironing board but you can imagine what it looked like to Alex Ferguson.

He ordered everyone out of the house except Giggsy and me, and stood at the front door clipping them all round the back of the head, even though he didn't know most of them, had nothing to do with them. It probably took ten minutes to clear everyone out, with them all grabbing their shoes and handbags and scurrying out of the door, and Giggsy and I wringing our hands in the living room, knowing what we'd got coming.

He came back in, sat us down, Giggsy on the end of the settee, me in the armchair a few feet away, then subjected us to the father, no, the grandfather, of all hairdryers. It was industrial strength; he could have dried the hair of a battalion of the Chinese army. His face was an awesome colour; you wouldn't know a face could turn that crimson. He leaned into us so he was an inch from our faces and tore shreds off us.

The main message to Giggsy was that a lad of his talent did not want to be throwing it all away going to Blackpool when he'd been told by the manager to stay in. We weren't taking it seriously; there were older players who were married with wives and families and they were completely focused on trying to win medals and achieve their goals. But we didn't give a shit and were just tossing it off, we weren't bothered, we were just having a laugh and doing our own thing.

As ever, he had a point; I can see what he meant. The fact was we didn't have the same attitude as the married lads. But it was rubbish to say we didn't take our football seriously; we loved it, we worked hard at it, it was our lives, completely. Of course we wanted to win the title. But we were also young lads, having the time of our lives, playing for Manchester United, fulfilling the dream of every young boy. I was still only twenty, Giggsy nineteen, and now three nights before a football match, as club rules allowed, we were going to go out and have a few drinks and a good time with some mates and some girls. We'd still be ready on Sunday, fired up, nervous as hell, determined to play our best; it was just that we didn't have a wife and kids to keep us occupied and staying in. Quite the opposite: we had mates and cars and half the young girls of Manchester to go at. Looking back, he was right; we weren't taking it quite as seriously as he was, or Robbo or Brucey or some of the other older, married men who had waited their whole careers to win something. Maybe it was happening too early for us, so we didn't appreciate how tiny a proportion of footballers ever get to win anything, let alone a League Championship. Maybe we were too young, too lighthearted, to think how enormous it was for Manchester United, to get that title back. Let's put it this way: of course it was important, we didn't need telling how huge it was, but our way of coping with that wasn't to live like monks until the season was over. Perhaps he needed to give us a talking-to.

I had to wait my turn. In his mind, I was the ringleader – which, again, had a certain truth to it. I liked to be the good-time boy, I was older, but it wasn't the whole truth, certainly not in Giggsy's case, who had his own ideas of fun. The Blackpool trip had been his idea anyway. Not that I would say that, or say anything, because I had some personal haranguing to take now.

'You're losing your fucking pace,' he started in on me, his face so close to mine I could feel the heat. 'You're going down the pan, but the worst thing is that you're not just taking yourself down, you're dragging all the young lads with a bit of talent down with you.'

I sat there and took it. I didn't say a word. I'd learned not to.

He had a thing by now about my lifestyle: he hated my car, which was a Vitara jeep, bright blue, a bit flash; I loved it. Giggsy played the game better than me: he had a Vitara too, but he used to leave his at home and drive the boring club car to training. Fine image, according to the manager. Then I used to turn up happy, with a smile on my face, highlights in my hair sometimes, with the music playing in my jeep. That did not mean I ran any slower or trained with any less effort than the other lads – I always enjoyed training and was at the front in the running. But I did it with a smile on my face, which was silly. Going about looking happy, like you're having fun, like you enjoy being a footballer not a welder, isn't what managers like to see. They want to see that you think it's hard, grim, serious work; that means you're dedicated. Smile, and you can't be.

He used to tell me not to knock about with people we met around Manchester because they were hangers-on, but I was in a city to which I'd moved purely to play for the club, so take those people out, the first team were all a lot older than me, so that left Giggsy and the young lads, yet somehow he thought I was a bad influence on them. He started looking round the house, saying he'd have me out of it.

'You can get rid of your car,' he said. Then he looked up, through the patio doors, and behind them was a big chrome set of drums, because I was getting into drumming. He just shook his head in utter despair and sort of moaned and screamed at the same time: 'What the fucking hell are they?'

I was almost ducking. 'They're, er, my drums,' I said. 'I'm learning to play.'

So he lost it with them, screaming: 'You can get rid of those fucking things too.'

I sat there thinking: right, right, I'll get rid of everything, everything I own, if you just stop ranting at me and get out of my house and go home. I thought we were going to be sacked in the morning; I thought it was all over for me at United. We must have had ten, fifteen minutes each, before finally he tore himself away and stormed out. We just sat there shell-shocked, pulverised, with that horrible, sick, humiliated feeling in our guts. Giggsy was trembling, shaking all over. He just got up, white as a sheet, and drove home.

Then I heard footsteps on the stairs. It was a young lad, Raphael Burke, who was in the youth team at the time, with David Beckham, the Nevilles, Nicky Butt and Paul Scholes, a really good player who never made it. He'd been upstairs when he heard the manager arrive, and all this time he'd been hiding under a bed. He tiptoed down when he heard the manager leave, gave me a look, part sympathy, part terror, and legged it.

I rang my dad. 'I think I'm going to get sacked in the morning.'

I didn't, and in the morning Alex Ferguson was almost back to normal. He gave us another bollocking for going to Blackpool when he'd told us to stay in, and said he expected us to give it everything now at the club. Then we went to Liverpool on the Sunday, and I wasn't even on the bench. He left me out completely, although Giggsy was in, on the left wing. Alex Ferguson was always good if he was leaving you out: he'd take you to one side and talk to you, give you a reason, not leave you to find out when he announced the team to everyone. He told me, assured me it was nothing to do with what had happened, it was just the formation he wanted to play, and I accepted it, but I've always believed something changed in his attitude towards me. The team lost at Liverpool, the third defeat in a row. Too much tension, the yips. I was on the bench for the final game of the season when we beat Spurs, but Leeds pipped us to the Championship, meaning another year to wait, and the manager wasn't a happy person.

My dad always believed afterwards that that night stuck in Alex Ferguson's mind. It needled him that the team was chasing a title but Giggsy and I went to Blackpool, then when he came round he thought there was some kind of orgy going on at Sharpey's. Dad reckoned it changed the manager's attitude to his one-time blue-eyed boy, and he was never the same again towards me. It was the beginning of the end – unfairly, I think, because nothing was going on and we weren't breaking club rules, even if the Blackpool trip had gone against his orders. My partying was always tamer than he thought, but he was from a different generation. Bursting into my house was counter productive, because I really resented it. I still do, actually, can't help it, and it made me more defiant in little ways I could get away with. I pushed back when he had a go at me. Perhaps it worked on Giggsy, terrified him at an impressionable age, and so he played the game from then on, learned it was best to have his fun on the sly. Then the story got out, with a very simplified cast list: Giggsy playing the wide-eyed, impressionable youngster, Alex Ferguson the concerned guardian at the end of his tether, and me as the good-time Charlie. Which went a long way to fuelling those myths, for all three of us.

CHAPTER 10

My drugs shame

The story of my downfall is one that everybody knows, don't they? My George Best-like plummet, from football stardom to the doldrums, from dancing round corner flags after scoring to what we were forced to describe as a 'serious illness'. Nudge nudge, wink wink. Everybody knew. It was Manchester in the early 1990s, Madchester, the twenty-four-hour party city, the Hacienda, baggies, pills, thrills and bellyaches, and there was Lee Sharpe, always out in the middle of it all, the young football starlet, dancing in nightclubs, a grin on his face so radiant it made the era's smiley icon look like Alex Ferguson after a 1–0 home defeat to Middlesbrough.

What always amazes me about the 'true story' of 'my drugs shame' is not just how many people think they know all about it, but how they think they're the only ones, they've got the inside track, they're in the know. More than that, there seem to be thousands of people who haven't just heard that it was the acid, coke, speed, ecstasy, even heroin shooting through and carving up my beautiful body and effortless ability; they actually saw me at it, they'll swear to that. So many people claim to have seen me in a toilet somewhere, down in the bowels of the Hacienda or some other club, furiously drilling a line of coke up my hooter, or feverishly running around the place to find who was dealing, to get the gear which could keep me dancing and clamp that smile to my face. Poor old Alex Ferguson, the father figure – so the story goes – tried everything to keep me on the straight and narrow, but like dads and granddads everywhere, what could he do with his young boy against the chemical tide sweeping through the nation's youth? He even had me living with him, everybody knows that, but in the end I was a party animal lost in the wrong city at the wrong time, and I drowned in the trippy sea, my body too riddled with chemicals to run and fly down the wing as I had in my pre-drugs innocence. One of the cautionary tales, I am, of clean-living athleticism, sport and the care of well-meaning elders, against the temptations of wild living. Chalk me up with Bestie, Gazza, Greavesie. Where did it all go wrong? The rebirth of Manchester United met the reinvention of Manchester the city, and down I spiralled.

I can put my finger on where the story started, too. It was straight after we won the Cup Winners' Cup in Rotterdam. Ralph Milne, the Scottish winger signed by Alex Ferguson in 1988 – who hadn't played more than a handful of games before Danny Wallace arrived, then I came through, then Giggsy – had been let go after Rotterdam, because his three-year contract was up. I liked Ralph, got on with him, as I pretty much did with all the lads, but I was never great friends with him, never went drinking or socialising with him, so I thought it was funny when he rang me and told me he was selling his story to a newspaper.

He sounded uneasy, talked really fast, telling me that his contract was over, he was having to move house and faced an uncertain future. Which all sounded pretty bad, not where you want to be at thirty with your career almost completely behind you, but I wasn't sure why he was telling me. He said he didn't want to do it but he just had to.

I said: 'OK, look Ralph, that sounds miserable. You do what you want to do, it's your prerogative, mate. Good luck.' I didn't think anything of it at all; just that it was funny he should even mention it to me.

So Ralph did this little piece in a tabloid, which I never even read, which apparently 'blew the whistle' on United's young pros 'taking drugs' in Holland at the Cup Winners' Cup final. I don't think it mentioned anyone by name, certainly not me, otherwise I'd have been told, and I'd have sued, so it left people to read between the lines: who would this be except the flash, nightclub-haunting, smiley-faced one? Put two and two together: a few spliffs in Holland and Sharpey on the left wing always grinning and doing silly little dances, looks a bit high on life, and now I was making sense to people. Who were the other candidates for drug-taking young pros? Lee Martin, who used to go home to his mum and dad in Glossop after training; Darren Ferguson, who really did have a serious father figure to lead him down the right paths; Mark Robins, the six-yard-box poacher with the spotless Vauxhall Nova and his policeman father? I don't think so.

From what I heard, Ralph and the paper either got what happened wrong or kept it vague. He wasn't in the first-team squad at that point, so he'd travelled over with the reserves. They'd gone to Amsterdam on the Tuesday, not Rotterdam, and they had a night out there the day before the final. A group of young footballers, out on the town in Amsterdam before a European final the next day, which they would only be watching, not playing in: might they have had a few drinks and even – shock, horror – a few joints? Well, maybe they did. It's legal there anyway, isn't it, so I'm not sure I can see the problem; I might have joined them if I'd been with them. But – fact – I didn't, because I was in Rotterdam; I was playing. I spent my days before the match shitting myself about the football, my heart weeping over Debbie, then getting fantastically drunk with the lads till 6 a.m. the morning after the final. I was in the Man U bubble and I didn't get a chance to go out and sample the relaxed attitude of the Dutch towards soft drugs.

I'm sure that started all the rumours, though. Then, when we got back, I had the groin problem, so suddenly the golden boy wasn't in the team, and the gossip spread like a wrap of whiz unfolding in a Manchester gale. I was still going out with my mates, usually with a flock of girls chirruping around us, me at the centre grinning, talking, dancing, flirting, so it all made sense: like a lot of young men my age in Madchester at that time, I was E-d up, sailing away on the love pill.

I only came back patchily that season when we were pipped by Leeds, and my form wasn't great, then the 'Blackpool incident' and other bollockings about my so-called wild lifestyle stoked up the image of a young man out of the control of his exasperated manager. The following close season, the summer of 1992, I contracted viral meningitis and the rumours were all confirmed. Everybody knew what that really meant, or thought they knew. Viral meningitis: a likely story.

Unfortunately, though, it was true. I wish it wasn't, wish

it had been a cover for something that was a lot more fun. It was violent, horribly painful and, at times, terrifying, because nobody knew how long it was going to last. It attacked me after just two days' pre-season training. I'd bought a St Bernard dog – I liked my unusual pooches at that time – and gone up to north Manchester to pick up a tiny Rascal van from a friend, which I was going to use to get the dog home. I got back to my house in Timperley, and felt pins and needles in my foot. I was shaking and stamping my foot to get rid of it, but it travelled up my leg, right up my left side, then down my left arm. I was watching TV and I kept dropping the remote control because I couldn't feel if I had hold of it or not. That went on for about an hour, then suddenly I started throwing up, really violently, chucking up everything; I couldn't get off the toilet for hours.

I rang the club doctor; he came over right away and said it was food poisoning, I should see whether it worked its way through by the next day. He left, but I kept throwing up, all through the evening and night, plus I had a migraine, an awful, pounding, piercing headache, and by about eleven o'clock I rang him back.

'Listen, I'm still struggling; I haven't stopped throwing up since you left and my head's thumping.'

He came back and decided to get me into hospital, the Bupa one in Whalley Range, south Manchester, which United use a lot. They checked me out and diagnosed viral meningitis. That, I can now exclusively reveal, was the true, shocking revelation behind the story United then put out that I had viral meningitis – I did. Hold the *News of the World* front page. Or don't.

It was another dampener to my career, actually, at the

wrong time; another interruption I didn't need when I should have been maturing to my peak as a footballer. It was a horrible illness, too. Viral meningitis hits you when the red and white blood cells in the coating of your brain are out of balance, and mine, they told me after doing various tests, were way out. One of the worst things about the illness, as bad as the attacks themselves in a way, was the dread of them. When I felt that first tingle of pins and needles in my foot, I knew exactly what was coming, could time it almost to the second: half an hour for it to spread up the whole left-hand side of my body and into my face, then my speech would start to slur. Half an hour later it'd be gone, and I'd have this terrible hour of nothing happening, the lull, where there was nothing to do but batten down the mental hatches and wait for it to hit. Then the attacks would come, countdown to the worst migraine you can imagine and the most violently, retchingly sick you can be. I used to sit, when I wasn't in the toilet, in agony, my head drilling into me. I'd have to hold my eyes because they ached so much: it hurt to close them, it hurt to keep them open. I'd think the hell would never stop, but then, finally, it did. All the time, for weeks, I knew that if I did too much in a day, tired myself out, I'd get that tingle in the bottom of my foot. It was the signal that I had two hours, almost to the second, until another furious attack.

In the hospital, they put me on a drip because I couldn't keep any food or water down. Alex Ferguson came to see me – just what you want when you're laid up in bed, him staring at you. No, only joking; he was good like that, always used to go and see any player who was in hospital for an operation or treatment. He was never one of these managers, all too common in football, who ignore players when they're of no immediate use. He told me to get myself right, then he was looking forward to having me back. I was like, yeah, I'll see you when I get back to work, gaffer; bye then.

My mum and dad were up a lot, sitting by my bed. After a couple of days I asked if I could get out and have a bit of fresh air. The doctors said OK, but not to do anything at all strenuous. So there I was, quite seriously ill, the invalid, walking painfully slowly round the shrubbery and car park of the Bupa hospital with my frantically worried mum and dad, when suddenly a guy appears clicking a camera and some woman reporter's straight in my face, saying:

'What's your reply to people who believe this is a drugs-related problem?'

'Print it,' I said. That was it. 'Print it. Please, please do go and print it, because it will make my day and it'll also make me a very rich man.'

I never categorically denied any of the drugs stories, not publicly anyway. At one point when the rumours were really rife my dad did ask me if I was clean. I told him I was, and he said: 'Well, that's good enough for me, son.'

To the papers, though, I never did. I just dared them to print it, and they never did. Still, around Manchester, the country, the world, everybody knew – or thought they knew – I was a victim, the first footballer to tangle too far with the edges of youth culture, another young lad with his whole life ahead of him, another basket case fallen to the flipside of E. I suppose I helped the stories along, at the time, because out in town on a Saturday night I didn't think they did my image any harm. I was bumping into some heavy-duty people, a few proper big-time gangsters who we'd see about and nod to and say hello. That started right back in digs, when we'd go up to the snooker club and some of Salford's finest would be up there, always keen to know the young United up-and-comers. Then there were local hardnuts, men on the fringes, wheeler-dealers, hangers-on, and also just gangs of lads, football supporters, most of them my age, out and about in Manchester. I thought all the stories doing the rounds gave me a bit of street credibility. I was one of the lads, a good-time boy: I was out on the pitch scoring goals and putting crosses in on a Saturday with the biggest club in the world, holding my own in Fergie's team with Robbo and Incey and Brian McClair, but then on a Saturday I was out with everyone. I had a drink, and all the talk of coke and E made me seem pretty cool, too, that I was partying with the best of them.

I think I was accepted as a good lad to have about the place. I don't think it did me any harm, which it might have done if I'd come out and made some sort of Just Say No, drugs-are-bad-for-you statement. So if someone came up to me in bars and clubs and offered me a line of coke or whatever it was, I didn't go off my head, tell them to fuck off, that I was a footballer, one of Alex Ferguson's finest, role model to the Nevilles, the clean-living, upstanding son of Leo and Gail Sharpe of Halesowen. I didn't want to be some stiffy little kid in the corner at every party, so I'd give them a bit of leeway. I'd say, 'Not tonight, mate,' or 'I'm all right, I'll just have a drink,' and quite a few must have gone back to their mates and said they'd offered me some coke and I hadn't said no outright, just not for now, and thought it meant I was part of the gang, a face. That suited me fine.

With the papers, I didn't see why I should deny it outright, and I also thought it could be tricky if I did. It'd give these stories credibility: I'd be associating my name with hard drugs in the headlines, even if the word 'NOT' appeared in it somewhere. Then some people might come out of the woodwork and say they'd seen me, or they'd done it with me in some club somewhere. I get that a lot, not just people who heard off a friend of a friend that some bloke once knew someone who saw me, but people saying they've actually squashed into a toilet somewhere with me and we've snorted coke together. Then I'd have to deny it, and it'd go on and on, and there's no smoke without fire and all the rest of it. Ultimately, I was quite serious about wanting them to print it, because I wanted to see if any of them had the bottle. If they did, I would have sued them and, as it wasn't true, I would have cleared it up once and for all and made a lot of money.

One of the worst things about the meningitis – well, it was grimly funny too – was that a girl I was seeing at the time chucked me while I was in hospital. She was called Jo, I think, and was an air hostess; she had big boobs so we called her Jugs. She was a good laugh, a bit of a ladette, happy to be out late knocking about and drinking with the lads. She used to be flying for half the week so she'd come round my house and stay for a couple of days then be off again. It wasn't serious, we were drifting apart anyway when I came back from my holiday that summer, but then I had the meningitis, was in hospital for two or three days, and when I got home, all sick and worn out, there was a note from her saying that I'd changed since I'd been on holiday and she was getting out of there. She'd see me around, she said.

My mum saw the letter when we got back from the hospital. 'That's not very nice, is it?' she said, shaking her head.

It wasn't a good way to get dumped, while I was on a drip in hospital. To be fair, she thought I only had food poisoning; she didn't realise I was nearly dying. I'm not sure I did ever see her around.

It took me a long time to recover – from the meningitis I mean, not Jugs. I went home to Birmingham for a few weeks, so my mum could look after me, and I had to make sure never to do too much or I'd have an attack. I couldn't train at all, but they wanted me at the club to be in kit in the pre-season squad photo, so my cousin drove me up to Manchester, because I wasn't well enough. I did the team photo and talked to a few of the lads, told them I was sick and it was bloody awful. Then my cousin and I drove into town, walked round the shops, had a bit of lunch, got back in the car to drive to a flashy car showroom in Cheshire somewhere to look at the motors. We had a look round, then he drove me back to Birmingham and on to my mum and dad's couch. That night, I had a terrible attack, my head being crushed, my eyes throbbing, my stomach trying to escape out of my throat, my mind in pieces, just from that little old man's outing.

I'd been home a few weeks when the *Sport* newspaper turned up at the house. They had a letter, on Manchester United notepaper, signed by the chairman, Martin Edwards, which had gone out apparently to all the newspapers, saying I had retired from football because of a fierce addiction to drugs. There was plenty of detail in there, the usual spiral of decline, from a life of such young promise, I had experimented with cannabis, then dabbled in speed, cocaine and ecstasy, until finally the dreaded poppy, heroin, had claimed my mind, body and soul and I was a wreck in need of treatment.

All the other papers must have known it was a fake: when you looked at it the Man United heading was all wrong and photocopied, and Martin Edwards's signature was a ridiculous forgery; reporters have since told me they arrived in all their offices and were chucked straight in the bin. But there was this *Sport* reporter at the front door in Halesowen, wondering if they could have a picture of me reading this letter and a few words of me denying it. I said, no, I wouldn't have my picture taken, but there was another guy at the bottom of the drive who took a photo of me holding this letter, and it did actually go in the *Sport*: Lee Sharpe denies he's on drugs; it's viral meningitis, I'll be back soon, blah blah blah, and that really was the only piece that ever went in any paper actually naming me in connection with any hard drugs, and, as I thought, it probably did me more harm than good, just putting my name up there in association with it, even though I was denying it.

To be fair to the manager, he never gave these stories a moment's thought. He never wanted clarification; he was smart enough to know it was crap. He was worried enough about me just going out, about girls; he didn't really think the dark rumours had any truth in them. But I sometimes wonder whether it all did me damage around football. It's a very small world, really: the game has a massive profile, with millions of fans, but there are really a very few people involved with it, and at the top level there are twenty managers, that's it. I've often wondered if they heard the stories and believed them, most of them knowing nothing about drugs anyway, and I became a player with a bit of risk attached to me. I used to get the odd player asking me if I knew where he could get some coke – not United players, but one or two who I met on holidays or tours – and I'd have to say, no, I haven't a clue, mate.

Here are the facts, though. It wasn't true. I never took drugs. Never. Here's where the real world, what actually happens in life, bumps up against all the silly fantasy stories people want to believe about the so-called high life. I was nineteen, twenty, I'd developed a taste for going out with the lads in Manchester, drinking, and pulling women, which was starting to become very easy for me. We didn't go out that much, Saturdays and midweek on the night we played. The weekend was the big night. I'd be out with six or eight mates, but we didn't go to the Hacienda or clubs like that in the house music scene; we moved in completely different circles. We went to cheesy places where people were dressed in shirts and chinos, highlights in their hair, pop, chart, smoochy music in the background, where the girls were in white, dolled up, not wearing much at all, standing around sipping drinks through straws, waiting for gangs of lads with bottles of Sol with quarters of lime – how sophisticated did that seem? – to chat them up and maybe take them home. If you were a young Man U player with lots of confidence after a couple of drinks and getting a bit of a reputation for yourself as a love machine … let's just say I was usually in with a chance.

People might say drugs were everywhere, but they're mistaking the Manchester places that made the cover of *Newsweek* with most of the dressed-up bars in town.

In JW Johnson's, Cheerleaders, Discotheque Royale, Piccadilly 21, I never came across drugs, of any kind. How's that for a blow to my credibility? In the early nineties, I think you still had to go looking for drugs, or go to places where you knew they would be. Now it's different; everyone seems to be on something. Old boys in the golf club come up to me, give me the wink and mutter conspiratorially:

'I had a bit of the old white marching powder on Saturday night.' Fifty-odd-year-old blokes, tapping their noses. 'I had a bit of that, got a Viagra down me, and was banging the missus all night.'

Back then, it was different; everybody wasn't at it, it was still quite underground with an air of danger. We didn't go to the house and rave clubs. I didn't like those places; they weren't my thing. I went to the Hacienda only two or three times and I found it dark and a bit threatening, out of my element. None of the lads I knocked around with were into drugs, mostly none of us had ever even tried anything, and we had a cracking time without them, a non-stop party when we were out.

I never fancied it, that's the awkward truth. I wasn't the streetwise huckster who could do it all: play football for Alex Ferguson in front of 45,000 people then do E and coke with the happy crowd on a Saturday night. I was actually quite scared of it. I was worried about what might be in it, washing powder, bleach or whatever, and I was scared of taking something that would make me hallucinate. I didn't want to start jumping off buildings and all that.

Plus, I used to think: I don't need it. I don't need anything to make me feel happy. I'm high as a kite, I play for

Manchester United, we're becoming the best football team in the country at a time when the whole game is on the up. I play at Old Trafford, we might beat Arsenal or someone, my mates are all with me, I drink a few ciders, the room's full of lovely girls. Why would I want something to change my mood?

I still get people saying it now, all the time. Some of it comes from people seeing me out who can't believe anyone could have a smile that wide and seem to be having such a good time without something exciting my head first. Some of it seems to be the pure power of urban myth; stories become so settled in everybody's minds that they come to believe they've actually seen me at it. I usually ask these people for a bit of detail and the stories crumble; come to think of it, they didn't see me. I was in a club coming out of the toilet, but, no, they hadn't actually seen me snorting anything, but somebody said I had – or whatever.

Simple truth? I never have. Not speed, ecstasy, coke, heroin or acid. Not my scene. Dope, some weed? Well, yes, but that's a different story, a few years later, when I was living in my next house in Hale Barns with another long-term girlfriend, Lisa, and we were all domestic and cosy and I smoked the odd joint on the couch watching a movie. But the truth about the drugs stories of 1991–92 was that when Manchester was Madchester, the centre of the music world, reinventing itself as a city, rediscovering its panache and confidence with those name bands and a scene which pushed the frontiers and changed youth culture for ever, I wasn't part of it. The young football starlet was 100 yards up the road from the Hacienda in some cheesy, brightly lit theme bar, sipping a bottle of cider, having a laugh with my mates, wondering which girls might come piling back to my place that night. Maybe this isn't good for my image; it looks a bit square, doesn't it, in Manchester, at that time? So that's it, my hard drugs shame: I never took any.

CHAPTER 11

A medal in the loft

The other strange aspect about all the rumours that clung to my image at that time, the Boy Wonder who blew it all, was that I went on to have four more seasons at Man U after the meningitis, playing the best football of my career. I got back in the England side, and won three Premier League titles. The following season, 1992–93, we finally did it, won the Championship after twenty-six years, the culmination of all Alex Ferguson's fuming, furious drive to make Man U the nation's top club. We'd worked our nuts off to do it, from the days of the fledglings, who'd nearly all been shed by now, the FA Cup win of 1990, the European Cup Winners' Cup the following year, and pushing Leeds so close in 1992. For me it was strange, though, because this final arrival at the wine bar of success didn't feel like happiness to me, but was the beginning of the end of my love affair with United. When I look back at the records, I'm actually surprised at how much of a part I played in it, because I remember being on the fringes, the manager starting to move me around in the team, to centre midfield, where he fancied me for a while, back to the left, occasionally on the right – occasionally left-back, or at least defensive left-side in front of Denis Irwin, who was a machine in that position. Gradually, I felt I was becoming one of the players not included for the important games, but played in the easy wins while the big-name players were rested. It was the reverse of what used to happen, when I might be rested but brought back for semi-finals and key matches.

So it's quite a surprise to look back and realise just how many games I played, how important I still was to the team, when we won the Premier League in 1993, and then, in 1994, the Double. I must have worked really hard to come back from the meningitis, because in 1992–93, once I was back in, away at Villa at the beginning of November, I played in every game but one. This was my second golden spell. By March, Graham Taylor was picking me for England again; I came on as sub in a 2-0 win against Turkey in a World Cup qualifier, almost a full two years after my debut against Ireland. Funny that I don't have happy memories of this period, that if you'd asked me without looking it all up, I'd have said I might have played half the games, that I was being moved all over the field, and the manager was cracking away at my head. I was twenty-one, coming up to twenty-two, I had a ridiculous four full seasons at United behind me at that age, plus the Torquay Murder Ball initiation, so I was probably easing into some sort of prime. I had filled out, which meant I lost a dab of pace, but I was stronger and more of a presence, and I can remember Alex Ferguson saying in the press that I looked in good shape, like a middleweight boxer.

Giggsy had come through the previous season, a genius the minute he was out there, weaving up the left, swerving at a leggy pace I'm not sure the game had seen before. People look at our careers and think I must compare myself with him and wonder where it all went wrong for me, but there is one very simple difference to start with: Giggsy's better than me. He has to be one of the best left-sided players in the world over the last ten to twelve years, one of the most outstanding of his generation, one of the great Manchester United players of all time. From when he was young, the left wing was his; that was it, he played in his own position all the time, which helps. He's a Manchester lad, and although he was at City as a kid, he was the first product of Alex Ferguson's own youth system, coached by Eric Harrison, having done his time in the youth team and reserves, not just thrown in without much coaching, like me and some of the other fledglings in that generation just before him.

Giggsy and I drifted apart in the end: lads' stuff – he went on holiday with his mates without telling me, after a couple of years of them all using my house in Timperley as a doss-house and knocking shop, so I was a bit put out. But before that we had been really good mates, the two bright young faces of the new Man U. Giggsy was the first youngster to come through since I had; in fact, with Russell Beardsmore gone, Mark Robins gone and Lee Martin out injured, Giggsy was the only 'home-grown' player in United's team, barring Mark Hughes, who'd been to Barcelona and come back. Giggsy played the manager expertly too, giving Alex Ferguson the poker face more than I ever learned or wanted to. He was a local lad with all his mates around him, and I'm sure he went out more than I did. He was into the Hacienda and some of that scene which was too heavy for me, he liked his girls and his flash cars, but somehow to the manager he appeared the deadpan, dedicated young professional, who had to be protected from being led astray by evil influences, including Sharpey, the loose-living, Vitara-driving, manically grinning, hair-highlighted wild thing.

One day off during that season Giggsy and I were mad enough to accept an invitation from our esteemed club captain, the great Bryan Robson, to help him promote a new greetings card shop. Ron Wood is a big Man U fan who owned the Birthdays card factory in Bury and shops all over the country; I think Robbo was in business with him, having quite a few of the franchises, and they were opening one in Dublin, so he thought it'd be good if Man U's two young starlets put in an appearance at the launch.

It must have been an official day off, no playing or training, so we said we'd do it, and we were probably paid a few bob for it, but it turned into a nightmare tour of a day in the life of Bryan Robson. It was just an ordinary day off to him, leisurely. We got to Manchester airport in the morning, and Robbo got the beers in, a few bottles to set us up. On the plane over to Dublin we had a couple of cans just to pass the time, chatting, enjoying the ride. Then we landed, went straight to the shop in the city centre, and suddenly I was stunned by English football's massive popularity in Ireland; Manchester United's in particular. We were absolutely mobbed; it was like the Beatles touching down in New York in the sixties. There were thousands there, screaming girls pressing their faces up to the window of our car, Giggsy waving out of the window as if he was the world's number-one teenybop heart-throb. Which, of course, was my job – but I let it lie.

When we got to the shop, we were cutting the ribbon,

meeting and greeting. There was a fridge full of beer, so we cracked open a couple of them, then Giggsy and I went downstairs to sign autographs for a while, make the girls' day. We had a good time, then after a couple of hours we were driven back to the airport but the plane was delayed, so we had three or four beers in Dublin airport while we were waiting. We had another couple on the plane, then when we landed we went to Mulligans, a favourite United players' haunt in the Four Seasons Hotel in Hale next to the airport.

Well, we had a drink or two in there, and by this time I was really quite half-cut, merry, you could fairly say. We'd had a few hours off without a drink while we were signing autographs, but we'd been drinking from quite early morning. We had a few in Mulligans and suddenly, around eleven o'clock, I was really gone. It all hit me; I was absolutely smashed, pissed, couldn't see properly. I was staggering about, the floor rising up to hit me in the face. The room was swimming around me, and somewhere around its rim I could make out Robbo, up at the bar, older than us in his slacks and shirt, just chatting, to blokes he knew or punters, having an ordinary night out, a few beers. They were going on to a club and I seriously was not in any shape to do that, but there were only Giggsy, Robbo and me and it wouldn't do for me to bow out just then, so I did go along to some club where I swayed about, until 12.30 or so, when our day out to Dublin with Bryan Robson caught up with me. Next minute, I was downstairs in a toilet cubicle, the young footballing crush-magnet, throwing my guts up, lying on the floor with my head in the bowl, doubled up, thinking: get me out of here. Get me to bed. I want my mum. Robbo, meanwhile, was upstairs, perhaps a little bit tipsy by now, but right as rain, enjoying himself, chewing the fat with a few blokes at the bar, the night yet young. Just an ordinary day off. I think he poured me into a cab, sent me home to crawl under my duvet. The following day I needed a crane to get me up, but Robbo was there, at the front in training, running faster, harder, than anyone. Truly, madly, deeply frightening.

United was a plc by now, the ground was becoming all-seater, it was the start of the big-money revolution which Roy Keane would later blame on the prawn-sandwich brigade, but we were still at that time a group of blokes which most football people would recognise as an English football team. Robbo was still organising sessions out for the lads. It wasn't just a good time to him, a bit of a relax; he believed in it. It was an important part of a club, for the players to bond, and also it was all about seeing the inner characters of the players once the beer had drowned what guard they might have. He used to tell the manager we were going out for the day, make sure all the reserves were there, clear the ground rules: what time some of the young ones had to go home or whatever – the main thing was to stay just the right side of trouble and make sure there was nothing that would end up in the papers.

Eric Cantona joined that season, in December. Everyone knows the difference he made on the field; he had that gift of dragging space around, of having time on the ball, and the vision to find openings and angles which no other player would have seen. He made a lasting impact because he had a kind of mysterious foreignness, he was exotic, and he played up to it, with his trawlers and fishermen and refusal to conform. Off the field, though, to me, he was just one of the lads, a footballer, who liked his drink and to go out and be with the team.

We had a Christmas do that year, which I think Robbo was at the forefront of organising, a skill I learned from him and which would make me famous at other clubs. As usual, we had a meal at the Four Seasons, in an area separated off for us, then we went to a bar or two, then that night we had part of a club boxed off; I think Incey knew the owner. We had a show with strippers, which was pretty normal for a Christmas do, and the lads were told that if anybody wanted sex with the strippers they'd have to pay them extra on top. It wasn't really my thing, to pay for it, but later on in the night I was sitting near the end of the bar and I heard this tremendous grunting, pumping, 'UGH! UGH!' coming from behind a door. I went with another of the lads to investigate, we pushed open this door, couldn't see anything, walked in and round the corner was one of the customers shagging this girl so hard it was a miracle she ever managed to walk out of there.

Alex Ferguson indulged Eric; he was the eccentric French genius, this artistic temperament which had to be nurtured or he'd blow up and flounce off. Which was probably true – but it pissed me off. There didn't seem to be similar allowances for me, or a special way to bring me on, little thought of how I might react or what I might need. I think there were two things going on with the manager and me: bollockings, which were designed to 'keep my feet on the ground', but actually undermined my confidence and turned me into a rebel I wasn't. The other was that I felt Alex Ferguson always saw me as that sixteen-year-old kid with the tie tight round his scrawny neck in the boardroom at Torquay.

There were times when the different treatment Eric got was laughable. I'd turn up, and my clothes, hair and car were fair targets for some personal dig, but Eric could wear what he wanted and pretty much do what he wanted, and be indulged. At the end of the season, after we won the title, we had a reception at Manchester Town Hall with all the dignitaries and directors and men in suits about the club. It was the close season, summer, so it was hot, but we all had to wear suits and be smart young men to meet the Lord Mayor of Manchester and Lord Mayors and Lady Mayoresses of all the different districts of Greater Manchester. We had to turn up at seven for a seven-thirty meal, and when I got there, all the lads were in dark navy or black suits, proper conservative, respectful gentlemen's attire. I picked for the occasion, out of my extensive wardrobe of the time, a tasteful olive-green silk suit with a rust-coloured silk shirt, the outfit completed with a green and rust silk tie. It might sound horrendously loud, but actually it was a pretty cool summer suit, well made; it looked quite smart, none of the lads thought anything of it at all and nobody gave me stick.

The manager came straight up to me: 'What the fucking hell have you got on?'

'Well, I thought we had to wear a suit, so I'm wearing a suit.'

'Yeah, but the lads have got black or navy suits on; they all look smart.'

I was sighing. 'Well, if you'd told me to wear a black or navy suit I would have done. But you told me to wear a suit, so I've got a suit on.'

He was at a loss with me again, over something so small, so nothing; he was on about fining me. He was shaking his head, exasperated: 'It's ridiculous wearing that sort of suit here.'

I looked over to my left, and there was Eric. He had on a black suit, fair enough, but with a white shirt, the collar wide open, no tie, and on his feet at the end of these black suit trousers were a pair of bright red, canvas Nike trainers.

We both just stared for a few seconds, the manager stuck for words. I said: 'Are you going to be fining Eric, then?'

Alex Ferguson almost screamed. I swear he gave a sort of 'Aaargh' before he stomped off.

It sounds like nothing, pretty funny really, Eric saving the day with his bright red trainers in the middle of some over-the-top function room in that massive Victorian town hall. Eric got the leeway, that was him, he had to express himself, he was French, but I thought the manager couldn't help but forever think of me as the wide-eyed kid he'd met off the train five years earlier. I became convinced the manager didn't like me, he'd had enough of me, he was just going to sell me. I was wrong, as it turned out: he never did try to sell me.

There was another one on a pre-season trip to Dublin. The manager had a sergeant major-ish, Victorian Dad-style hang-up about short hair; he was always telling players to get their hair cut if it was long. I decided I fancied shaving all mine off completely and having a skinhead, so on one of those long nights in the hotel with nothing to do, I asked one of the young lads, John O'Kane, who had clippers, to shave my hair. I wanted a number two, fuzzy, not completely gone, but it looked awful, like a soggy tennis ball, when he'd done it, so he shaved it all off on the basis that it'd grow again in a few days' time. He pressed hard on my head, so it really was a bonehead.

The next day I came down for breakfast and I can picture the manager's face now. He was eating his breakfast, he looked up at me and practically dropped his cutlery, just stared at me in total exasperation. So I was looking at him, he was looking at me, another put-down was heading my way, when Eric walked in behind me, with his head bald and shiny: he'd had a complete skinhead. Alex Ferguson saw him, shook his head, then just looked down and carried on eating. Saved by Eric again.

I ended up doing things on purpose at that time, wearing a loud shirt or a loud tie on a match day, messing about with my hair, anything to wind him up. I was pushed, so I pushed back. It might sound silly now, but it was a survival tactic, a way to keep my character intact.

When Eric karate-kicked that fan a couple of seasons later at Crystal Palace, it was astonishing. Nobody had ever seen anything like that at a football ground; we just could not believe he'd done it. We drew 1–1, and we came off still mostly in shock at what Eric had done. The manager came in and we had no idea what he'd say about it; we were practically diving for cover before he started. It never came, though. He was a bit busy, saying he wasn't happy we'd only drawn with Palace, and he tore into a few people for playing rubbish. Someone had given the ball away, another hadn't tracked back, someone else should have scored; whatever, the usual. We should be coming to places like this and winning.

Then he just turned to Eric, and said, really mild, no shouting, no raising his voice: 'And, Eric, you can't go round doing that.'

That was it, that was all he said to him. We could not believe it. Now I think he said afterwards that he hadn't seen the incident, so maybe he just meant the fact that Eric had been sent off for kicking Richard Shaw all over

Selhurst Park, but even so, if anyone else had done just that, he'd absolutely have slaughtered them. Then when Eric got his long ban, he ran off to France and started talking about retiring, so Alex Ferguson went over to bring him back, went to his house in Paris to talk to him and plead with him to return. He was showered with praise, then, for standing by Eric through Eric's ban, when he was working with underprivileged kids in Salford, but he was terrified Eric would flounce off, as he did at the end of his time at United. With Eric, he had to watch his feelings, mollycoddle him because he was supposedly an off-the-wall genius who needed to be treated differently to get the best out of him. It was one set of rules for him and one for the likes of me. Yet in the press, the manager was praised for treating Eric differently. You still hear people saying that he tailored his management to individual needs. But I don't think he adapted his style for me.

That season we didn't start too well. I didn't come back from the meningitis until November, when we were tenth. Eric joined three weeks later, and we went on that tremendous run, losing just two after that, winning the final seven games of the season, making it to the top by the beginning of April and not losing after that. We won it, finally, without playing: Villa lost with two games to go, which meant they couldn't catch us, so we were champions, even before we were due to play Blackburn at home the following night.

It was an epoch-changing moment for the football club, the culmination of the careers of some of the older lads, the threshold and platform for all the success that would come for United through the nineties, but for me, well, I just didn't feel that great. I couldn't get hold of anyone, I didn't know where the action was so I went down to Old Trafford, where crowds of fans had gathered, and I ended up getting lifted up in the air and thrown around. The fans were ecstatic and that was brilliant, but the security people brought me into the ground for my protection. Finally I managed to get hold of some of the lads. They said they were at Brucey's, so I went round there and everybody was half-cut, music playing, the wives all there, all the players getting drunk and slapping each other on the back. I was off the pace, we had a game the next day, I thought I'd steer clear of the manager having a go at me, let them have the bollockings the next day, so I went home quite early, one, two o'clock, something like that. Some of the lads were there till four or five, toasting United's first League-title win for twenty-six years.

Before the Blackburn match the next night, the manager went easy about the drinking: 'I don't even want to know what went on last night,' he said in the dressing room. 'It's congratulations. I know you were round at Brucey's, but I don't want to know what's gone on.'

You could see how chuffed he was. How relieved, how fulfilled, how it was everything to him. How proud of his boys, how huge it was to him, the culmination of a lifetime's work, the arrival on the plateau where he'd always wanted to be.

'Just make sure you go out and win tonight.'

Robbo had played only a few games all season because he was injured, and his time was coming to a close; he'd been sub for weeks, while I'd played every game. The manager made Robbo sub again for the Blackburn game, but he wanted him to share in the glory.

'I'll be watching carefully. Someone will come off for

Robbo, because he's coming on to play the second half.'

He was still the team captain, the great warrior who'd helped drag the club to this, and the manager, fairly, wanted him on the field the day United won the league. But the second he said it, my heart sank. I thought: yeah, and I can tell you now, whatever happens, who it is that's going to be making room for Robbo.

We went out, and 40,000 fans were there, completely and utterly beside themselves, hailing this moment they'd waited for, many of them, all their supporting lives. It was carnival time at Old Trafford, and there was me, who'd been there since I was seventeen, from a different era really, playing my part in a new side – only me, Steve Bruce, Brian McClair and Mark Hughes, besides Robbo, had played that day I'd run out in the sunshine for my debut against West Ham. Yet somehow I struggled to revel in my part in the triumph, because the whole of the first half, I knew Ferguson would be hauling me off. Football's a team game but any player will tell you, you're only happy when you're playing, and playing well. So at the pinnacle of my career, the end of everything I'd worked for and devoted myself to, everything I'd given to the manager, the club and my team-mates, half time came, I was off, Robbo was on, and I had a sour taste of disappointment in my mouth. We beat Blackburn 3–1, it was a real party. Robbo deserved to be on, don't get me wrong, but I felt not fully there. I was one of those with mixed feelings, coming off the sidelines in my tracksuit, trying to celebrate with the lads. It's strange, that I remember it as so bitter-sweet, because the facts were that I'd recovered from a desperately awful illness to play every game but one, and I had a Premier League medal, deservedly so, which should count as a great achievement.

Yet there it is. I gave the medal to my dad, he put it up in the loft at their house in Birmingham, and it's associated in my head with the growing, sinking conviction that I was on the edge of it all, no longer one of Alex Ferguson's important players. I felt I was becoming expendable. Strange, in a way, having been so important to dragging United up, that the start of the decade of success was the beginning of my own disenchantment.

CHAPTER 12

Is this all there is?

The following season, 1993–94, United went one better and won the Double, establishing the club's place at the top of the English game; and there's me again, without particularly good memories of it, feeling I was sidelined. Yet, again, look up the bare statistical record of the season, watch the video highlights, and they show that I was absolutely flying; it was my best season in football. I was strong, fit, fast, playing in a team full of good players who knew they could win, and, while it was true that the manager did move me around, he included me in most of the games when I was fit – I had a hernia at the beginning of 1994 – and I mostly performed, smacking the goals in without a thought, running straight over to the fans afterwards and giving it plenty from one of my repertoire of daft dances. For all that, whatever the video shows of my part in a Double-winning side, I remember having more fun off the pitch than on it.

Life had taken a turn for the better because Roy Keane had arrived. From what I heard, Alex Ferguson asked Robbo, perhaps Steve Bruce, one or two of the senior players, who he should sign that summer. They told him that Roy Keane had been the best player in the league the previous season for Forest. That was another quality Alex Ferguson had: he asked the advice of his senior players, which many managers never did.

Keaney and I got on straight away. He's got his dark side, as everybody knows by now, but he and I are the same age, he was company for me, who'd been one of the youngest in the team, and he's incredibly funny. People don't realise that about him, because he comes across so aggressive and he's got these Damien eyes that would kill you as soon as look at you. But he is really quick-witted, mostly in a savage, cutting, ripping-the-piss-out-of-people sort of way. The trick, which a lot of people haven't grasped over the years with him, is not to take it personally; instead, the obvious answer to his brooding, menacing, fucked-up ways, which came to me naturally, is to laugh at him. In training he used to rip into people. If they hadn't given him the right pass, or not tracked back, or just slipped up in some aspect of the life-and-death business of playing football, he'd carve them up, dissect them and leave them in pieces. He used to start in on me sometimes, and I just used to look at him, smile, say, 'Come on, this is me now,' and he'd shut up, shake his head and growl away again.

In the dressing room, we were a double act, sitting next to each other to get changed at the Cliff, messing about like a couple of kids, taking the piss out of the old gents in the team, their clothes, shoes, crap hairdos, anything they ever said, giggling away like a couple of hyenas. Players would come in and we'd be straight into them, no mercy. Gary Pallister was one of the best. He was a good mate of mine, Pally, still is, but he really is a very sensible person, with his side parting and sports jackets and brogues. By then a lot of the lads were being sponsored, and Pally always used to turn up in all his free, sponsored, Reebok tracksuit and gear, even though he's so tall and his legs are so unfeasibly long that the stuff never fitted him. So Pally would walk in for another day at the office and we would be straight at him, ripping into him for his style bypass, calling him tight for not spending his own money. Paul Parker couldn't take it at all; he used to call Keaney and me 'Piss and Shit'. He'd see us together in there and be like: 'I'm off. I'm not staying here with these two,' and he'd go and read the paper upstairs somewhere.

Roy Keane has become one of the most written about, psychoanalysed people ever in football; he's a bunch of myths more than a man these days. But I knew him before he made the decision somewhere deep within himself that he was going to sack the drink, the going out, the life he led really, and just burrow deep into himself as the obsessive footballer. That was the deal I was never prepared to make: I worked hard, I loved the game, still do somewhere within myself, but it was never going to be the be-all and end-all of my youth.

My take on Roy was that he was a great lad, a great mate; he loved a laugh and to go out, but he had this blackness inside him I suppose I never understood, and it came out when he drank. He'd turn more than aggressive; nasty with it. He could walk into a bar and take an instant dislike to someone who caught his eye, then they would have him coming their way if they stayed around. There was no reason to it; it was part of him, a part he indulged, that there were good guys and bad guys. He's talked about all that himself, who are fakes, who are real, all that black and white stuff which I, drifting along thinking what will be will be, have never shared. I think we got on and he trusted me because I was his laid-back opposite, yin to his yang, balm to his fury. For some reason, it's an aricle of Keaney's faith: don't trust anyone, your colleagues aren't your friends, they're just work acquaintances. Which is mostly true, in football teams; we're all looking after ourselves, and the laughs and friendships can be only as deep as the thickness of the team shirt, or, with some people, not there at all. But it's no way to think if you want to enjoy life. Keaney has got his family, his brothers, and they're a clan, it's them against the world in his mind, and he's got kids of his own for whom he's the snarling protector. His attitude to the rest of the world's population, particularly when he'd had a drink, was often hatred. I was always pulling him out of black moods, his instant dislike of somebody standing at the bar minding their own business, and I used to do it mostly by laughing at him.

I remember when it kicked off with some of the Liverpool lads in their Spice Boys, white-suits-for-the-Cup-final heyday, the kind of lightweight fluff which was truly not Keaney's idea of football men of backbone. One Saturday night we were in Alderley Edge, which we used to grace with our presence regularly. Brazingamans is a nice nightclub, which has had plenty of money poured into it, and Keaney, who'd started drinking in the players' lounge straight after the match and hadn't eaten anything, was in there absolutely smashed. I'd seen one or two of the Liverpool players in the place, might have said hello, but didn't think anything of it and was up at the bar chatting away, when somebody, it might have been Jamie Redknapp, tapped me on the shoulder and said:

'Will you come and get hold of Keaney. He's kicking off with Babbsy.'

Keaney didn't like Phil Babb, a fellow member of the Irish squad: he was another in Roy's 'No' camp. Christ, what's he up to now? I went over there and he was in one of his evil pissed states.

'Who the fucking hell do you think are, Babb?' Keaney was saying.

Phil Babb was just trying to get away, trying to remember what you do when backed into a corner by a rabid dog: arms at your side, look down, no eye contact, go mumbly and humble.

'Fuck off back to Coventry,' Keaney went on.

So Phil Babb tried the gentle talking method – 'Come on, Roy, we're only on a night out, we don't want any trouble – which didn't work at all. John Scales was there and he tried to act as peacemaker: 'Whoaa, Roy, we're just chilling out and relaxing after the game.'

Then Roy was straight into the limitations of John Scales as a person and a footballer: 'You, Scales, you're fucking rubbish an' all, with your England B cap, you're nowt, you're rubbish.'

So then Jamie came up with his nice smile and boyish twinkle and said: 'Come on, Roy, leave it, man; there's no need for all this.'

So the frothing Alsatian turned to him, too: 'You, Redknapp, are you happy with your Under-21 caps? What the fucking hell have you ever done in the game?' All of which I thought was pretty funny.

Finally I stepped in and put my arm round the unfortunate young man with the devil's own eyes and said, 'Come on, Roy, let's take you away now,' steered him out, found him a cab, apologising to the three lads: 'Sorry, boys, he's just a bit pissed.'

We got out into the Alderley Edge night air and Keaney was giving me a great big cuddle: 'I love you, man. I fucking love you. You're the fucking best, Sharpey.'

And I was like: 'Roy, I love you too, you mad bastard, now get in that cab and go home to bed.'

He trained like a maniac, played with every last bit of blood in his body and will in his crazy head, then we'd go out after matches, to bars in the centre of Manchester, or out in Cheshire footballer-land, and he'd get into all sorts of trouble, wanting to fight the world. He had a proper drink problem at the time, which I never had. He's acknowledged it; it was obvious. I just wasn't into heavy drinking in that way; I went out to enjoy myself, to chat, have a laugh with mates, pull women. I remember Eric Cantona coming up to me in the middle of some chaotic night out once, saying: 'Sharpey, you're the man.' I protested: 'Eric, everybody knows: you're the man.' He said: 'No, no, I've just been talking to these girls; all they want to know is where Lee Sharpe is. You're the man.' And I was like: 'Well, shucks, I dunno…'

Gary Pallister gravitated into a threesome with Keaney and me; we knocked about together, went out drinking quite a bit. The manager used to have us in his office every now and again if he'd heard we'd been out, asking why we couldn't stay indoors. Why couldn't we all go round to Pally's house for a few beers, why did we always have to be out? 'What are we expected to do round Pally's house?' we asked. 'We're young, we're footballers, we're not going to just stay in on the night of a match.'

The three amigos split up, though, after Pally and Roy

started fighting in Marbella on a mid-season break. Those few days were supposed to be a chance for the players to chill and get away from the pressure, but we went in November, the place wasn't exactly jumping, and we used to end up sitting in empty bars on our own, killing time. We'd been there three or four days, training in the morning, then maybe some golf, going out at night, but Marbella was dead. One night we were in some excuse for a club, there must have been half a dozen people in there apart from a few Man U players, and Keaney started really winding up Pally. He was going on about Pally being under the thumb – which is funny now, seeing as Pally isn't even married to his partner and Roy's a family man to his volcanic core.

Eventually, Pally decides he's had enough: 'Right, I'm going back to the hotel.'

Keaney's not ready to let him: 'Go on then,' he says. 'Ring your missus, go on, wash that thumbprint off your head. You don't want to be with the lads, do yer, 'cos your missus might not like it.'

On and on, nailing him about his missus and being under the thumb, whereas Keaney's his own man. Pally is a mild, laid-back lummox by nature, but even he reaches a point where he's had enough.

'Keaney, leave it now,' he says. 'I've had enough. I'm tired, I'm drunk, just leave it.'

But Roy keeps going, non-stop. He's even annoying me now. I'm thinking: God, Keaney, just shut up, man, but he won't stop needling away, so in the end Pally just says: 'Right, I'm off,' and walks out on his own.

The club's rubbish, nobody's about, it's so off season the tables and chairs are bored, so twenty minutes later we call it a night too and leave. Fifty yards up the road there's a little snack hut doing kebabs, tapas and stuff, and Pally's there, waiting for his kebab. Keaney, the devil in him, can't help but start in on Pally all over again – 'Give your missus a ring, make sure she's all right, don't you worry about the lads, you ring her, you're so under the thumb' – and this time Pally hasn't got any patience left. The next thing I know, Pally has turned round and swung for him. A great big haymaker. Roy's moved out of the way so it doesn't take his head off, but Pally's hit his wrist, Roy's watch has come undone, and he's protesting:

'See that? He's fucking hit me! I haven't done anything and he's gone and hit me. Are you watching?'

'Keaney, you've been bugging the shit out of him,' I say. 'Just leave him alone.' But the next minute they're at it again. So I jump in between them: 'Whoa now, come on, that's enough, don't start.' It's a bit of a struggle, but I manage to send Roy away before Pally and I stagger back together, sour and pissed off.

They didn't speak for months. Not a word. They were like a couple of teenage girls, each waiting for the other to apologise; it was mad, weird even. It must have been six months at least before they talked to each other. They've never been the same since, never mates again in the way we were, a threesome knocking about together. All over absolutely nothing; just because we were stuck together a long way from home with nothing to do, a bit drunk, and one evening just went on too long. It can work both ways, the time you spend together in a football club. It's not all laughs and banter; it can curdle with footballers as with any group of lads on a night out. You win some, you lose some.

Alex Ferguson wanted young men who didn't get up to

this sort of thing, who ate, drank, slept football, with no other interests or sides to them which he would see as trouble. He was getting a couple of those coming through now: the Neville brothers. Straight, football-obsessed, clean-living, the game was the be-all and end-all to them. I remember one of the first times we ever noticed Gary Neville. We were at the Cliff after training. A few of the old lags were up in the canteen, having a cup of tea; Robbo was there, Steve Bruce. I'm much closer in age to the Nevilles, Nicky Butt, Paul Scholes, David Beckham, the great young players who were coming through, but I was really not their generation, not at United. I'd been schooled in the ways of team spirit according to Bryan Robson. They'd been coached, disciplined, nurtured, harnessed, kept on the straight and narrow under the excellent tutelage of Eric Harrison. I'd been thrown in to discover Manchester myself. So, that morning, we were up in the canteen, drinking our tea, chewing the fat, when we saw this strange sight over near the high wall of the gymnasium.

'What the fuck's that?' somebody said.

We peered over, and it was Gary Neville, on his own, throwing the ball against the gym wall, as hard as he could, over and over again. Practising long throws, Gary Neville's idea of fun.

When we used to go out on one of Bryan Robson's sessions, the round, starting at the Bull's Head in Hale, used to be: twelve Budweisers, six Beck's, a couple of shorts, a bottle of champagne for Eric Cantona, and two Cokes for Gary and Phil Neville. I remember on one of those days out we were about to go to a nightclub, but Gary Neville said he was going home: 'I don't like nightclubs.'

'Sorry?' I said. 'Run that past me again, Gary. You don't

like nightclubs? In nightclubs there's beer, decent music, women: what exactly is there not to like?'

But he was insistent: 'No, I don't like nightclubs. They're not my scene.' And off he toddled, with his brother.

Alex Ferguson wanted that attitude, I suppose, although he had to tolerate the drinking and didn't mind it when it was his generals doing it. Keaney was coming to take Robbo's mantle and that, for quite a while, extended to the drinking. Except with Roy, the drinking showed. One night we were at a huge black-tie do at the Midland Hotel with a European trophy-winners theme, with some of the old players from Matt Busby's 1968 team and a core of the players from the 1991 Rotterdam side. You can't get more respectably Man United than that, and it was a huge formal dinner, with 500–600 people there to raise money for charity.

The current players were all on the front table, including Keaney, who that day had gone straight from training to the pub, eventually got home, grabbed his tuxedo, got to the do and then carried on drinking, so by the time the meal was over and the charity auction about to start, he was struggling. The whole crowd could see it and they were loving it. They started singing: 'Keano! Keano!'

Then the charity auction started and Keaney decided to bid, though he wouldn't have had a clue what it was for because I doubt he even knew where he was. It turned out to be for four nights in London with tickets for shows and hotel accommodation, but Roy just slurred out that he'd give £200. Well, the old guy who was bidding against him, who quite fancied these tickets, was a great guy but with a formidable reputation, not that Keaney knew that. We had our heads in our hands as Roy, no idea what he was doing, proceeded to chuck his money away to outbid one of Manchester's finest. I think the guy let him have them when he'd got him up to £500.

After the meal finished, some of the punters left but there were still 150 or so people carrying on in a VIP room afterwards. I was chatting away, enjoying myself, when Steve Bruce came up and said: 'Listen, you'll have to come over and sort your mate out.'

It was always me who had to haul Keaney out of all his scrapes. It's all I did some nights. Keaney didn't like it when fans came up to us wanting to talk when we were out. I don't mind it – I'm sociable and I like it – but there's a line that gets crossed when people are in your face too much. Quite innocently usually, they want to talk to you, talk through the game; they think because you're a Man U player and they're fans we've got loads in common. Normally we used to manage with a nod and a smile and a thanks. Keaney couldn't stand that. It was his personal space, his dividing line between work and being out with his mates. His attitude was that he had given everything he had to the game, and that was his bit for the fans, too. Then, when he was out for a drink, he'd say hello and do his bit but he really didn't want to be talking to people. There were times when I could see him reaching popping point, Demon Eyes beginning to sparkle, and I'd have to ask people to give us ten minutes on our own. For their own health.

But I didn't want to be Keaney's minder every night of my life. I said to Bruccy: 'Is he not your mate, too?'

Brucey just shrugged. 'Come on. He listens to you, doesn't he?'

So I went over and it was the usual story. Some pretty

harmless blokes had done something to seriously annoy Roy; he'd got into one of his moods and he was about to kick off. So I went in again, scooped him up, shepherded him out, told him I loved him, he told me he fucking loves me, I'm a fucking brilliant mate, I put him in a cab and he disappeared down Oxford Road, the performance over.

Next morning, Roy woke up with a steaming headache, a rough throat, and tickets for a four-night trip to London. When he got to training, we told him who he'd bid against to get them.

Alex Ferguson's attitude was that he wished Roy didn't drink like that, but he was able to understand it, I think, more than the way I went out to have fun. Robbo could drink anyone under any table, but he was an awesome football man. I wasn't a big drinker like Keaney, but the manager, I think, didn't get me; he didn't understand me being out in the clubs doing a young man's thing. With Keaney, though, it was a genuine, old-fashioned, working-class drink problem, and that he could relate to. I don't think it ever made him question Roy's attitude if he was up a back street in an Irish pub all day, because he could understand that. If I was out dancing, though, being a bit flamboyant, the manager was convinced my head wasn't on the football. His attitude to the drinking culture was actually rather more subtle than wanting to ban it outright.

I still wasn't sure: does he like me, does he not like me? I'd be regularly on the phone to my mum and dad, saying he'd bollocked me again, and they were finally beginning to think he was going over the top. But then the manager would still pick me. I was playing really well when my confidence was up, but it wavered, came and went in waves; I could never work out a reliable method for preparing mentally for a match.

In that period, even though it is now remembered more for farce than football, being picked for England was a real pleasure, a mini-break from the intensity and pressure at United, where I was now one of the big-game players expected to perform. It was the dog end of Graham Taylor's stint; I'd played in the dreadful 2–0 home defeat by Norway in June, then gone straight on tour to play some friendlies in America, to promote a World Cup we now looked like we weren't going to qualify for. On the way, there was a bit of silliness in a nightclub. Nothing went on but some girl went to the papers, all the married players were getting screaming calls from their wives asking what was going on, and the papers had a field day about England players living large after a defeat. I was just chuffed to make the front page of a tabloid, another feather in the young man's cap: Look, I said to my mates, I really have made it now.

When I came out flying into the new season, scoring two away at Villa which took Man U to the top of the league, Graham Taylor picked me for the final two matches of England's horrible qualifying campaign: the first a 3–0 win at Wembley over Poland, who were out already; the next, a month later, 13 October 1993, away to Holland. Did we not like that game. It will, of course, always be remembered for the manner of Graham Taylor's exit – which isn't fair, really, because he was a lovely guy. I still don't understand why he agreed to a fly-on-the-wall documentary of the car crash which was our qualifying campaign. People forget how badly the luck went against us in that match; we had to win and we gave it a real push. Paul Merson was ripping into the Dutch and he hit the post a couple of times. What really upset Graham Taylor was Ronald Koeman bringing Merse down when he was through. He thought he should have been sent off. As it was, we hit the post from the free-kick, and then Koeman came up to our end and dinked the ball over the wall to score a free-kick for them. We all knew what we would get for England failing to qualify for the World Cup. Graham Taylor knew his time was up, but, knowing the cameras were on him, should he really have allowed himself to follow the linesman up and down, saying again and again: 'Tell your mate he's just lost me my job'? Like everybody, I love it and hate it. It's funny, you can't help laughing, but it hurts. I felt sorry for him when he did immediately lose his job; then when the TV programme came out, he got butchered again. He was good to me, and it was a genuine honour to play for England at the time. I think he was just too normal in the end, too much an ordinary, decent man, and the press were merciless with him for it.

However grim the football, the England trips were still like little holidays for me, the pressure beginning to build as I became one of Man U's more important players. The Sky millions were in, the Premier League was taking off and United were the club for the new era, surrounding the team's success with superstores, merchandising, all the packaging of a football business. As players, that meant we were becoming mini-industries; always balls and stuff to sign, a hubbub around the players' entrance at Old Trafford, the Cliff, more press, magazine interest – and also more money for us. I didn't have an agent, and we weren't keen on agents taking a percentage of our wages, so Bryan

Robson negotiated a new contract on my behalf, and he did the same for Giggsy. We bypassed the manager and Robbo went straight in with Martin Edwards, the chairman, to thrash it out. He was really good. We all trooped in for the show; I just sat quiet, minding my manners. As players, we never had much to do with the board. Martin Edwards was fine; he was obviously shrewd and didn't want to give us too much. Robbo kept saying we deserved more, we were good players, we'd done well for the club. Martin Edwards had a figure in mind, I think Robbo bumped him up a bit, and in the end we did a deal: four-year contract, £250,000 a year wages plus a £50,000 signing-on fee every year. I was twenty-two years old. I'd just gone from a contract my dad had negotiated which delivered £52,000 a year to one that was to pay me £300,000 a year.

Giggsy and I just danced out of there. I was high-fiving, whooping, laughing, jumping about, not knowing what to do. Except, in the words of the play, spend, spend, spend. We bought Robbo a nice Gucci watch, a very expensive piece, as a thank-you for doing it. Top, top man, what a guy, the way he looked after the young lads. Then I went out and bought myself a lovely, juicy big house in Hale Barns, proper footballer land, half a mile down a country lane, backing onto the golf course. It was a gorgeous house, big dining room with a pool table and a bar, lovely spacious living room, four bedrooms, half an acre of land; idyllic. On a Sunday morning we'd sit in the kitchen drinking tea, reading the papers, and ramblers or horse-riders would trot past the house. Sometimes I'd nip out the back and go onto the golf-course greens and do a bit of chipping and putting.

In January 1994 I was out of action with a hernia, went on holiday to Tenerife for a week, and met a girl, Lisa

Crute. Not long after we got back, she moved into that house with me. She was a window dresser, with an eye for design, and she did the house up beautifully, built for a boy to have fun and domestic bliss. In that time, cuddling up together, I'd smoke a bit of weed. It made me mellow, just chilled out; I didn't get out of it, giggly and mad, and I never got really smashed. I'd just have a couple of joints occasionally, on the sofa with a cup of tea, watching a video or whatever. I never used to drink in the house at all.

My best mate for a long time was Mark Russell, a guy I met when I lived in Timperley. He was a male model, a very good-looking guy, and a good golfer; we met on the driving range. Mark, tragically, committed suicide years later; he had attacks of schizophrenia that he never shook off, and it was desperate at the time. He and I were so close; we went out together, played loads of golf, went on holiday, got into scrapes, had laughs. Mark liked a spliff too, and we used to smoke a bit, then put the golf on the telly and practise a bit of putting in his front room – without a golf club. He'd virtually give me golf lessons in his living room, and because I was a little bit stoned, I seemed to really get the message; I was relaxed and it seemed to focus everything. I learned more about golf techniques in Mark's living room with the help of the odd spliff than I did on any driving range in the wind and rain. Then I'd go home and go straight to bed at eleven, twelve o'clock and sleep like a dream, so the demon weed seemed a lot less harmful than going out and guzzling a gallon of beer.

I never went and bought any dope; I never got that far into it, never even rolled the joints, because I couldn't, but I did enjoy it for a while. I never smoked when we were going for a night out, as that's a completely different vibe;

I'd have been well off the pace if I'd been stoned, because it just used to relax me.

In March, we played Arsenal at Highbury on a Tuesday night, which was my first game back from the hernia and niggling injuries; I'd missed nearly three months in all. The team was flying down to London in the morning, so we were at home the night before the match. Lisa and I had sat in, hung out, I'd smoked a couple of joints, and we'd gone to bed early. The following day we flew down, went to a hotel, had a bit of a kip, some lunch, got ready, in the coach, down to Highbury. It was another match when Eric started kicking people and got himself sent off. Funny how you do well against some teams and not so well against others, but I always did well against Arsenal, scored two that night, and we drew 2–2. A cracking return for me, and after a couple of spliffs the night before. So that made me think, it really can't be as bad for you as people make out.

When Chris Armstrong tested positive for dope at Spurs and was banned, I quit completely. I wasn't risking that. I was never going to be a Fabulous Furry Freak Brother, but I enjoyed it while I did it. That was the sum total of Lee Sharpe's life in drugs: cuddling up on the sofa with my girlfriend watching videos, drinking endless cups of tea, or playing imaginary golf with my mate. It wasn't exactly rock'n'roll, but I liked it.

United were champions again, and won the Double when we beat Chelsea 4–0 at Wembley. I'd played every league game when I'd been fit, scored nine in the season, fourth highest scorer behind Eric, Giggsy and Mark Hughes. You can see me in the video, banging them in, carefree, doing a Sharpey shuffle every time, the fans loving it. The manager was just putting up with it by then, but I genuinely wanted to celebrate my goals, show the fans that it was as great as they must think, scoring for Man U at Goodison or Villa Park, scoring winners at home against Tottenham.

The most I remember about the Cup final is that I was sub, and Alex Ferguson brought me on for Denis Irwin, to give me a run with just six minutes to go, when we were already 3–0 up. The fans were in song, the players were cruising, Chelsea were on their knees, the turf was lush; it was all a dream. I went on and knocked the ball about with the lads, Brian McClair scored in the last minute to make it four, then the final whistle went and we all piled on each other. Success poured on success. The dreams of the child with the ball and his boots in bed with him, to win the Double for Manchester United, at Wembley, with your team-mates all around you and the crowd having the time of their lives.

In the dressing room afterwards elation was in the air. Then I heard the manager behind me, poking me in the back and asking: 'What the fuck do you call that?'

I'd had a tattoo done and I really did not think it was any of his business. Nor did I think now was the time and place for him to play the pissed-off father. Plus, I was twenty-three by then, not the sixteen-year-old kid in the tracksuit, nervous as a rooster.

I remember one night around this time at my house at Hale Barns. A lad I was mates with, Jonathan Stanger, a goalkeeper, came back to the house with Lisa and me after we'd been out. The house had scaffolding up because we were having work done on the roof; it was warm, we made a cup of tea when we got back, and Jonathan and I decided, at three o'clock in the morning, to climb to the top of the house on the scaffolding. Up we went, with our tea, up, up, to the top of my lovely house looking out on the golf course, the farm next door, the garden, the still, starlit Cheshire night. We perched ourselves somewhere at the top, looking down, and I thought: it doesn't get much better than this. Look at you, Lee Sharpe from Birmingham, with a nice house and a couple of big cars, a beautiful girlfriend, you're playing for Man U, you're famous and the money is pouring in; sometimes dreams do come true.

Then, I remember, an empty feeling started to burrow its way into the pit of my stomach. The moment of peace and serenity didn't last very long at all. There I was on top of the world, and I felt faintly uneasy, dissatisfied. Was this really it? Had I arrived? Was this the end, the pinnacle, was this all there was? Still, years later, I have never quite worked out what that feeling was; but the constant pressure from the manager was part of it. It was also something to do with having worked so hard to get all this, coming back from illness, injury, striving with all the lads and great players to win that first title, then doing it, then getting my first proper fat contract. I'd done it, at twenty-three: achieved my goals, fulfilled the dreams I'd had since I was a boy. Now I was really here. So what happens now? It was something to do with having had more fun getting there, working up to it all, than being there.

Somebody said to me: people spend hours, days, years, struggling to climb a mountain, overcoming all challenges to get to the top, the crags, the ice, the storms, the jagged rocks. When they finally haul themselves up that last gruelling stretch and onto the summit, it's their ultimate achievement, the culmination of everything they've worked for, elation, incomparable, unbelievable, and they can't take it in. They sit down, shades on, snow flecks in their beard, gazing out at the magnificent freezing blue of the top of the world, awestruck. It's truly wondrous, but, after just a few minutes, a bit chilly, too. Slowly they realise they're hungry, they need the loo. Gradually they run out of things to do: they've seen the view and it's great, but they can't stay up there all day. So, they look around them, gather up their stuff, and begin the journey all the way down again.

CHAPTER 13

Flying the nest

I suppose it might seem a bit weird, that of all the things to do when the great club I joined eight years earlier went on to win the Double again, the Double Double, I asked for a transfer. But I did. I had to get out by then. Manchester United was becoming a dynasty, a power, a massive business, the unbeatable machine which the manager had been implacably determined to create since the day he turned up. But that – winning, the silverware – was never what I had in mind; I really did want to enjoy my football. I didn't want to take the big, ballooning direct debits into my bank account, be a model pro, a squad member, play twenty-five games a season in different positions, collect the medals for a glass cabinet in the living room. I wanted to be in every match, on the left wing, beating full-backs, scoring goals, doing daft celebrations, playing with a smile on my face.

I had played most of the games the season before, 1994–95, when we just lost the title to Blackburn at the very end, and were beaten in the Cup final against Everton when we didn't perform. I broke my ankle in the third round of the League Cup at St James' Park in October 1994, so was out again for three months, but apart from that I was in the side, mostly playing midfield again, but sometimes left-wing if Giggsy was out; once or twice filling in at left-back if Denis Irwin switched to the right. The manager kept telling me he wanted me to play a defensive position, but I never fancied it at all. He didn't take the time to explain why, his word had to stand, and questioning it, or just asking him for a reason, was exactly what you didn't do. So I had run-ins with him over that and we grew more distant. I remember Giggsy and I taking a fearful bollocking at half time at Anfield, with him playing in front of me and neither of us being able to pick up the runs from their five-man midfield and overlapping full-back, Rob Jones. We used to have trouble against Liverpool even when we were winning everything.

Being moved around, I felt I couldn't get going; my confidence was still erratic. I was picking up injuries, then having to work back to form afterwards, but I was played in different positions, so I didn't get enough of a run anywhere. I do think, looking back, that at this time in my career I began to suffer from the lack of a foundation of proper coaching. I was a confidence player, and without that bedrock of technique, all the moving around, injuries and occasional bollockings were eating away at me. Now, the clubs have psychologists – I read somewhere that Bolton have three of them. Bolton! Back then, nobody at Manchester United was available in that role. When I filled out, I lost half a yard of pace, so maybe we needed to reassess what position would be best for me. I could do everything well, so that meant Alex Ferguson fancied me as a playmaker in midfield, or he could have talked me into playing left-back; after all, we played all those years with Denis Irwin, a right-footed left-back, and I found myself filling in all over the park, trying to do my best with my own resources.

I didn't have any techniques for mental preparation, either. I still used to feel incredibly nervous before every game, driving to Old Trafford at twelve o'clock, smelling that sweet, hoppy smell on the way, thinking: Christ, I've got to go through it again. I still always brooded on my performances, accentuating the negative, burrowing into myself with self-doubt. If I scored, it was lucky. If I missed, yeah, well, I was being found out. That's how my mind would work after games if I wasn't careful. I never worked out how to prepare myself before a match, so I never knew if I'd play well or not. Some days I'd focus everything on the match, block everything else out, take the warm-up desperately seriously, focus in the dressing room, walk out strong and determined, then when the game started it would fly off the side of my foot, I'd give it away, I wouldn't find my man. If I then got criticised, it only added to my self-doubt.

Then other days I'd drift into Old Trafford with the music on, light-hearted. My mates from Birmingham would be in the stands and in the warm-up I'd find myself thinking about them, the good night we'd have afterwards: we'd go to my local pub and get something to eat, then back to my house to get changed and order the taxis. I'd think about all the different bars we'd go to and where we'd end up and who we might see and how good it would be. Then when we played the match, it'd be a dream, everything going right, I'd score, celebrate, beat my full-back, play every ball to feet, work hard, we'd win and the manager would love me again. I spent most of my time for four years worrying that he hated me, that he was going to sell me, but he never did. Then I'd play well, he'd give me a smile and a pat on the back and I'd think he might like me after all.

You spend your time looking for the zone. You play your best not when you're tense and psyched up, as they call it, but relaxed, at ease, in tune with mind and body. Your vision is at its widest, you see everything clearly, you have time, everything happens in a manageable way and you can choose what you're going to do. One of the best goals I ever scored was against Barcelona when we drew 2–2 with them, Nadal, Romario and all. The ball came across from the right when I was arriving at the edge of the six-yard box. It was all clear and perfectly in place: the way I was running with my marker, the ball was coming just a touch behind me and my guy was in front of me and I could see exactly where the keeper was and would be, so I let the ball run on just that bit further past my left foot as I ran in and stroked it in with a flick of my right. It bulged the net in the corner and, if you look at the video now, you can see after that one I absolutely did not know what to do with myself, it was so perfect, an equalising goal against Barcelona in the European Champions League at Old Trafford, and it was a back flick, at pace, with my right foot, so what should I do? I had to do something. I ended up pretending to shag the post, didn't I? I was sort of pumping the post which was holding the back of the net and even at the time I was thinking: what on *earth* are you doing? I was ecstatic, truly; those are the moments you work your life for, and which you never get back again, and which you miss when you've retired, so when they happen, you want to enjoy them. Afterwards, the papers said it was cheeky but actually it wasn't. It was the only option available. It was probably the best goal I ever scored. It was professional football at the highest level, perfection.

Yet sometimes I'd go out against Coventry or Wimbledon or Middlesbrough and I couldn't control the ball, I couldn't beat a man, I couldn't find one of ours. I might get a bobble in the first few minutes, and suddenly feel tense, start a debate in my head about what I'd do next time it came, suddenly I was chasing it and consciously trying too hard, and the zone was something that only other people found. Suddenly it's all escalating and spiralling and I'm thinking I'm shit and I can't play and at half time the manager confirms that that is indeed the case, and I'm so far in a hole I can't remember how you start to dig yourself out. And all the while I suppose I look carefree because that's the way I am.

I went through a locker, kit bag and suitcase full of pre-match routines and thoughts I dreamed up for myself, putting my left shin pad and boot on first, going out fifth or sixth in line, but I never really believed in any of them. I'd try the relaxed, thinking-about-my-mates technique one week and do well, then have a nightmare the next. So the next game I'd try another method, to clear my head, go out, play naturally. Sometimes it worked, sometimes it didn't. In fact the truth was, as I was forced to admit to myself, none of it made any difference, and I had to sack the superstitions and pre-match rituals.

The squad was getting bigger, too, which obviously made it more difficult for me to have a place every week. When I was first in the team, there were only two or three left-side players at the club, and one of those was Ralphy Milne, so I wasn't competing with too many for a place. By now,

Giggsy had claimed the left wing, and the manager also signed Jordi Cruyff and Karel Poborsky. Gradually, the young pups of the awesome youth team were coming through, and in the first game of the 1995–96 season, we went out for the first game, away at Villa, with Gary and Phil Neville both playing and another couple of lads who Alan Hansen had clearly never heard of – Nicky Butt and Paul Scholes. I played in that game, on the left wing because Giggsy was out; Roy Keane played, Pally, Peter Schmeichel, Brian McClair – what a side. We lost 3–1 and Hansen came out with his brilliant, unshakeable judgement that you 'win nothing with kids'. Maybe not, as a rule, but we'd seen these kids come through and we had an idea they were pretty decent. On the bench that day, with John O'Kane, one who didn't make it at United, was David Beckham, who had been reared as somebody special from the age of thirteen and was part of the furniture. Becks was popping into the first-team dressing room as a kid, the manager ushering him in to talk to the lads, so we had known him, and his parents, for years. Then we'd watch the youth team play and see Becks sitting in midfield, pinging sixty-yard passes straight to people's feet, striking the ball in that beautiful, clean way of his, curling it, crossing it, and we knew he had a very special talent. The players would say hello to him and by the time he was sixteen he was comfortable with them. We weren't some out-of-reach superstars; we were just the first-team lads to him.

The buzz started to go round that we had a special group of kids once they started getting in the A team. I'm not much older than them, just two or three years, but I was an experienced campaigner from the drinking-culture days by the time these athletes were calmly playing their way to stardom. There was no jealousy towards them; you didn't have gnarled old pros trying to keep the kids down. The older players liked to go and watch the young lads when they could. It was exciting to see how good they were, to pick out who was going to be special. It cheers everybody up to see young talent blossoming; like spring blooming between the cracks of the grey pavements of Salford. If ever we were playing on a Sunday or Monday, we might do some training on the Saturday and we'd catch the end of their game as we came off, or have a shower and watch the second half. Sometimes when they played in the FA Youth Cup, some of the first-team lads would go to watch, take their own kids with them. Often we'd see that these kids were, quite simply, better than we were. I'd watch Becks and know he had ability I'd never have. He was a different class technically, but perhaps a bit lightweight, so they sent him to Preston on loan to toughen him up. Deepdale for him was Murder Ball to me.

The Nevilles were footballing machines, Alex Ferguson's perfect graduates. Nicky Butt was sound: rough and ready, got stuck in on the pitch but a genuine, nice lad, self-confident but not loud, slice of Mancunian wit on him, really good to have around, and an excellent player. He improved, too; at first he used to give the ball away a little bit cheaply but he worked on his passing and uses the ball well now. Pelé himself said Butty was one of the best players in the 2002 World Cup. I think Alex Ferguson made a mistake letting him go; I think United miss him now.

Paul Scholes was the archetypal Salford kid with not a lot to say. He was never, let's face it, going to trouble Magnus Magnusson on *Mastermind*, but he had only to walk over a touchline onto a football pitch and he was instantly transformed into a brilliant athlete, with a great sporting brain. Towards the end of the first year of his apprenticeship, Scholesy wasn't the most fancied of the group and they were even considering letting him go, then one day after our training the manager and a few of the senior lads were watching the youngsters play an A team game. Scholesy picked the ball up on the edge of the box, as millions have watched him do week in, week out, for a decade, skipped round three people and smashed the ball into the bottom corner. Everybody on the line was like: ahem, I think we perhaps ought to give this boy more time...

What I've said here about my experience of Alex Ferguson might shock a few people who believe, because all these lads came through, that he must have been an expert handler of difficult young talent. You could point to these lads and say it must have been me, my partying, drinking, my attitude, that I was the one who got away. Yet, thinking about it, as I have, I reckon it's a lot more complex, and there are a few more difficult questions for United to answer. For a start, as I've said, out of my generation, the lads holed up in the boarding houses round Salford in my time, the fledglings, the Sean McAuleys, Shaun Goaters, Wayne Bullimores, crowds of them, hordes of them, I was the only one who made it. The rest were shipped down to the lower divisions without even a footnote in the official histories. And then look at the ones who did make it later: they were all local boys; they all lived at home with their parents. Except one. Becks. Giggsy, the Nevilles, Nicky Butt, Paul Scholes, they did their training then went home to their mums and dads and got to be themselves. They weren't with a group of ten apprentices, larking about but

Lee Martin, Russell Beardsmore, me, Mark Robins and David Wilson –
the first batch of Fergie's Fledglings on tour.

Bryan Robson with some of the young United players. He was a leader in so many
ways, on the pitch and off it. (*Popperfoto*)

Top: The bachelor pad, c1990, with all mod cons – even a phone!

Above: The drums didn't go down too well with the boss either.

Right: The date: 28 November 1990; the venue: Highbury; the score: 6–2 to United, and a hat-trick for me; the result: I got the full hairdryer treatment. The goals were a twenty-five-yard curler, a header and a right-foot finish. (*Colorsport*)

Bryan Robson and Mark Hughes are intensely focused on the task ahead, against Barcelona in the 1991 Cup Winners' Cup final. Meanwhile, Paul Ince tries to knock me over with his knee, as we share our own private joke. (*Colorsport*)

Let's party! Ryan Giggs and I celebrate beating Forest to win the League Cup in 1992. (*Colorsport*)

Twenty-six years of waiting are over, as Brian McClair and I celebrate winning the Premier League title in 1993.

A rueful Fred the Red looks up at me after he's been mugged. (*Colorsport*)

Bryan Robson and I
warm up for the
recording of United's
number one hit 'Come
On You Reds' with Rick
Parfitt and Francis Rossi
of Status Quo. A true
classic! (*Popperfoto*)

David Seaman does not look best pleased as I score one of my two goals past him in a
turbulent 2–2 draw at Highbury in March 1994. That season I was really flying.
(*Colorsport*)

Backheeling the ball into the net in the Champions League against Barcelona in 1994-95 – one of my all-time favourite goals. (*Colorsport*)

Celebrating the goal in a style that always infuriated Alex Ferguson. Well, sometimes he may have had a point, though the fans seem to appreciate it. (*Colorsport*)

On the way to another Double as I score against Manchester City in February 1996. (*Empics*)

The embarrassing 1970s-style bath shot after winning the 1996 FA Cup. Denis Irwin, Ryan Giggs, David May, Gary Pallister and I enjoy the moment. (*Getty Images*)

really in permanent competition, driven half mad with boredom, struggling to grow up. Even in their FA Youth Cup-winning team, which Eric Harrison shaped, coached, trained, none of the boys from outside Manchester made it. With the exception of Becks, and he was an exceptional talent.

There are a few parallels between my progress at United and how Becks got on. As a kid, he was a bit of your classic cockney. He wasn't the sarong-wearing global fashion and lifestyle icon he's become, not living in digs in Lower Broughton anyway, but he still had a bit of a glint and an edge; not loud, but self-confident. Bit flash, I suppose, which came out in the way he played, pinging balls all over the park, doing ridiculously confident things with free-kicks and set pieces. He was a good lad, though, polite, humble, came from a nice loving family not that different from mine. What you see in the media all the time isn't really him, or it wasn't then; really he's pretty quiet, likes his clothes, cars and all that, but loves his football. He was always a nice, genuine lad.

I think he looked up to me when he got there as an apprentice, when I was in the first team but he was just struggling for a bit of strength and not sure he was going to make it. I was friendly with him, probably showed him the ropes a bit. I always remember the time he was at a loose end one Sunday, so he turned up at one of my fan-club afternoons. The Lee Sharpe Fan Club, eh. One of the first of its kind for a footballer. Pure class and glamour. Once I'd hit the big time with my hat-trick at Arsenal and my little dances, suddenly thousands of letters were pouring in, 95 per cent from girls. There was so much that I wasn't managing to answer any of it, so in the end my mum decided we'd set up a proper fan club: she'd do the admin, and Keith Fayne, a friend who did the DJ-ing at Old Trafford, said he'd run discos for all these little groupie darlings of mine.

We commandeered the supporters' coaches, doing different pick-ups all over the country, and we brought these girls to Manchester – we used to get 2,000 turning up. They would be taken round Old Trafford first for a guided tour, round the museum, and then for the grand finale Keith would do a disco for them at Discotheque Royale, the club I practically lived in on Saturday nights with my mates. We'd had plenty of time to get to know the manager there, so he used to open it up for us. We'd have a couple of bands on, a DJ, a raffle and I'd make a little speech, tell them all to have a brilliant afternoon. They'd scream their heads off and then afterwards I'd sign autographs for all of them.

The time when David Beckham came, he was standing shyly off to the side, as he did in those days; sheepish, awkward, nobody knew who he was. He was a young lad, living in his digs, working his way through the reserves, with endless time to kill. I remember my dad talking to him, giving him a real gee-up: 'You keep working hard at your game, David, and you'll have all this,' pointing to the Sunday afternoon disco and the fourteen-year-old girls queuing up for my autograph.

Becks shook his head, looked down at the ground: 'Nah,' he said, 'I never will, no chance. Sharpey's a legend.'

You've got to say he was right. OK, so Becks broke into the first team, he scored his wonder goal against Wimbledon, he met his popstar missus, he's become quite famous on billboards and TV screens all over the globe – do they say he's the most immediately recognisable face on the planet? – made a bit of money, I shouldn't wonder. All well and good, but has he ever sold out the Discotheque Royale in Manchester on a Sunday afternoon? I think not.

We're so close in age, but what stardom entailed when we each came through was completely different. Football had exploded by the time he made it; gone a little beyond features on the inside back pages wearing three top hats. Still, even though his presence in the Man U team launched him into global celebrity and mega money, there are similarities between his experiences of Man U, and Alex Ferguson, and mine. He was better than me, don't get me wrong. He was by rights one of the best players in the country; they won the European Cup, the Treble, with him skipping up the right; he didn't drink loads, he looked after himself, he was a completely dedicated and brilliant professional footballer – so why did he have so many issues with the manager? And what was it if not the same old stuff, that strange allergy Alex Ferguson had to 'lifestyle' – clothes, hairstyle, girlfriends, what you were doing in the press? The difference was that in my time, the lifestyle issues, the antics which made Alex Ferguson feel he was losing control and that I was losing focus, were a few puny interviews in the odd magazine, fan-club Sunday afternoons for young girls, and going out with my mates to cheesy bars like Cheerleaders on a Saturday night. By the time Becks married Victoria and hit the big time, his entertainment of choice was a film premiere in Monte Carlo with Elton John and an entourage – but at its heart it was the same stuff.

Alex Ferguson also wanted to control everything I did on the commercial side. He said he hated agents, and he even arranged my first couple of endorsements, of boots and shin pads. By this time, though, I had an agent, Jonathan Marks – looking after sponsorships, not the football contracts with United – and he secured me a column in the *People* and work for Barclaycard. There was some modelling, magazines wanted my face on the cover; I was still an appealing face of born-again football, weeding the soil ready for Becks, you might say. One day, the manager called Jonathan, asking what the hell he was doing, telling him: 'Everything goes through me here.' Then he had me in his office, wanting to know who Jonathan Marks was, saying he was trying to destabilise me and get me a transfer. I told him that was ridiculous, he wasn't even doing my football contracts, so if he got me a move there was nothing in it for him, and as he was doing my image, my commercial endorsements, what could be better for him than me being at Man U? The manager was concerned, yet I was only doing the completely reasonable thing of employing an agent to find me work. Later, Alex Ferguson would be criticised for the closeness of the links of his son, Jason, with the agency work at the club.

Becks coped with it better than I did, the bollockings, the hairdryers, once they started, but he had a team of PRs and commercial people handling all his affairs. After the incident when the manager kicked the boot and it whacked into Becks, there was David in his car with his plaster on for the paparazzi; he played the publicity war very cleverly. It must have been horrible in the dressing room for him for a while, but he danced and skipped round the manager and in the end outmanoeuvred him, got his move to Real Madrid, and whatever the overkill of his *galáctico* life with Victoria, most people believe United have missed him, that it could have been handled differently. It wasn't like that for me. I only had my dad advising me really, and he, naturally, just thought it was magnificent, unbelievable, that I was at Man U, and spent a few years telling me Alex Ferguson must be talking to me like that because he liked me. It was only in the last couple of years, when my dad was perhaps less starstruck and used to it, that he thought I had taken enough, and perhaps I should move on. When it came to me and Becks, the manager, with his tough background in Glasgow, found our lifestyles alien, fluff and froth, and he believed it was getting in the way of the football. Which it wasn't; not in my case, and I'm sure not in David Beckham's. It was still my talent, my life, the one thing I'd always been good at, what I enjoyed most. I feel what I needed was some coaching and management, particularly on the mental side; not bollocking me for enjoying myself off the field.

I found it difficult to stop being disillusioned with it all. The injuries got me down. None of them were things I could have helped, broken ankles, hernias, groins, but it's always a long way back without playing, then I was sub for quite a stretch in the November of the win nothing-with-kids season. It was bitty, a struggle, and I might have drowned my sorrows once in a while. Then I was back in, but in different positions, so I had a few run-ins with the manager about that. I didn't play against Newcastle, who were flying then; I was sub against Arsenal, and suddenly I felt as if I was one of the squad players covering for others in the easy games. I had a decent run in January when we hit tremendous form. I scored the only goal against Blackburn at home, then Eric went on a ridiculous scoring run to take us top of the league. It was the kind of finish to the season which Alex Ferguson's Man U teams became famous for: invincible, unbeatable, coming strong as others faltered, that experience of stalling in the run-in with Leeds back in 1992 always standing us in good stead. Still, I didn't feel a central part of it. I played more than half the games, came on as sub for ten more, I scored four goals, and from January, in that fantastic run-in, I was involved in every game but one. I scored the winner against Man City in the FA Cup fifth round, scored against Southampton in the quarter-final, played against Chelsea in the semi at Villa Park, but I still had that feeling I was expendable, that I could be rested, brought off, moved positions, and it niggled my confidence and sapped my enjoyment.

What made me decide to go in the end was feeling that I was filling in for other players, that I was only a part of the squad, not a vital member of the team. You're in football to play, or I was, not to be part of some corporation that wins trophies, in which you serve your honourable best. Sorry, no. You want to be out there. I decided I needed to go elsewhere, to a club where they would rate me as a left-midfield player, where I could express myself and work on my game, carve out my own way again. I thought it was time to jump out of the Man United cocoon after eight years, see what life was like in the real world. I remember saying to my mum and dad: I'm playing here there and everywhere, I want to leave now. And in the end they said I was right, it was time to move on.

Because I hadn't played regularly and had been moved around the pitch, because of the rumours about me, people thought there was some problem at United and that ultimately the father figure, at the end of his tether after all he'd done for me over the years, was forced to send me from the bosom of the family. It wasn't like that and he didn't tell me he wanted me to go. My memory of those three years, when United finally hit the plateau of success, was that I spent it all plucking up the courage to go to see him and ask for a transfer. I still think that's quite brave, that it only took three years to go up those terrible stairs, into the scary corridor and knock on his fearsome door.

Perhaps we both could have handled the situation better. I was twenty-five and should have been coming to my peak; maybe I should have gone to him and sat down and asked if we could assess where we were going and what would be best for me. But I couldn't see Alex Ferguson getting into that sort of discussion. As far as he was concerned, I was happy, I'd signed a contract, I was an important part of the squad, and the bollockings were his way of dealing with me. Perhaps it'd shock him to know that players take it to heart, that they might need more encouraging and motivating and some more complicated work than that at times. I felt that the manager thought I was a party animal, that football wasn't my main priority. It was the same mistake he'd make later with Becks, for the same reasons. I could have stayed and had quite an easy time of it in some ways. The team was supreme by this stage and I had a couple of years left on my nice fat contract. I just needed to keep myself fit, play my twenty, thirty games a season. But that wasn't for me. It wasn't my thing. Once or twice after I'd been brought in and done a job in midfield or left-back or somewhere, the papers had called me a 'utility player'. Nothing fills me with more dread and disdain than becoming a utility player – I still wanted to go out there and master my own game, make a difference. I'd tasted it and that's what I wanted from football. I know Phil Neville stayed and did it; Ole Gunnar Solskjaer was the master of being a squad player. I'm sure they both have a big safe for all their medals, but like I say, medals weren't what I was in it for, and nor was being part of a squad. I wanted to feel the wind in my ears, the full-back hitting the deck behind me, make goals, score goals, be fully involved.

We won the title at Middlesbrough that season. I played on the Wednesday in centre midfield and did well; we beat Forest 5–0. Becks scored two, Giggsy got one, Scholesy and Eric the others. There were nearly 54,000 people having a nice time watching it. Steve Bruce had been captain all year, but he'd torn his hamstring, so he couldn't play on the Wednesday, or at Middlesbrough. Before that game, the manager took me to one side and said he was going to play Nicky Butt, because he's more defensive than me and we needed to contain Juninho bombing forward. I was like: fine, yeah, no problem.

We did the team talk at the hotel, then we went down to the ground. I walked into the dressing room and there were three subs' kits out, but mine wasn't there. I said to Brian Kidd: 'What's happening here?'

'You're sub, aren't you?' he said.

So I went and asked the manager and he said he'd put Steve Bruce as sub, not me, because he wanted him to be in his kit when it was time to receive the trophy and pick his medal up. I was out, not even on the bench. It really hit me, that one. Fair enough for Brucey, I could see that. He was Alex Ferguson's new warrior, new leader, great captain, great bloke, so fair enough that he wanted him picking the trophy up in kit. But – minor issue – he could barely walk. He couldn't have come on if we'd needed him. And I'd played my part too; I'd been involved in nearly every game, scored, helped us get to Wembley, yet there I was, not involved at all, not even sub. I felt a million miles away. We won 3–0, Brucey lifted the trophy, they all went parading it round the pitch and I just stayed in the tunnel with my suit on. Bobby Charlton came down and asked me what I was doing.

'You should be out there,' he said. 'You've done your bit.'

I was like a sulky teenager: 'Nah, I'm all right. I'll just stay here,' I said.

When we went to Wembley to play Liverpool, Phil Babb, Jamie Redknapp, John Scales and the rest in their ridiculous white suits, I was sub. He left Brucey out completely, so he told me he thought I'd be happy with that. He did attend to detail, he did know how players might be feeling, but he misjudged me with that Middlesbrough game: that hit me hard, and being sub in the Cup final was no great consolation. Of course I loved it when we won, the old thrill came back when Eric scored that volley to win us the Cup and the Double. You can see me on the film of his goal, because I was behind the goal warming up, jumping up and down like crazy when the ball went in.

Then we had the open-top parade, the town hall reception, the plaudits, the crowds lining the streets, but I felt detached from it all, a bit of a fake. I didn't see the point of medals if you weren't enjoying it. Perhaps I'm different from some of the others: when I used to dream about football as a boy, medals, winning cups, had nothing to do with it. Flying down the wing did, as did being a poster boy on a million bedroom walls, the fame and the girls. But taking a medal home when you haven't played? Er, not my idea of fun.

It niggled away at me through the summer. I remember coming back and working hard pre-season, but after a few weeks I just decided there was more to life than another season on the fringes, that I ought to go and find a club where I'd play every week, a new start and a new experience.

That was it, the moment had come. I braced myself to go to the manager and tell him I wanted to go. I didn't have an agent to do this sort of thing for me, so I went round to Gary Pallister's house for him to help me write out a transfer request.

Pally opened the door to his house in Wilmslow and I told him what I wanted to do.

'Are you sure?'

'Yeah, yeah, that's it, I've made my mind up, just tell me what to write.'

Pally looked at me really concerned: 'Are you sure you want to do this? You don't need to go.'

I said: 'Look, I'm not playing regular, I'm getting nailed all the time, I've been here a long time and I think it's time for a change for me.'

Pally just looked at me. 'But who am I going to play golf with?'

Spoken like a true footballer. As for my feelings, my reasons, my career, what did he care? So I told him to shut up and just tell me what to write. He dictated something, an official request. The following day I went out to buy some half-decent notepaper and wrote it out in my best handwriting.

The next day at training I told Keaney I was going to hand in a transfer request, and he told me not to, to talk to his solicitor first. It was Michael Kennedy, something of a legend among a lot of footballers; he's been passed around on recommendations for years. So I spoke to him and he told me if I handed in an official request I'd lose the signing-on fees they owed me in my contract. I said I wasn't bothered about that, I just wanted to leave, but he said I might as well leave with a few quid if I could, so he called the manager first and talked business with him.

The next day, I made my way up the dreaded stairs. Shitting myself, I believe is the phrase. I knocked and walked in, and there he was, with his window looking out over the pitch, his desk with the TV and video, his trophy cabinet with his manager of the month awards. I went and sat in front of him and, clearing my throat, told him that I'd been thinking about it over the summer and I thought it was time for me to move on. I didn't know what he was going to say, how he'd react. I wondered if he might even punch me.

It didn't take long for my time at Manchester United to come to its end. He was very composed and in one of his paternalistic moods.

'Are you sure?' he said, and I just looked down at the floor.

He told me I didn't have to leave, that I was in his plans, that I was part of the squad and he'd like me to stay. That's the truth for people who think Alex Ferguson had to get rid of me in the end because I wasn't performing or was some sort of bad apple. He didn't and I wasn't. He asked me again if I was sure and I said I was.

'Well,' he said, 'if you've made your mind up, it's your choice.'

I wondered if he was glad really.

Brian Kidd, who'd replaced Archie Knox and was always

close to the players, trusted, a good guy, told me later he'd told the manager not to let me go, that I was still one of the best players at the club and I'd be in the side more than I thought. But I told him I couldn't be playing the odd game and covering for other players: it wasn't for me.

I thought, given the time I'd been there, Alex Ferguson might not put too high a price on me, so I would have the choice of more clubs. There was interest from France and Deportivo La Coruna in Spain. I really fancied going to Spain for a while, thought it'd suit me in every way. He said, well, I was a good player, and I obviously thought I was good because I thought I should be in the side, but I shouldn't worry because there wouldn't be a club in the Premiership which couldn't afford me.

He was good with me – I can't say he was devastated but he was dignified and decent. He told me I'd been tremendous for the football club and I'd always be welcome back. 'Are you sure?' I said, and he smiled.

In the time I was there he'd transformed United from a great club sagging under the memory of Matt Busby's teams to one which won Doubles and would win a Treble. When I made my debut on that sunny September day in 1988, there were people with their hands through railings round the side of the pitch, who'd paid one or two pounds to get in and stand up on the terraces, singing and cheering the team on, United in the blood. It was a privilege to be part of it, and it was an unbelievable dream, that I ever got the chance to do that, but it was all about football, really, the love the fans have for the game. In midweek, a few kids or football obsessives might turn up at the Cliff to watch us train. The players were giants of the game but they liked a drink too; we had some great nights out.

By the time I walked out of the ground and drove away from the forecourt for the last time in the summer of 1996, Old Trafford had become a constantly expanding all-seater stadium and in the school holidays we had 3,000 kids held back behind a rope at the Cliff, screaming for autographs. I used to do them, drag Giggsy or someone out, do a marathon autograph session, let them leave happy. United was a football business, where people came to a match from miles around, from overseas, for a day's very expensive entertainment which they'd pre-booked. The old fans were still there, loyal, those who could afford it, but a large part of the ground was full of new people every week, sitting quietly with their shopping bags, taking in the show. There were more foreign players, most of whom didn't drink, didn't have the English banter, and that changed the balance in the dressing room, turned it from what everybody would recognise as an English football team into more of an athletic enterprise. Within a couple of years Roy Keane would go teetotal: that's how serious things were getting.

I had no regrets leaving; it wasn't the place for me any more. As it turned out, it was all downhill from there, but I didn't regret it then, and I don't regret it now. I had to get out. But since I packed the game in completely in 2002, finished with football at thirty-one, disillusioned, confused, I think for a while truly depressed, I've worried at times that I've become bitter. I'm the free spirit, smile on my face, what will be will be. Bitter is not a part of me, or how I have ever seen myself; it's the opposite, it's for hard, sour men, bunched up with resentments, not me, not Sharpey. Yet I find myself thinking about Alex Ferguson a lot. How he came to get me at sixteen, how he met me at the station that day, showed me round Old Trafford, behaved like a father figure, but also how he threw me out of my house, barged into my next house, chucked everyone out and bollocked Giggsy and me, how he stamped on the greatest week of my life, and now it's over it's hard for it not to eat away at my insides, at my head. He moved on, he was given ever more money to spend, he won the Treble, more League Championships, he was the manager, and it's in the nature of things that he probably never thinks of me. Players come, players go, it's the current team he has to think about, the business of football, of winning. Yet to me, it was my whole life. He was my authority figure, my boss, the man I put my trust in when I arrived and for eight formative years, so I can't help thinking about him, round and round in my head. I'm angry, frustrated, still making sense of what happened there, and what happened after that, so quickly. I made mistakes, I wasn't perfect, I know that. I went out, I wanted to live a life I enjoyed.

In some ways my dad agreed with him. He would ask: 'Why can't you just stay in and live a quiet life, then go out when you've retired?' I would say: 'Because by then I'll be in my thirties and I'll want to be settling down, married with kids. I want to go out now, while it's enjoyable; I want to make the most of life.'

I know that was my choice. I could have played the game more, not been so stubborn, done what the manager said, played where he wanted me, never had an interesting haircut, worn sombre clothes, kept a po-face when I scored, kept a lid on all my emotions, then maybe I'd have lasted longer and we wouldn't have had so many run-ins. It just wasn't me, though. And I do blame him for a lot, too. There could have been more talking and coaching, more allowances for who I was and for the fact that I had to grow up as well. I don't ever want to be bitter, about anything, but I can't help thinking that in some fundamental way, in those eight years at Old Trafford, Alex Ferguson changed me forever.

There were no emotional goodbyes, not really. I stay in touch with Gary Pallister, I'm friendly with all the lads when I see them from time to time, but Roy Keane was right, although too black and white, about footballers: we're acquaintances – rivals, probably, underneath – not truly friends, however much we lark about in the dressing room like kids, and have the banter. I was going, and for everyone else, life was moving on; there was another season to look ahead to for Man U.

After a few days, Alex Ferguson came back to me on the price he was charging for the kid he'd picked up from Torquay for £185,000, who gave him eight years' faithful service at the highest level and had already repaid him ten-twenty-fold. In the end, my fee was to be £5m. It was goodbye La Coruna, farewell South of France. Those clubs had money to pay good wages, but they didn't have that sort of cash to put into transfer fees. A few Premier League clubs were interested – I was still a big star, after all, and had just won the Double with United – but most had spent their transfer funds by that time in the close season. So there were few with the money to pay the asking price, and that was how I ended up going to sunny Leeds.

CHAPTER 14

George's executive club

In Leeds, football fans don't have the blag or the patter of the Mancunians: they talk very straight. If they want to know something, they usually ask a direct question. I still live in Leeds; I like the place, always have, so I meet the fans all the time. They're friendly enough, they've always been all right with me, but the one question most of them always ask is this:

'How come you were so good at Man United, then when you came to us you were shit?'

Simple question – and I wish the simple answer was true: Fergie had had enough of me; it was a lifestyle thing. By the time I got to Leeds the heroin habit was out of control. I was shooting up on the coach on the way to matches, behind the card school and next to the drinks machine. I didn't train because I was always at all-nighters off my head on E. How great it would be to explain it away so simply. What a story for football lads to lap up: it was all my fault; I threw it all away.

This is a real-life football story, though, so it's all much more complicated and dismal than that. I didn't blow it; I went to Leeds to work hard, determined to make my name again at a club which really wanted and believed in me. But football isn't about individuals alone – players want to play, we're only happy if we play well, but we can only play well in a team. The game is about teams, clubs, managers; players are only a part of it. I'd asked for a transfer so that I could discover what life was like outside the bubble of Man U. I did, and learned from my grim journey, by default, how well things were done at Old Trafford.

In any case, that I didn't perform for Leeds is another of those myths that don't quite stand up when you look at the details. The first season there I played pretty well, finishing joint top scorer with Brian Deane despite missing two months with a groin problem, and despite the fact that it was miserable because we were managed by George Graham. Now, I'm a laid-back person; I've got on with just about all the footballers I've ever played with, all the different personalities. I give everybody a chance, I look for the good in them, I usually find it, I like to be friends with everyone. So I can honestly say that, being generous and balanced about it, taking everything into account, I didn't find a lot to like about George Graham.

He hadn't signed me and he never seemed to particularly like me, even though I'd always played well against his Arsenal sides. Perhaps that was why; I don't know. Howard Wilkinson had signed me, for what was big money at Leeds, £5m, and all the signs at first were that it was going to be a great move. Lisa and I went up to Yorkshire on a beautiful sunny day and had a wander round Harrogate, which looked stately and gleaming. Michael Kennedy was negotiating my contract, and kept phoning throughout the day, saying: 'This is incredible; they really want you, they're throwing a lot of money at you.'

Leeds at the time had their famous crop of kids coming through the youth team. The club was in transition after their Championship win four years earlier, but the first team had some very solid, good players, lots of internationals, some of whom, like Tony Dorigo, Carlton Palmer, Rod Wallace, I knew from England trips. They had Tony Yeboah and Brian Deane up front, Gary Kelly at the back, Lucas Radebe had joined, the previous season they'd had Gary Speed and Gary McAllister in midfield, although both had left. Leeds had started well that season but lost 3–0 to Villa in the League Cup final, then had an awful finish in the league, ending up thirteenth. As a statement of intent – another sleeping giant trying to wake up in the new Premiership era – they'd given Howard Wilkinson a lot of money to spend. So my transfer fee, a Leeds record at the time, was partly PR – Howard Wilkinson showing he could sign a top player from Man U. Michael Kennedy calmly ploughed that field of willingness for me until he called me and said he'd got them up to £10,000 a week, a half-a-million-pound-a-year pay package. Thank you, I told him, sitting in a nice restaurant with my beautiful girlfriend, the sun streaming through the windows, where do I sign?

My dad came up when it was time to meet the chairman and do the deal because he loves all that, being on the inside and going round the ground. He embarrassed me fussing on to the chairman and manager about which squad number they were going to give me. Then I came into Leeds' pre-season training absolutely flying. I was fit, free of Man U, as if a weight had dropped off me, so eager for the new start, keen to make a good impression and also, probably, although I didn't know it confidently enough in myself, full of good habits from eight years at United and playing in a team that had just won the Double Double. Howard Wilkinson also signed Nigel Martyn in goal, Lee Bowyer, and Ian Rush, who, the plan went, would play his final couple of seasons as a striker then start on the coaching side, bringing some of the Liverpool ways, the style and consistency, to Leeds. It was all very promising.

At first I travelled over from Hale, doing the M62 every morning to training, but I didn't want to seem like some big-time tourist. I wanted to be fully part of the club, and before I bought a house in Leeds, occasionally I'd stay in a hotel and the players would all go out, have a drink and get to know each other. They were good lads: Carlton Palmer was a bit flash, Gary Kelly is absolutely hilarious, completely mad, Rushy was a legend; we had some good nights. The club was smaller scale than United, but they were trying to be a big club, trying to do everything right.

Howard Wilkinson's plan was for us to play three in midfield, with me wide left where I could get on the ball but also have the chance to run at full-backs and get crosses in. I enjoyed the training straight away; I felt confident, I was scoring goals, flicking it here, lobbing it there, stroking the ball about, smile on my face, loving it.

Howard Wilkinson came up to me in training after a couple of weeks: 'Look,' he said, 'obviously I knew you were good because we paid big money for you, but I didn't realise you were this good. I want you to just get that ball and play your game. It's up to you how good you want to be. You're fit now, but if you get really fit you can get better and better.'

Which, to me, was music, joy, freedom, motivation. Here was what I'd wanted: a manager who believed in me, rated me and was prepared to tell me so, play me regularly, give me free rein on the left, to pass and move, run at players, get forward. I attacked the season, thinking it was going to be superb – and it lasted just a single, solitary, enjoyable month before they sacked Howard Wilkinson, appointed the great George Graham, and it all turned to misery. We started reasonably well, drawing 3–3 at Derby in the first game, losing to Sheffield Wednesday away, but then I scored the only goal to beat Wimbledon and we beat Blackburn away next, a good result. But then we played United at home and they battered us, 4–0.

The United fans chanted my name as I lined up against good old Gary Neville and Becks full of optimism, only not to get a look-in all day. United were dominant at this stage; they were on the way to winning the league again and they just played us, a new team of decent players yet to gel, off the park. Brian McClair came up to me afterwards and told me I looked like the only player who knew what I was doing. But here is my problem with what happened next: what is the point of giving a manager all that money to spend on signing four or five good new players if you're going to give him only five games and then sack him? It isn't as if we'd done that badly. United were the best team in the country; they were beating everybody out of sight. It wasn't a fair test of where we were up to, so how much of an over-reaction was it to sack Howard Wilkinson? At United, that didn't happen. The fans were calling for Alex Ferguson to be sacked during my first and particularly my second season there, but the board had given him all the money to spend in the summer of 1989; even after we lost

5–1 to City and were in the bottom half of the table, they gave him time to see if his team would work. Now, he was cleaning up. Here at Leeds, you had a club, becoming a plc like so many of the others, so aspiring to be a serious business, giving the most important employee the authority to spend millions, then sacking him a few weeks later. Sorry, I don't get it. We weren't in crisis, we were ninth in the league. There were twenty clubs, so if my maths is right, five games in we were in the top half of the league, having got the most difficult game of the season over with. It was only early September and they went and sacked the manager who brought me to the club.

George Graham swept in, gloom in an overcoat. First minute, first team meeting; a group of good pros, the makings of a decent team, internationals, some who won the title four years earlier, who wanted to bounce back from their disappointment against Villa in the Cup final the season before. George Graham looked us up and down and said:

'Right, lads, we're going to avoid relegation.'

That was us condemned, relegation scrappers. The crucial thing, he would insist, was to defend properly. When I'd heard he was coming, I'd thought it might turn out all right. I expected him to be a disciplinarian, to take no nonsense, but I'd lasted eight years with Alex Ferguson, so I thought it could work, as long as he gave me the licence to play. But suddenly, under him, my game was tracking back. His tactics were that every player had to man-mark a specific opponent until we got the ball back, which often meant players didn't work as a team, didn't help each other because they thought if they left their man, to attack or defend, they'd get dropped. He took Rushy to one side, told him he knew he had some sort of understanding with Howard Wilkinson, but that was finished now, he was just another player. Rushy was like: fine, I understand. But he had Rushy, at the tail end of his great career, playing right wing-back. What he got from playing Ian Rush at thirty-five, thirty-six, whatever he was, running from corner flag to corner flag in a position he'd never played, I will never know. Perhaps he was trying to show him who was boss. But I used to think that we had one of the greatest centre-forwards in the history of football here, he was often played out of position and only scored three goals: who's the mug? Then George Graham had me playing everywhere: on the left, centre-midfield, right-wing, left wing-back if we had five at the back, which seriously got me down.

Next, he said: 'All this drinking, team bonding, nights out, that's pure 1980s, that doesn't happen any more. You're on too much money. You're on executive salaries, you're expected to be acting like executives.'

I'm not saying he didn't have a point – perhaps beer had soaked its way too far into English football, and as the game became more serious it all had to fizzle out – but the way he said it struck me as wholly negative. He didn't say we were going to do anything instead, to help team bonding in the afternoons and evenings and days off. That's a clever line, about footballers getting executive salaries, and many fans and pundits would support it. But at no club are we treated like executives. Executives are asked to make use of their knowledge and experience, but we were just footballers, there was never any thought we might be consulted or that we might have some expertise to offer ourselves. We were the players and he was the boss.

After that first team meeting, we went out and did a defensive training session: closing down, getting tight, one-on-ones, two-against-twos, marking exercises and drills, all for defenders, getting low, shadow play, how the full-backs should show the wingers inside. I felt he killed much of the enthusiasm, drive and ambition of the dressing room within minutes. He talked much less to the players than other managers I've played for. Unlike Alex Ferguson, for example, he dropped or picked players without advance warning, just dumped it on everyone in team talks an hour and a half before a match. He's not the only manager to do this, but I don't think it helped anyone who was surprised to be in or out of the side. At half time he might shout a bit, but usually he wouldn't say much; he'd just haul people off, say he was making a change. There were no explanations, no debate.

George Graham was rebuilding his career, we all knew that. He'd won the league twice with Arsenal doing that: defending, little flair or expression, everybody in fear of the gaffer. But this was the Premier League, a different era, and those methods weren't going to work, but he kept his old style. He'd had very few foreign players at Arsenal, and rarely signed players from big clubs – Ian Wright came from Crystal Palace, Alan Smith from Leicester. Then he'd been caught out over the £425,000 – as he would have it, the 'unsolicited gift' that John Jensen's agent, Rune Hauge, had given him, so he was banned for a year. Leeds just had to be the ones to give him another chance.

We clashed, in an unspoken way, because we were very different people and in some way he seemed to feel I cramped his style. I was buzzing, enjoying a new club, a new city to explore; my reputation went before me, I was a big signing from Man U, famous before I got there.

My mate Mark and I were in the Flying Pizza one night, a favourite footballers' hangout in Leeds, and we bumped into a couple of older women. They said: 'We don't like your manager very much.'

They'd come away feeling that Leeds was just a stepping stone to a bigger club. He brought in honest grafters like Robert Molenaar and Gunnar Halle, people who'd owe everything to him, so would do what he said. I was shocked at all this political stuff, because for all Alex Ferguson's temper, he was always dedicated to doing the best for Manchester United.

I'd put down a deposit on a new house in Leeds, but I put it straight back on the market, I was so sure he'd get rid of me. We started to play this dreary game of his, not allowed to express ourselves, tracking back, showing wingers the inside. He used to show us videos on the way to games, of today's opposition firing the goals in during previous matches, just to show us how awesome were the giants we were up against. Then on the Monday he'd show us a video of all the defensive errors we'd made, so we could see how really, truly bad we were. Sure enough, we went on a horrible run: we lost to Coventry, Newcastle and Leicester in his first three matches and were down to seventeenth, so under him we were going to be battling relegation.

There, and later at Bradford City, I discovered the art of enjoying yourself as a team off the pitch while the football was miserable on it. Carlton Palmer was one of those annoying thin people who can drink all day and be running everywhere in training the next morning. Maybe it's some West Brom thing he shared with Robbo. We had some good nights, and days, out with Gary Kelly and Rushy – he wasn't going to let someone like George Graham upset him; he just said he'd stay and collect his money, it was the manager's loss.

Howard Wilkinson had signed Mark Hateley, too, and we all used to take the piss out of him. We called him 'Topper', because everything you'd done, he'd done twice as well and twice as fast the week before. Tony Dorigo was once talking about his cars, a couple of Porsches he had, so we all then had to sit back and listen to the garage history of Mark Hateley, the supercars he'd had, the way the whole car industry had relied on him and his wallet. If you'd climbed Everest, he'd done it in half the time. You had to be careful calling him Topper, though, as he didn't like it.

One afternoon out, Rushy, Mark Hateley, Gary Kelly, a young lad called Mark Ford and I had lunch in the Flying Pizza, then went to a pub for a few pints and a few games of pool. I suppose I was feeling brave because I'd had a few, and after he potted a ball I just called out: 'Good shot, Topper!' The next thing I knew, Topper whacked me on the head with his pool cue, with Rushy in hysterics behind.

We got through George Graham's regime by laughing at him. Graham had this way of saying 'Supeeerrrrb' in his Scottish brogue in training, and Gary Kelly did a great impression of him. We had a do at a TGI Friday's, where, after a few drinks, Gary sucked the helium out of a balloon and did a whole George Graham 'Supeeeerrrb' routine on helium, and everybody fell about.

Graham brought in David O'Leary as his assistant manager. At that stage, he was very inexperienced in the coaching role. He'd be setting cones out and collecting the balls, handing out bibs, then occasionally Graham would say he could take a session and he'd come up with some weird ideas. He'd be like: er, right, well, put the ball on top of a cone then volley it off, and we'd be looking at each other, talking out of the corners of our mouths: 'Volley the ball off a cone?'

O'Leary would be very friendly with me and the more senior players, very chatty: 'All right, Sharpey, what d'yer get up to on Saturday? Oh, out, right, yeah, I went up to Harrogate for dinner, yeah it was smashing, how's the golf...?' How was this and how was that, all fine and dandy.

Our football was really dour, and even George Graham admitted it. It was so defensive, we hardly scored a goal – twenty-eight all season. We ground out a couple of wins, I scored against Sunderland and Southampton, then we had three goalless draws on the trot; the fans were going home and watching *Night of the Living Dead* to cheer them up.

Then George Graham fell out with me when he fined me a day's wages. He was always fining people for so-called breaches of so-called rules: wearing baseball caps with your team tracksuit, not having the right tie on, timekeeping, all of the petty building blocks of ridiculously childish football club discipline. In my case, I missed a day's treatment on an injury. I wasn't playing, I'd been out in Manchester on the Saturday night for some special occasion; I think it was Lisa's birthday. I woke up on Sunday morning, felt a bit worse for wear, and thought there was no way I was driving from south Manchester to north Leeds to be put on a machine for twenty minutes by a physio, so I called in and said I couldn't make it. George got to hear of it and fined me a day's wages.

I was on £10,000 a week, so a seventh of that was, according to the calculator, £1,428.57. He wanted the fines in cash. I counted out £1,500 and took it onto the team coach. George Graham wasn't on it, so I tossed it onto the table in front of David O'Leary and said: 'Tell the manager to keep the change.' Paddy was like: OK, no problem.

Next time I saw David O'Leary, he said: 'The manager wants to see you. He's not happy with the way you paid your fine; he thinks it was disrespectful, the way you threw the envelope down.'

How demeaning is all this? We then had to have a mind-numbingly serious chat about the need for me to be more respectful. He kept the change, though.

It set the pattern for stretches of my next six years in football: depressing on the field, having a good laugh off it. The senior lads at Leeds could get away with more than the Man U players, who had the media all over them. We'd get the odd surprise day off and Carlton Palmer would stay over, Paul Beesley, a defender, a Scouser, would come out, Rushy, Gary Kelly, maybe Topper sometimes. We got snowed in one night and all ended up crashing in a hotel. Then there was a night we went to a local pub in Tadcaster. Some of the lads were letting off fire extinguishers when they were pissed, and to make up for it Carlton Palmer bought a bottle of peach schnapps and took it round the whole pub, the old fellers having a break from their pints of mild for a shot of peach schnapps.

Mark Ford knocked around with us quite a bit. He'd come up through the ranks, was a simple, barmy, local lad, a hard-tackling midfielder who played fifteen first-team games before they sold him to Burnley for £250,000 at the end of the season. One night we went out and he ended up sleeping with one of the women who worked at the club and helped look after the young lads. Leeds were one of the first clubs to have a dedicated centre for their apprentices. She was late twenties, early thirties and Fordy really fancied her. The next morning at training, Fordy came in with a huge smile on his face because he'd managed to sleep with her, and he was bragging all about it. They'd started kissing, he said, he'd loved it, then they'd gone to bed and got down to it, and it was great. Fordy was making love to this woman he really liked and she cried out, on the brink of ecstasy: 'Talk to me, Mark! Talk to me!'

Mark Ford was a straightforward Yorkshire lad; he wasn't quite sure what she meant. But she cried out again: 'Talk to me, Mark! Talk to me!'

So Fordy, struggling to think of anything to say at this point, said: 'Why is there no Vimto in the drinks machine?'

Why is there no Vimto in the drinks machine! Magnificent. Yorkshire pillow talk.

Next day, Fordy came to training and there were two bottles of Vimto waiting on a table for him. Somehow, when I think of my time at Leeds in the George Graham era, I always think of that: Mark Ford and the Vimto in the drinks machine. It seems to sum everything up.

To make things just that bit worse for me, I strained my groin, quite seriously. I was out for a couple of months – but it turned out to be one of the best things that ever happened to me. I was in the gym, doing some rehab, weights, and Richard Jobson was in there, also injured and working out. He'd made his reputation as a defender with Joe Royle at Oldham, and he happened to mention to me that they'd done a psychology course there, which had been really effective: they'd gone on a seventeen-game unbeaten run and taken Man U to the replay in the FA Cup semi-final when Sparky Hughes saved United with an equaliser right at the end. Some players laughed it off as hocus-pocus, he told me, but he'd found it really worked wonders. He gave me the woman's name: Claire Howell. I rang her up, met her, she persuaded me it was worth a go and I paid five grand to enlist for the course – my first schoolwork since school; or, some of my ex-teachers might have said, ever.

It was a good, very professionally run course, designed for corporate managers, about the power of positive thinking and motivation, and it was thorough – an academic approach to psychology beyond O-level and up to A-level standard. The principles, though, were almost heartbreakingly basic, once I understood them. It was really quite sad that a sport like football, with all the millions washing through it and all the pressure riding on it, leaves its young players floundering, has such a primitive approach to motivation and relies on bollockings, which, confirming what I knew from personal experience, I was told were counter-productive. We were taken through textbook psychology: the subconscious holds everything you know and learn, your creative subconscious holds what you need for your work, so to drum positive habits into your conscious mind, you need to bypass your creative subconscious and lodge them directly in your subconscious. It will then transmit positive, confident messages to the creative subconscious. That sounds too sophisticated for the average footballer, but really the methods were very simple: it was about affirmation, reinforcement, literally writing down positive statements, sending powerful visual images, over and over again, to the subconscious, making you genuinely confident so you can do the right things repeatedly.

I told Claire Howell what we did at Leeds – sitting on the team coach watching videos of teams we were due to play scoring bucketloads of brilliant goals; being hauled in on a Monday to watch replays of goals we'd conceded – and she was staggered that this was done at one of England's great football clubs. She said that it was a downer on everybody's confidence, making us feel bad while building up the opposition in our heads.

The techniques of the course were basic, but a revelation to me. Mostly we wrote positive affirmations, which triggered a strong visual picture to breathe confidence into the subconscious. So:

My feet are velvet cushions. Every time the ball comes it lands softly on the velvet cushion and I have it under control.

There would be some simple positive statements, which I'd write down and repeat to myself a couple of times a day:

Every time I pass the ball I find a team-mate.
Every time I shoot I hit the target.
Every time I pass, it goes to a white shirt.
I'm fast; when I run with the ball I beat full-backs.
When I go out I'm full of confidence.
I enjoy playing.

Positive, positive, positive. Not:

I'm rubbish, and I'm dragging everyone down with me.
My legs have gone, I can't pass.
I'm a little cunt who should get his feet on the ground.

Strangely, that's not what professional motivational psychologists suggested as the prime way to get the best out of a young sportsman. It was so simple: be positive and you feel positive, which makes your confidence grow.

I enjoy the work.
I enjoy training.
I enjoy doing weights.
I enjoy eating a healthy diet.

I'd read and repeat these affirmations before going to sleep at night, because that's when the subconscious is at its most receptive, vulnerable to the messages. You write them down, rather than just say them, because the sight of the words creates a strong visual picture. I found it worked beautifully: it changed my whole perception of myself, how to think about being a player, gave me a surge of belief in myself, in the things I'm really good at, in a calm, certain way, for the first time ever. All the bollockings drilled it into your mind that you are crap, so when you play well you think it's a fluke. The psychology course showed me that what people mostly need is to be told they're good. Accentuate the positive, then you come to believe it and you have a well of confidence to draw on. It really worked: in training my touch and control came easy, instinctive, I was finding my men, passing accurately, crossing, shooting, not giving the ball away, playing the game I could play.

I got fit and back in the team at the end of February. The previous match the team had lost 4–0 to Liverpool at Anfield. The course had confirmed that George Graham's management tactics were demoralising, and as I was enjoying my football so much for the first time in a long time, I decided to take no notice of them whatsoever, just prepare as I had learned to, then go and play my own game. When he showed the videos, stressing the superhumans we were up against, the failures we were, I never watched them. I used to read a magazine or put my Walkman on, just look away. I used to tell the lads not to watch them, and I meant it: 'No, seriously,' I'd say, 'you should *not* be watching this.'

It worked for me. The first game against Sunderland, we won 1–0 and I played well, my touch was in. The next was at Elland Road against West Ham and I scored the only goal, 1–0 again, two minutes into the second half. I even remember the thrill of a daft celebration. Then we played Everton at home and won again, 1–0. Claire Howell was doing bits of work with Everton at the time and Joe Royle, who was their manager then, told her I was the best player on the park. My control and vision were back, I was making passes, I felt quick, strong, my crossing was good, my game was back together. A few simple written statements accentuating the positive, and look at me. Amazing, the power of the mind. I hear now that Sam Allardyce does this at Bolton, has written affirmations around the dressing room. I did it at Leeds a few times: wrote a positive score up on the whiteboard, Leeds 2, West Ham 0, or whatever. Of course, it doesn't guarantee it's going to happen, but it means people have that idea in their minds, that we could end up winning, rather than being sure the other team is better than us and we'll have to work 110 per cent to grind out a draw. Amazing, really, that in a career in top-flight football in its boom years, when I was a multi-million-pound asset, this was the first and only work I ever did on mental preparation, and I had to enlist and pay for it myself. I do wonder, sometimes, what might have been, if I'd ever had a manager who had motivated me positively, and knew how to encourage me to bring out the best. What I might have achieved. It's something else I'll never know.

We were still digging in. In fact, we didn't win again and had a run of draws, including four more 0–0s – they had to keep a watch on high bridges for Leeds fans chucking themselves off after matches – but we were up to ninth after I scored again against Sheffield Wednesday in a 2–2 draw in late March. The last game was a 1–1 draw at home against Middlesbrough, which sent them down. Brian Deane scored our goal. Otherwise I would have finished on my own as top scorer with my prize haul of five goals. Brian had five too, so we were joint top scorers. It was dour, but we'd pulled it round to some extent and, personally, I'd come on dramatically. So I feel it simply isn't true that I didn't play well for Leeds. In a transitional team, with a manger gone after five games and a new one who played a style which didn't suit me at all, in a difficult, forgettable season, I struggled, grafted, was injured, but came out marauding and did reasonably well.

I came back pre-season fired up again. I was twenty-six, confident, fit, determined to go on. I wasn't going to take much notice of George Graham, but, to be fair to him, he'd seen the difference. Before our last pre-season game, against Forest, he came up to me and told me I'd been Leeds's best player by far, different class, supeerrrrb, all the rest of it: 'You're doing really well. Let's get your reputation right back up there,' he said, 'let's get you back in the England team.'

I'd finally won round George Graham, who was giving me the positive encouragement I needed, and I was all set to fly. So then I went and snapped my cruciate.

CHAPTER 15

In Paddy's field

It happened after twenty minutes of that final friendly, against Forest, before the season was due to start. The pitch was dry and the grass was long. I went to nick the ball away with my left foot and as I put my weight down, my studs caught in the grass, my knee twisted and I heard a clear pop.

It wasn't even that painful, just uncomfortable, disabling. I came off, then later my knee swelled up like a cannonball. During the week, as the lads were preparing for the season to start, I was having scans, then the specialist came in shaking his head and telling me it was confirmed, a snapped cruciate.

'That's it, I'm retiring,' I said to the physio, nearly in tears. I poured it all out: every time I was getting somewhere I got injured or ill; I'd had to work my bollocks off, done a psychology course, I'd finally got fit and won the manager round, gone into pre-season full of the joys, and now I was struck down. A cruciate means a season out. It means the long, slow misery of rehab. One minute you're right up there, happy as you can be in football, the next you're sunk.

'I'm sick of it,' I was saying. 'I'm sick of getting injured when I'm playing well, then having to fight my way to fitness, prove myself all over again. I'm fucking retiring.'

Dave Swift was the Leeds physio in charge of the programmes for the lame and injured. He was a nice enough bloke and he'd seen players in despair before. 'No, you're gonna be fine. We'll get you fit, you'll do your work, and you'll come back.'

They don't operate straight away. Three per cent of people can function without a cruciate – this is the kind of interesting stuff you learn when your life becomes centred on one of your knees for a year – so they put you through four weeks of weights before they get the scalpel out.

My head was in bits. I told Dave Swift I needed a couple of days' break, that if I came in straight away I'd just piss everybody off. I rang my mate Mark, who was playing in a golf tournament.

'Hiya, I'm on the leader board!' he said.

I just mumbled: 'I've snapped my cruciate. I'm going to be out for a year, and I need a drink.'

'I'll be there in two hours,' he said.

So Mark bombed it back at 120 miles an hour on the motorway and we went straight to his local, the Dexter. We'd drink all day, stagger home, crash out, then wake up the next morning and go to the pub again. A couple of nights, we went on to clubs in town, going home early in the morning. After three or four days of it, I presented myself at Leeds, grim-faced, head sorted about it all, ready to start.

I had five weeks of weights, exercises, to build up my quads, but it was clear I needed the operation. They slice off part of your patella tendon, a chunk of bone from your kneecap, then they drill straight through your knee. It's twelve weeks after that before they even know whether your body will accept the reconstruction, so you come in every morning, a million miles from fitness, while the lads are outside bantering and training; your leg's in a brace, and your day's work begins by stretching your leg onto a tray, then, agonisingly, trying to bend the knee. A few weeks later, you can gingerly get on a stationary bike. You do that all morning, a few weights, you talk to nobody, then you have a light lunch and do it all again. Then you come in the next day with that ahead of you again.

After four months of it, they let you have a gentle jog. It hurts. You go to home games but you don't feel part of it; you're alone, fighting your own battle, you hardly see your team-mates. You have to go through endless pain barriers. You're out shopping with your girlfriend and you catch your toe and it sends shockwaves through your body. You despair that it will ever be right. You mope in your own little world: you, your sore knee, your self-pity. You know there are worse things going on in life but you're a professional footballer and you haven't kicked a ball in months.

You drink and sulk and miss the banter. You snap at your girlfriend, then you go on holiday but you row and it escalates, and she wants to know if you're fully committed to the relationship and the truth is you have a problem with that anyway and this is really not the best time to confront it and in the end you just say, OK, we've grown apart, let's call it quits.

Meanwhile, without me, Leeds were improving dramatically, with Jimmy Floyd Hasselbaink scoring freely, probably their best ever group of young players beginning to arrive in the first team, and eventually they finished fifth, qualifying for the UEFA Cup. In my position was Harry Kewell. I had been at Man U just a couple of years before with Giggsy bursting through behind me, and now Harry Kewell, a quiet, unassuming young lad with world-class talent in his left boot, was dancing into my place at Leeds. I wasn't bitter; I just wanted to get my knee right.

George Graham was OK while I was injured. He'd say hello, talk to me, but no manager has any use for you when you're injured. He did give me time off to present a couple of TV shows, which was great, and has stood me in good stead for a career in TV now I've retired. It was a chink of pleasure in a year of toil. You work and work, then, finally, you start to feel stronger, you can kick a ball without the knee complaining all night, you can run a bit more, you start to move back to the fringes of training with the first team. A whole season, 1997–98, gone, but then I was still only twenty-seven.

I was finally fit, my knee healed, in time for pre-season 1998–99. On 15 August 1998, George Graham even put me straight in the starting line-up for the first game of the season, away at Middlesbrough. A goalless draw, what a shock. But I was still feeling my way; you can't just burst back after an injury like that. Then I had a thigh strain, so I went back in the reserves for a few weeks. Suddenly, for the first time in my career, I was in the stiffs, the undead; I was starting to find out why Graeme Hogg had been such a misery when I first arrived at Man U, starstruck by the Tango footballs. Then, in October, the call finally came for George Graham to take his true place back at the centre of British life, and he left for Tottenham. Nobody cried when he went.

David O'Leary took over as the caretaker manager, telling us, telling the media, he didn't want the job. We all thought he'd go to Spurs with George Graham. He played me in early October: we went to Leicester and lost 1–0. I had a good game, though; I felt sharp again, quick. I passed accurately, made some runs, attacked. Second half he played me behind the front two and I had a bit of space there and threatened them. The paper talk was that Martin O'Neill, who was Leicester's manager then, was the favourite to come to Leeds, and after the match he came onto the pitch, right up to me, grabbed my arm, and said: 'Well played, son, different class.'

I thought: great, he likes me, he's seen me play wide left and behind the front two. If he comes here he'll believe in me and I'll be able to play. Then Leicester refused to allow Leeds to talk to O'Neill; David O'Leary stayed on and eventually Leeds appointed him full time. He never played me again in the league. Not one measly game.

We went to Forest for the next game and I wasn't even on the bench. By now I was old and grizzled enough to go and have a word about it, so I went to find David O'Leary at the training ground. He pulled me into one of the smaller dressing rooms; it might have been a referee's room, it was all cramped and scruffy. He didn't make much eye contact, but he was perfectly collected. I asked him why he'd left me out after I'd played well against Leicester, and he said: 'I think you need a change.'

'Sorry,' I said, 'how do you work that out? I've missed a whole season, I've got fit again, played a couple of games. How do you mean, I need a change?'

'You're not getting down the wing like you used to.'

'Er, you've only played me in one game, and the second

half I played behind the front two. How do you get down the wing when you're playing in the middle?'

'Well, even in training you're not getting down the wing like you used to.'

He was really losing me. 'We play five-a-side in training, or seven-a-side. How do you get down the wing in those games? I've been out for a year, I'm hungry for the ball, I want to get on it, I don't want to stand right out on the line…'

'Well, I just think you need a change.'

I didn't even get a game in the reserves for three weeks or so. Don't ask my why: I never knew. Somebody told my dad – rumours, rumours – that I was considered too much of an influence on the younger lads. I don't know about that; it's not as if I took them out drinking or anything like that – Lee Bowyer and Jonathan Woodgate would show the world a couple of years later that they knew how to do that well enough themselves. I bleached my hair once; the management didn't rate the hairdo but the kids did and one or two of them had theirs done. Maybe it was the old story: smiling too much; laughing and joking and being friendly round the place. I was friendly with people in the commercial department; I used to go and chat to them, have cups of tea. He must have the wrong attitude.

The team had gone to Roma in the UEFA Cup and lost 1–0. I hadn't played at all for three weeks, then on the day of the return leg, with no build-up, David O'Leary told me he was going to play me. Right. So you've told me I need a change, you've left me out completely, even out of the reserves, even though I was still building up after the cruciate. I'm not match fit because I've played only two games all season, and you want to send me out in a European tie against the best full-back in the world, Cafu.

Why? You tell me. He can't lose. If I play well, it's a masterstroke. If I don't, it justifies him having dropped me and wanting me out of the club. I felt as though I'd been hung out to dry.

I didn't have a chance, but I went and tried and had a complete nightmare. It was my last chance, a massive game, and partly I dug my own hole by trying too hard. Nothing went right, my head was all wrong, my touch wasn't there, Cafu was strong and efficient. Our fans started giving me stick: 'You're shit!' 'Fucking rubbish!' I think O'Leary brought me off before the end and I just felt like crawling away into a dark room and never coming out. That was the last time I played for Leeds United, so perhaps when the fans think I lost it there, they're remembering that one game, when I had no chance.

The Leeds lads used to tease me in the first season, about how friendly Paddy was to me when he was the assistant manager, said he must be my long-lost brother or something, because it was Sharpey this and Sharpey that and what did you do Saturday night, Sharpey? Then, when I was coming back from injury and needed some managerial help, it was different. In the year I was out, the kids came through and when I was fit he didn't need me any more, or thought he could do without me. So he went from being a mate to telling me I needed to leave.

Personally I think he was lucky at Leeds. He had great kids just about to come through, who had been groomed by Paul Hart and Eddie Gray years before Paddy arrived. Eleven days after the Roma game, Alan Smith came on as sub, aged eighteen, and equalised against Liverpool with his first ever touch in the first team. When George Graham left, everybody breathed a sigh of relief and began to express themselves, but the discipline and work ethic he'd insisted on had made them strong. David O'Leary rode his luck into the period when Leeds went on to challenge and live the dream. Then he wrote his book just after the Bowyer–Woodgate trial and it all fell apart. I see him now at Villa and I think he'll fail. Maybe I'm wrong, maybe he's different with players he wants around the place, but that's how he was from what I saw. We'll see how it works out for him.

I was in limbo. No club was racing to come in for me when I'd been injured. The game had moved on, I'd already missed the first three months of the season, then been booed off the pitch in a European tie on the TV. Now I really found out about life in the stiffs, one of the walking dead, quiet, withdrawn. Marking the first team at set pieces in training; a brick in the wall. There were kids, like I had been, running around in dreamland, and suddenly I was one of the older first-teamers having his heart broken by the beautiful game. It was all a vicious circle: your spirits drop, your form with it, you don't play, your morale drops even lower, you end up having a few pints with your mates, your fitness slips, down and down you go.

I'd started seeing another woman, Joanne. She'd been with Noel Whelan, another Leeds player, and Lisa and I had met them in Barbados the year before when Joanne was pregnant. I ran into her during pre-season. We'd just played Wolves in a friendly and Steve Bull had caught me accidentally and I had a black eye. I must have looked truly appetising. 'Hi,' I said, 'how's Noel? How's the baby?'

She said: 'Oh, we've split up. How's Lisa?'

I shrugged. 'We've split up.'

We went out a few times. It was difficult because she had been with Noel and had his son, Ellis, and it's the biggest no-no to go out with another footballer's ex, but we did like each other a lot. Then a guy I knew in Manchester because I bought clothes from his shop, Phil Black, who was working as an agent, called and said David Platt, who was managing Sampdoria, wanted to sign me. I knew Platty from England duty. He called, asked if I was fit. I told him I was injury free but nowhere near match fit. He said: 'We need a half-fit you. Come over here.'

Fresh start, a godsend. Platty had played with me, he knew what I could do. He'd tried to get Arsenal to sign me when he was there. He signed me on 1 January on a six-month loan, with a view to me getting a contract if all went well. I went from the stiffs at Leeds to an apartment in a beautiful little village, Nervi, all tight little streets and gelateries, twenty minutes outside Genoa. I thought it was going to be a great move, but again it wasn't that simple. Sampdoria's glory days with Lombardo, Vialli and Mancini were gone; they were in the bottom four when I arrived. Platty was in trouble because he didn't have his coaching badges. It was a big stink in the papers because it was compulsory over there; and within the club, not that I had a clue at the time, there were people trying to force him out.

Ariel Ortega, the great Argentinian striker, was there, but there were no other big names. The players were friendly enough but as I hadn't a word of Italian when I arrived I was a banter-free zone. Still, the games were a great experience, intense, and although the pace of Italian football looks slower and more thoughtful, they actually close you down really quickly. Technically the players were better. The first game I played was against Bologna, and I did all right: I was quite energetic, up and down, put a couple of crosses in, nearly scored. That won a few of the players round and one of them who spoke a little English told me I was what they needed. It all had some promise.

I enrolled for Italian lessons twice a week, I was trying to get fit, my room-mate invited me over for dinner with a couple of his mates who spoke English. That was nice. I still missed the banter but I didn't miss the stiffs. It was magical really. I used to go down to the sea and sit there, although it was winter and freezing, have a toastie and a cup of tea from a café, wonder about the twists of fate which had brought me here. Then after just four weeks, Platty was finally forced out. He left without seeing me because I was already out knocking a ball about before training when he held the team meeting. The new manager came in and told me I was his second choice in my position, so I was back doing shadow play in training. Being away from home and all my mates would definitely have been bearable if there was a future for me there, but there wasn't, so it dragged.

I stayed a couple of months but it was limbo again. I was desperate to get back to England. I had a year and a half left on my Leeds contract, but I didn't want to go back. Phil Black put me in touch with Joe Royle, who was managing Man City. They'd dropped down to the Second Division and he was really keen to sell the club to me, take me on loan till the end of the season. Another agent, Dave Sheron, knew Paul Jewell at Bradford, who were in with a chance of winning promotion to the Premiership, and he wanted me, too. Everybody was in a rush because by now it was March and the transfer deadline was looming. I went to City first and Joe Royle was really keen. I knew all about the club, of course, but City were only sixth or seventh in the Second Division, not even sure of getting in the play-offs. I went to Bradford and they had a good set of pros, the manager was impressive, and they were going for automatic promotion to the Premier League. I called Joe Royle and said I was going to Bradford. He didn't give in easily, said he felt hard done by, but I told him I didn't want to play in the Second Division if I didn't have to and I could get back in the Premiership with Bradford.

'OK,' he conceded, finally, 'but remember: we're a big club, we're going places, and we'd like you to be part of it.'

I was still not match fit, but Paul Jewell thought I might just give them that bit extra in the final push, to the promised land of the Premier League, the top flight, where humble old Bradford City hadn't been since 1922. He'd signed Dean Windass too, a great player, barmy off the pitch but really clever on it, technically excellent, fantastic vision, a proper footballing brain. Paul Jewell obviously hoped we two could provide the final little pep to get Bradford up. The club was third when I arrived.

We lost my first game away at Palace. Then, in my second, against Grimsby, I came on and scored a header – don't ask me how – in a 3–0 win. I'd worked hard in training, and after that Paul Jewell put me in the starting line-up. Dean Windass scored two to beat Bury away on Easter Monday, and I scored the winner at home to Portsmouth five days later. Happy days were here again. Lee Mills, a strong, battering First Division centre-forward, scored in a 1–1 draw at Port Vale on 13 April and we were second, in the automatic promotion place, with four matches to go. The lads were brilliant, solid English footballers. I had a few decent games, felt the confidence coming back and even that long-lost loving feeling for football again.

Manchester United were winning the Premier League,

and were about to win the FA Cup, then the European Champions League, the Treble, the total success which Alex Ferguson had lusted after, raged for, his whole life. For Bradford City, the match at Wolves on 9 May 1999 became a Double and Treble rolled into one, a great moment in their history. Paul Jewell pulled me in beforehand and told me he was going to leave me out. He said he was going to have to play conservatively, defensively, that the other lads had done it all season for him and he wanted to be loyal to them. It was disappointing, but also fair enough – and if a manager explains it to you, and gives you a reason which makes sense, you can live with it. So we went to Molyneux and the lads scored three, hanging on for half an hour for a 3–2 win, taking Premiership football to probably one of the most unlikely clubs in the glamour league's history. I even got to come on at the end.

The Bradford players knew how to celebrate, starting with beer and champagne on the coach back to Bradford, and you can never see too many times the local TV footage of a celebrating Stuart McCall falling off the roof of a car in the Valley Parade car park.

I'd done OK, and Paul Jewell wanted to sign me on a full-time contract. Man City had won their miraculous promotion to the First Division on penalties after Paul Dickov's equaliser in the last minute of the play-off final against Gillingham, and Joe Royle was chasing me again, also to sign full-time. Nobody from Leeds was ringing to beg me to stay.

I went on holiday with my mates to Ayia Napa. There, Michael Kennedy kept ringing me, saying that he'd told both clubs I was on holiday but Bradford were putting the pressure on for a decision. Apparently their chairman,

Geoffrey Richmond, had put something in the press about Lee Sharpe facing make-your-mind-up time, which I thought was out of order, considering I was on holiday. But Michael said, no, they insist they want a decision by 11 a.m. on Friday.

I sat down with my mates in our holiday flat, girls waking up all over the place. I had a sheet of paper, the names Man City and Bradford, and separate columns underneath each: pros, cons. None of my mates wanted to get the blame if it went wrong, so they mostly kept quiet. The most useful thing anyone came up with was that Man City had a better kit. I wrote that one down. The other pros for City were obvious: massive club, sleeping giant, on the up, could be a good time to go. The cons: they were in the First Division, and there was also the United reject factor, although I'd always played well against City and thought I'd win the fans over. At Bradford, I'd enjoyed it, it was a happy dressing room, I'd got to know the lads, we had some momentum. It was going to be a hard season, we were favourites to go back down again, but the most important thing in the list, the pro which sealed it, was that they were in the Premier League. City even offered me more money, two grand a week more, than Bradford were offering, but the clincher was that Bradford were giving me Premier League football, a chance at the top again. So I phoned Michael Kennedy and told him I'd decided to sign for Bradford. Could he please go ahead and do the deal with Geoffrey Richmond?

That was how I came to make the worst decision of my career.

CHAPTER 16

Closing time at the Dog & Duck

Every story has its extremes, its beginning and end. The Premier League, too, can perhaps only really be understood by knowing its best and its worst. I know English football through and through, because I did my time at the greatest club of the era, Manchester United, and I finished at the club anybody would pick as the prime one not to have been at between 1999 and 2002: Geoffrey Richmond's Bradford City.

At the end of my first full season there, we stayed up, clinging on, all nerves and edge, to David Wetherall's thirteenth-minute header for a 1-0 win at home to Liverpool in the final game of the season. The crowd came on the pitch, players had their kids with them, Valley Parade was in delighted shock. It was one of my most spine-tingling moments in football, after a season of slog, as good as winning the Premiership, having kept a little team like Bradford up in the top flight with the glamour clubs.

Unfortunately, that's not the chief memory I have of Bradford City. I remember the chairman driving around in his Bentley Azure with its personalised number plate while we didn't have a decent training ground. He had built one massive stand but the rest of the place was old, the dressing rooms were shabby, they had what seemed like the oldest weights room in the world. When I signed, Geoffrey Richmond, all smiles, rolled out his grand plans for the onward march of Bradford City: there would be a new training ground, a new gym across the road, top-quality players brought in, we'd be staying in the Premier League. Then, after our first season at the top, he had his famous 'six weeks of madness' in the 2000 close season when he made a series of signings that were to go horribly wrong. The main place we trained, Apperley Bridge, was next to a river, and if it rained hard, the pitch would be waterlogged and there'd be a rising stink of sewage. We'd train on that, then we'd get back in our cars plastered all over with mud laced with sewage. That's what I remember about Bradford City.

Paul Jewell saw out that first season; he'd done well to keep us up. We had some good players, but they were mostly seasoned pros who'd done well in the First Division or, like Stuart McCall and Dean Saunders, were coming to the end of great careers. Of course, I went over on my ankle pre-season and did my ligaments in, so I was desperate to play and Paul Jewell was desperate to get me in, and when I finally played for the first time, against Wimbledon in October, it was too early, so he pushed me back to left-back for the first few games. We beat Leicester, then went to Liverpool, where we lost but played well. There was one point where I had to chase Emile Heskey down, he never really got away, and afterwards Paul Jewell said: 'You kept up with him there, you're looking sharp, your pace is coming back.' It was getting exciting again.

We went to Leeds, which was interesting. The Leeds fans had decided they hated my guts. I'd be taking corners and they'd be shouting, 'scummer', 'red scum' – they don't like Man U much. I'd turn round and smile and mostly they'd laugh and give me a clap. They don't really mean it, I don't think. I only had trouble once, with a lad in a bar in my first season saying: 'Once a scummer, always a scummer,' and we had a bit of a stand-off. At the end of that first season, I saw the same lad, and he came up to apologise, said I was a good player and he'd seen me out and I seemed like a good lad, too. I liked that. I've always done all right living in Leeds, there are no hard feelings.

We went to Old Trafford, the first time I'd ever been back, and lost 4–0. United fans were brilliant to me. I know what I mean to them, because I played in a special time for the club, and I always feel a bond with them, from having watched our 1990 Cup run on the terraces, and enjoyed the return of the great days, the good times, with them. With Bradford, we did all right to start with, got stuck into United, tried not to let them play, played to our strengths, and held them for a while before they ran away with it.

Paul Jewell knew it was always going to be a slog. We were never going to play possession and have five options on the ball. Most times we tried to whack it long, see if Dean Windass could hold it up, scrap something out. It wasn't my game but I did my bit; I was coming back to some form. Then, in the New Year, I couldn't get a game. Even though Peter Beagrie was playing a similar role, I felt that Paul Jewell wanted to pick me, but I ended up being out till April. Not the most enjoyable period in my life. Joanne and I were living together by then; I used to drive across from my house in Leeds to run around on the shitty training ground, for a club where despite being signed on nice fat wages I felt I wasn't wanted. I got a game or two at the end of the season, was sub a couple of times, but then was in at left-back for that final game when we beat Liverpool and did the miraculous for Bradford City – kept them in the Premier League. Eleven days later, I was twenty-nine. Time was marching on.

Bradford was buzzing that summer. One night we had a party at the ground then quite a few of the players went to a club in town. We had a VIP room upstairs and the place was full of Bradford fans with their club tops on; they looked up, saw us and were clapping, cheering, singing everyone's name. It was Euro 2000 and at the end of the night I got the DJ to put on Fat Les's dubious classic, 'Vindaloo', and I went downstairs, climbed on the bar, took my shirt off, swung it round singing 'Vindaloo', and suddenly everybody in the place had their shirts off, swinging them round their heads singing 'Vindaloo'. Dean Windass was throwing ice cubes at me from the balcony. What a night.

Bradford had survived, the greatest moment in their modern history, and now the most unlikely club in the Premier League could go on, suck in all the TV money, build the facilities and infrastructure they needed, perhaps another couple of experienced players to strengthen the side for another battle. And what happened? Paul Jewell went out for lunch with the chairman to have a chat about where the club would go from there. From what he told me, he begged Geoffrey Richmond to withdraw us from the Intertoto Cup, a meaningless thing which starts in the heat of August, so you have to be back in pre-season training two or three weeks early. Jewell wanted us to have more rest for another slog of a season. Geoffrey Richmond said no, you're in it, we're not pulling out, get them back early. Fair enough. Then, while they were at it, questioning whether he'd had a brilliant season, taking him through a couple of games, like the 5–4 defeat at West Ham in February, when we were winning and ended up losing, giving him a good lecture. Jewell told me he went home, mulled it all over in his mind, and quit. He was a decent manager, shrewd, brave – which he has proved now, by taking Wigan up to the Premier League. At Bradford, he decided, the manager's job was impossible.

Who would we get as the manager at this most important moment in the club's history, a man who could try to establish Bradford City in the Premier League, survive another season, push on? Well, none other than Chris Hutchings. Who? He'd been a lower-division full-back, played at Chelsea when they were in the Second Division in the early 1980s, then at Brighton and Huddersfield. He'd been Paul Jewell's assistant manager and, from what I knew, had never played in the top flight, had little experience of management, and none in the Premier League.

In what other walk of life would a multi-million-pound company, which is what Bradford had become, have as its most important senior employee a man with so little experience of the job? I can't think of one. This was the other side of football for me, the world outside the Old Trafford bubble: chaos and amateurism. What followed was one of the most notorious periods in modern football history at any club, and I had the misfortune to be a player in the middle of it: Geoffrey Richmond and his six weeks of madness, when, with little investment going into where the club really needed it, Bradford City suddenly signed Dan Petrescu, Ashley Ward, David Hopkin from Leeds for £2.5m, and Benito Carbone, a gifted player at completely the wrong club, on his infamous £40,000-a-week wages.

The chairman, rather than Chris Hutchings, seemed to take much of the credit for these signings. Either way, it was ridiculous. If Hutchings was responsible, you have to ask how an inexperienced manager can be authorised to spend so many millions of pounds at such a crucial time? If Geoffrey Richmond was doing all the choosing of the players, presumably of glamour players whom he thought the fans would fall in love with and flock to see, well, it was no way to run a football club. A manager has to decide who will best form part of his team. It was a recipe for collapse.

I played in the first few games, in this strange team whose balance had been upset and whose manager had gone without ever explaining his reasons publicly, under a new manager who had very little experience. We started OK. We only just lost 1–0 to Liverpool in the first game of the season, but beat Chelsea at home, 2–0, on the Tuesday night, one of the Bradford fans' choice moments in the Premier League. Two games later, the first week in September, we were at Old Trafford. United had been champions again the previous season and they were going to notch another win on Alex Ferguson's bedpost in 2000–01: three medals on the trot I might still have been collecting if I hadn't decided to experience life outside United.

I'll never forget before the game I was out on the pitch warming up, trying to get my head on the game, and Malcolm Shotton, the old Oxford manager whom Chris

Hutchings had brought in as his assistant, came up and grabbed my arm: 'Hey, big man,' he said, looking all around him, at the great bowl of Old Trafford, 'what a great place for you to turn it on, what a great place for you to play.' He looked awestruck, like an explorer taking in the hanging gardens of Babylon, soaking in the atmosphere, loving every minute of it.

I know it was his way of encouraging me, but to me it was no big deal: I played there every week for eight years. You're looking for a game plan, tactics, good psychology, motivation, not the assistant manager acting like it's a privilege just to be there. Paul Jewell wouldn't have played at Old Trafford much himself – perhaps underneath he was wobbling with nerves when we'd been there the previous season – but he wouldn't have been gazing round like a tourist. He told us to keep it tight, give United no space to play, rough them up, try to break away and get Dean Windass to hold it up, nick one on the counter-attack. We'd done quite well the previous season for most of the game. This time, we lost 6–0. It's not in my list of favourite football videos to take to a desert island.

There were players at the club who'd been around and knew how shabby it was. Dean Saunders is a comedian from the cutting edge of football banter, a brilliant impressionist, and he used to do a magnificent take-off of the manager, which he'd do even when the dressing-room door was open and Chris Hutchings might hear. Can you imagine him doing that with Alex Ferguson?

Hutchings dropped me to sub for the next game, then I played against Southampton. We lost 1–0, but I played quite well. Then he didn't pick me again. Peter Beagrie, the man whose shimmies made him the fans' as well as his own favourite player, came back for a while instead of me. I wondered if it was the old curse, having a smile on my face? Whatever the reason, I was out in the cold, playing for Bradford City stiffs while being paid £550,000 a year. I wanted to play, I still could play, but although I was a massive expense, I was played in the reserves. Without me, the team got two draws in five games, were second bottom of the league, and then Geoffrey Richmond sacked Chris Hutchings. He hadn't a chance and was out in the first week of November.

Stan Collymore had arrived by then, and seemed more likely to please Geoffrey Richmond than some of the coaching staff. Obviously Collymore was a great player, different class, but not the sort we needed for a relegation dogfight. So he joined the party too, another crowd-pleaser for a crowd whose team was sliding out of the league, taking the whole club and its crumbling foundations with it. He played five games that season; we were nineteenth before the first one, nineteenth after the last one. Great decision.

Stuart McCall took over as the caretaker manager, but I had no joy with him, even though we lost, to Everton and Derby, in his two games in charge. Still no need for me, despite that. I was obviously crap and with my pedigree couldn't possibly make any difference to the worst team in the division.

By mid-November we were bottom of the league with seven points; we hadn't won since we beat Chelsea three months earlier. The chairman appointed Jim Jefferies as the manager, from Hearts. With the task already looking hopeless, his job was clearly to shovel players off the wage bill, ready for relegation and the complete and utter meltdown which was waiting in store for Bradford. Jim Jefferies turned out to be a proper manager – he even gave me a game around Christmas, calling me in from the wasteland of the Bradford stiffs to make me feel just a little like a footballer again.

We lost, 3–0 at Chelsea. I was still a long way from match fit, but then, out of the blue, Steve Claridge, who was managing Portsmouth, asked to have me on loan, and Bradford weren't going to say no, as it'd get me fit, and they'd get a chunk of my wages off their red bank statements. True to what I was learning about the realities of football, Steve Claridge was sacked almost immediately. Graham Rix came in, and under him, for four months from February to May 2001, I had one of my happiest runs in football. It was a struggle, at a club battling to stay in the First Division, but Rix was a pleasure to play for, the sort of manager I'd pined for.

Obviously he had pedigree himself as a player, so there was a respect for him in the dressing room. He was full of positive encouragement, and he talked to the players. He told me he wanted to extend my stay from the month originally agreed, and he wanted me to play deep in midfield, linking with the back four. He made me feel I was a good player again, that I had something to offer.

Then he did something which really shocked me. One day in training he asked to have a word with me, along with one or two of the more experienced players: Scott Hiley, the full-back who had been at Man City, Lee Bradbury, the centre-forward, Carl Tiler, the centre-half. Graham Rix asked for our advice. Come again? It was like he was speaking a language we couldn't understand. You mean you, the manager, gaffer, boss, are asking for advice from us, mere players, the lads? He explained, very matter-of-fact, that he was new to the club, we were in a relegation battle, he'd appreciate our views on who he should play and how we should play as a team. He was always going to have the last word, but just wondered what we thought. Incredible. Unthinkable. A manager who believes that players who have been around, in my case at the highest level for over ten years, might actually have something valid to discuss with him. Well, it was nothing short of a revolution. It also made us feel good about ourselves, that we were good pros with experience and ability, so much so that the manager wanted to hear our opinions. I think everyone responded. The young lads liked him, too, because he was full of encouragement and he was giving them a chance, and the team pulled together, everybody doing their best not to let the manager down. I was in the team, playing this central role, getting involved all over the field, pass and move, spraying the odd one out wide, or over Lee Bradbury's head, and I loved it. They were some of the most enjoyable games of football I ever played, which might be surprising when you think of the teams I've played in and the big-name managers who bossed them, and that here we were battling for survival in the First Division.

We played at Huddersfield at the end of March. I was all over the field trying to get on the ball, but we were losing and my touch wasn't in. I was giving the ball away a fair bit and so with around twenty minutes to go Graham Rix brought me off. I was disappointed, but then again he had to do something and it hadn't been quite happening for me, so I could see his point. It didn't work, though, and we lost 4–1. The next day, my phone rang. It was Graham Rix. He just wanted to apologise for bringing me off. I nearly dropped the phone. Sorry, run that past me again: you're ringing me up to apologise for taking me off? Is this the same game I've been playing for thirteen years?

'Well,' he explained, 'I've watched the video of the match now and you weren't having a great game, you did give the ball away, but I've seen now that you were all over the field, you didn't hide at all, you were working hard to get the ball down and play and do all the things we ask, so having thought about it I actually think it was the wrong decision to have brought you off and I just rang to apologise.'

'No problem, don't worry about it,' I managed to say, then spent the rest of the afternoon staring at the walls. A manager who apologised for taking you off because he'd seen the video and thought he might have made a mistake. Sorry, that doesn't happen.

It was still an awful battle. We didn't win for nine games; it came down to the last game of the season, against Barnsley. But we rose to it, beat them 3–0, and Huddersfield went down instead. Another season, another hugely dramatic and ultimately successful last game. Many fans might think I disappeared when I left Man U, and it was mostly an ordeal, but when you add it up, I helped get Bradford promoted, then stay in the Premier League, then helped Portsmouth just about stay up, so even in those grim years I was part of a kind of success. Bradford, of course, had never got off the bottom in the Premier League. Petrescu had gone, Collymore had gone, but the club went down as surely and predictably as a Bentley Azure rolling off a cliff.

Graham Rix wanted to sign me but didn't have big money to spend and couldn't get anywhere near what Bradford were paying me – up to £650,000 for my final season even though we'd be in the First Division. I was all for living in Portsmouth: it's a nice part of the world, the climate's a touch kinder than tropical Leeds, and I was knocking round with some good lads. Michael Kennedy tried to negotiate with Geoffrey Richmond, saying that if they'd pay me some of the money they owed me for the final year of the contract, he'd save Bradford the rest because I'd sign for Portsmouth, but for some reason Richmond wouldn't have it. He was going to keep me there on £13,000 a week in the First Division, but I was barely going to play a game.

I know it's a huge amount of money, more than the vast majority of people could ever dream of earning, and I'd admit that we footballers, of my generation, can be guilty of taking it for granted; money on that scale is our reality, our normality. But I went into football with my dreams of playing on the grand stage, because I loved the game, and I dreamed of the fame and fortune that went along with that. I still wanted to enjoy it; I didn't want to just take the money and not play. There are so many players who don't enjoy football any more, who treat it as a job, say they're going to bank the money and look forward to retirement, but for me, though the big money was rolling into my bank account from the regime of Geoffrey Richmond, there wasn't much joy in it.

The following season, back down in the First Division, it got really depressing. For quite a few of us, it became about trying to forget the football, because it didn't bear thinking about, and getting more enjoyment out of going out with the lads. That feeds on itself: the more you do it, the more you get to know each other, the more of a laugh you have. The football was the worst I ever experienced; everything about the place was wrong, but the crack we had was one of the best. At a lot of clubs you get groups of twos or threes knocking around outside training but at Bradford there was always a great team spirit despite the nonsense at the club. Even though people lived all over the place, they'd stay in hotels to have a good night out on Saturday or midweek in Leeds or Bradford. We'd organise a coach to pick us up from Bradford sometimes, and then maybe go to a pub where we knew the owner, who'd give us a private room; we might have some food laid on and money behind the bar.

Aidan Davison, the reserve goalkeeper, was a football animal, the biggest disgrace known to man. He'd only been there a week when we had a do and he showed us one of his party pieces: taking a condom, snorting it up his nose then pulling it out of his mouth. We're all looking at each other, thinking: this guy really is mad, doing this when he's only been here a week. There was worse to come.

I remember one of our many losing, chaotic, bumbling away trips, when they'd taken me along even though they had no intention of playing me. I was rooming with Jamie Lawrence. He was playing, so he was downstairs resting; I was upstairs with the goalkeepers, Aidan Davison and Matt Clarke. Aidey knew he wouldn't be playing and Matt had fallen out of love with football a long time before, so on the way back from wandering around in the afternoon we bought a couple of cans from the off licence. In the evening, we'd drunk them and wanted a few more, but we couldn't go out and get any as it was too risky to walk through reception because we'd get clocked. So I rang Jamie Lawrence downstairs and told him to grab a few cans of beer from the minibar in our room, and to throw them out of his window and up to ours. Aidan Davison got his goalkeeper's gloves on and leaned right out of the window, ready to catch these cans that Jamie was going to lob up. He couldn't get much leverage, so he was bouncing the cans up and off the wall. Aidey was nearly falling out of the window, but managed to catch three or four of them, bringing all his agility and years of experience to bear in the service of his team. Jamie lobbed up the last one, but it clipped the underside of the window sill. Aidey went to grab it, but he didn't quite get it and it fell out of his hands into a bush below the window. Well, that's it, we said, leave it, but suddenly Aidey was climbing right out of the window, hanging off the outside window sill, then he leapt off the first floor of the hotel, spun in the air and landed starfish-style right into this bush down below. There was a rustling and rumbling in the bush, then a minute later this goalkeeper's glove emerged from the bush like the sword from King Arthur's lake, clutching the can of beer, and everybody gave him a massive cheer and round of applause. Then Aidey climbed into Jamie Lawrence's room, and crept up the back stairs to our room. When he got in we were cheering and clapping him; he was kissing the can of beer and hoisting it above his head like it was the FA Cup. That's what we did for entertainment.

On 24 December 2001, Jim Jefferies was on his way out too, a special Christmas present for him and his family. The next appointment, another managerial great for the proud Yorkshire club, was Nicky Law, fresh from having wrestled with Chesterfield while they were in administration. I'd never heard of Nicky Law, I have to admit. He'd been a famous player at Chesterfield, and kept the team going while the club was in financial crisis with his assistant, Ian

Banks, who came too. They brought with them a fitness coach, Kevin Hornsby, who, to be fair, had latterly been Chesterfield's fitness coach and kit man.

To the players, we were already more a drinkers' club than a football club, and it wasn't going to change. Think about how clinically professional the game was becoming elsewhere, with foreign coaches and scientific attention on every area of the game. Our big joke among ourselves now was that we were the Dog & Duck: a pub team, bunch of dossers, training in shit with managers whose job seemed to be to get us off the payroll, and a chairman driving around in a big car like someone's dad. At Christmas, I started to talk about packing the game in. I was getting no enjoyment out of it; it was demoralising, not playing. My love for the game was ebbing away – or, let's be accurate, not the game itself. I love football, the simple, beautiful game, the feel of the ball when you're running with it totally under control, the camaraderie of playing as a team, the cleanness of pass and move, the perfection of a goal. But my love for it was curdled by the politics and amateurism that went with it – and with the simple fact that for all the money I was on, I wasn't actually playing a game.

Nicky Law did play me at home to Portsmouth in January; we won 3–1, I scored, and played really well. The following week was a local derby against Barnsley, and I played well again, scored and set up two very late goals for Ashley Ward to get us a point, 3–3. The goalkeeping coach told me afterwards that Nicky Law had been blown away, had said I was different class and was asking how he should treat me, what did I need to motivate me? They told him just to leave me, keep playing me and I'd do fine. We lost the next game but then we beat Grimsby, a good little run, but after that he left me out. From star man to reject in a couple of games – it didn't make sense to me. It was hard to care after that.

The thrill had gone. For the first time in a fourteen-year career, I used to wake up and instead of thinking how great it was to be a footballer, going into training with a load of silly team-mates acting like kids and having the crack, I didn't want to get up and go. I found myself making excuses not to go in, pulling the footballer's equivalent of a sickie, something I could never have imagined doing before. I'd always loved training, loved laughing with the lads; it was always nonsense that I didn't work hard because I had a smile on my face. Alex Ferguson knew that really. I loved training and I loved playing. Now, I couldn't face any of it. I do think I was depressed for a while. And, of course, nobody talked to anyone. The new management team didn't seem to me to have the necessary equipment. Their job was to ship players out; they were waiting for the best players to finish their contracts so they could get rid of them. The whole club was unhappy, on the slide, with players laughing behind their backs that we were the Dog & Duck, the joke team of the Football League.

On 16 March 2002, we played Rotherham away. They'd just been promoted to the First Division, which was massive for them. This was another local derby. We still had Ashley Ward, the ageing Stuart McCall, me and a couple of other big names – and they kicked us around all afternoon. Their fans were giving me loads of stick, about being a Man U reject and a Leeds reject and a drug addict and all the rest of it. I'd be going to take a corner or throw and they'd shout: 'Do you want any Es? Do you want any heroin?' I'd smile. 'Er no, you're all right.' The pitch was dry, bobbly, it was windy, the ball was being hoofed from one end of the horrible ground to the other, hoof, leather, foul, launch, barge, batter, elbow. It was a massacre of the game of football as we knew it. For the record, Wayne Jacobs scored for us, and we drew 1–1, but that ninety minutes of thuggery was no substitute for football. I came off bruised, battered, dejected. I was only sorry my mum and dad had had to witness it. After the match, my mum looked at me, all glum, sorrowful and withdrawn, like a ten-year-old boy who'd just taken a hammering for the Cubs, and she said: 'Do you know, I think it is time you retired.'

My parents had said at Christmas that if football was making me unhappy, then maybe I should get out. I'd worked really hard until the Bradford days, but they wanted me out and I couldn't see anybody much coming in for me. I shrugged: I wasn't carrying on for games like we'd just played at Rotherham. I pottered along until the end of the season, unwanted, detached, sub a couple of times. Geoffrey Richmond nearly made it to the end of the season, too, but in May he was suddenly up there announcing that Bradford City were completely and utterly insolvent and were going into administration with debts of £36m. I had only a fortnight left, so they owed me next to nothing, but Beni Carbone had two years to go on £40,000 a week. Ashley Ward, David Wetherall and a whole dressing room of others were on massive money, which the club didn't have. The administrators came straight in and announced they were sacking *all* the players, cancelling the contracts. They also sacked dozens of staff in the club's shops and offices. Nice people. You can't sack footballers, though, because the contracts are protected, so Bradford City were dragged through years of trauma trying to find the money to pay the debts. Then it all came out that in the previous couple of years, when Bradford were millions in debt, even selling players and leasing them back, mortgaging everything, Geoffrey Richmond had shared with his son £4m in dividends and been paid a £250,000 consultancy fee. Not a great surprise, really, a lot of things now made sense, but I did think it was a bit much, for the bloke running the Dog & Duck.

CHAPTER 17

Goodbye my beautiful game

In the summer of 2003, David Beckham finally decided to sample life in a football dressing room not equipped with Alex Ferguson's hairdryer, and helped himself to a decent move to another little club, Real Madrid. You might have noticed the story; it was bigger than the Kyoto Treaty. More journalists crammed outside the clinic for news of Becks' medical than had waited outside the hospital in Dallas in 1963 to see if the President of the United States was going to live. Becks – global *galáctico*, although he's still never sold out the Discotheque Royale in Manchester.

To be swamped with news of my latest career move at the same time, you'd have had to have been a reader of the local paper in a small Icelandic town, Grindavik. It was massive news there: LEE SHARPE SENT HOME. Right, you'll be thinking. Sharpey at it again. How the mighty have fallen: he can't even behave playing for a bunch of part-timers in Iceland. But again, underneath the headlines was the same old story: I really hadn't done much at all. I hadn't gone on a three-day bender, I hadn't washed up in some gutter or fjord, I hadn't snorted anything up my nose.

I was guilty of wanting to enjoy myself just that little bit; and, of course football, even at that level, is a Very Serious Business.

I went over to Iceland in the spring of 2003. I'd been out of the game for several months, and the idea was to get fit there because they play through the summer, and maybe see if I could get one more contract back in England for the following season. The season in Iceland lasts only four or five months, through the summer with its long hours of daylight. It was a nice enough little town, a bit of a gossip den where everybody knew everybody's business, but they set me up with a little flat. It was big news that I was coming, they paid me a few quid, so I thought it would be pleasant enough and couldn't do me any harm.

I had a few weeks pre-season, I didn't go out at all, I was getting fitter and stronger and it felt good. There was a Scottish player, Paul McShane, who lived there, working and playing part-time for Grindavik, and one evening I went round to his house. We had a few beers, watched telly, had a chat, messed about. Well, that turned out to be huge news locally. It was five days before a match – five! – but the manager pulled me in and said they had a curfew, no drinking seven days before a match. Seven days before a match? With a game every week that means not a single beer all season. The manager said that's right: it's a short season, so the players must not drink at all throughout. I told him they don't even have a regime like that in the English Premier League.

Then a mate of mine came over to check out Iceland; he stayed for ten days or so, from the Friday through to the following Monday. We planned to go out on both Saturdays. We were playing on the Tuesday and, the following week, on the Wednesday, so in English terms – no drinking two nights before a match – we were OK. We went out to Reykjavik and had a cool night; it was weird that it didn't go dark, very disorienting, but they like to drink and party and we had a good time. The next day, somebody had grassed me up, told the manager I was out. I said to the guy: 'Look, in five weeks I've not been out, I've sat round my house drinking tea, I've been to Paul McShane's once, then my mate came over and we thought we'd go out for a special blast.' The manager shook his head solemnly: 'OK,' he said, 'we'll let it go this time, but if you go out next Saturday, there will be some serious repercussions.' I enquired about airline schedules and came straight home. The idea hadn't been to live like a monk so I could dedicate myself to amateur football in Iceland.

That was pretty much it: the end. While Becks was becoming a global brand with his popstar wife – or has she retired now? – and his glittering team of internationals, his one-time idol at United was heading back from Iceland and packing the game in altogether.

I was bitter, disillusioned and it didn't suit me at all. I had made my decision, I'd quit football and never for a moment really considered going back on it, getting fit, and plunging into another lower-division war. But, stuck at home in my house in Leeds with Joanne and her son Ellis, I had very little idea what I was going to do. For fifteen years I'd played football, all I'd ever wanted to do; most of it, for all its bruises, at the top level in the English game. I suppose the way I finished made it more difficult, skidding to a dead end rather than going out at the top or in a glorious last flourish. It's not how you plan it, getting frozen out at Bradford. So, while I needed to look forward and work out what on earth I was going to do with my life, I spent a big chunk of the first two years of retirement wading through the past, the memories, trying to make sense of it all. It was harder, too, because even the good years, the dream time, the Torquay-to-Man U rise probably unmatched by anyone, is tarnished in my recall of it: the hat-trick at Highbury is associated with the bollocking Alex Ferguson served up straight afterwards; the Premier League wins a mish-mash of falling out of love with United. Obviously, you don't tend to dwell on the times you played badly, or on the six, or at least five, miserable years at Leeds and Bradford, but there are clouds over my good times, too.

I've always found it an ordeal to get up in the morning, but when you're playing football, you've got something to look forward to: training, kicking a ball about, the crack and banter with a group of overgrown kids in a dressing room, the feeling that you did a good session, worked hard, and the competitiveness, finishing off with a shooting competition for a fiver, and winning it and feeling like you can cut it. That's quite apart from match days, the weeks building up to the weekends, supplying great highs, like scoring against Barcelona, or deep lows, trooping off after being kicked about at Rotherham. Whichever it was, life was structured, dramatic, and always salted with humour and friendship and being part of something you always wanted to do.

All suddenly gone. You wake up in the morning and there is nothing to get up for. It's a long old day when there's nothing on, when you're kicking round the house, no structure, no banter, no getting out and coming back. Instead, you're just wallowing around the house and waiting for the phone to ring. As the weeks went by and that didn't happen, as I sank into the obscurity of being an ex-footballer, I'm sure I became genuinely depressed. I didn't shave, I slunk about, I was withdrawn, I went over and over everything in my mind: how have I ended up like this? And I drove myself mad wondering what I was going to do next. All that rubbish about drink or drugs. I was only ever a social drinker, out with the lads, for a laugh and a good time. But now, with my career over, I began to drink at home. I'd get a bottle of wine in, sit on the couch and drown my misery in it. I went out on a few benders, too, trying to forget what was happening, get pissed, grab a night of pleasure.

I didn't want to watch football; I didn't want to talk about it, think about it, play it. The game whose glories I fell in love with as a boy in Birmingham: I hated it. Bradford had sapped my appetite for it; the games people play, the politics, disappointments, egos, the chairmen, desperate managers, the months, years, piling up, lost. It's a short career, they say, and you can't afford to lose a year here, a year there, while you're injured, a club's in crisis, another manager doesn't fancy you, they play you too soon when you're coming back and think you've lost your form so drop you again and then you're trying to get fit and recover from loss of form and rummage inside yourself to find the confidence you mislaid a while ago. Even the memories of Man U, where I helped to put a smile on football's face, were tarnished. I reached the point when I didn't even want to keep fit, I didn't want to eat healthily, I didn't want to get up and do anything and it all went round in my head: how has it come to this?

When I pick my way through the detail of it, there are no simple answers. Why did I throw it all away? Er, I didn't.

Why was I good at Man U and shit at Leeds? Er, Man U were the best team in the country at the time and it was easy to play a part in that. You can't do it on your own in any team, but at Leeds I was one of the best players in my first season, then I was out for a whole year with a cruciate, then I came back and David O'Leary, in his first manager's job, didn't pick me. I helped Bradford City to win promotion to the Premier League – I must have done all right because they wanted to sign me after the loan period – but the club ended up in as much of a mess as Geoffrey Richmond's ashtray. When I finally washed up out of that one, I was thirty.

Football changed in my time, from a game a lot of English blokes played because they loved it and fans supported for the same reason, to a big business. The clubs are more clinical, athletic endeavours. I got into it because I enjoyed playing it, and I dreamed of the lifestyle that would go with it: plenty of money and a nice house, good mates and girls hovering about. I didn't dream of business and power trips.

I joined United at seventeen. Not one player from my age group and above really made it, so you can look at it the other way – how did it all go so right? When did anybody get signed from a Fourth Division club at seventeen, get thrown in with no coaching, and do so well for eight years? Recently I watched the video of it all, *Life at the Sharpe End* – the popstar footballer shows you round the beautiful home he shares with his beautiful girlfriend and talks about life at United – and I was actually shocked by how good I was, how I played, particularly in that second purple patch, 1993–94, with such speed and confidence, slapping the goals in and dancing the joyful celebrations which drove

Alex Ferguson to such fury. Becks is on the video, saying something about what a good lad I was to have around. Little Ellis, who's grown up with me in and out of the side at Bradford, then packing the game in, couldn't believe it.

'It's David Beckham!' he shouted, wide-eyed, pointing at the telly. 'David Beckham's talking about Lee!'

With hindsight, should I have stayed at Man U? I still say no, despite everything. I wanted to leave, see what life was like outside, and it was messy, muddy, not what it's cracked up to be, and showed me how, by comparison, Man U was a brilliant, professional club, and Alex Ferguson a quality manager. In football terms it looks like a disaster, but I wasn't going to stay as a squad player and not express myself while collecting medals. It wasn't part of the dream for me, not my idea of fun. In terms of growing up, experiencing life, I think I know a lot more for having been around and seen life at the other extreme. I'd still like to be playing regularly somewhere decent. I'd probably take the twenty games a season at Man U now, but not at twenty-six; I had too much ambition and drive and I believed I could establish myself fully somewhere else.

It didn't happen, but it's hard to look back and see where I could have done things differently. I suppose when it got miserable, at Leeds and then at Bradford, perhaps I could have dug in deeper, taken the medicine in the stiffs; maybe I'd have got a better move somewhere. But the game moved on so fast, the foreign players poured in for the money, there was no big club wanting or needing to take a risk on somebody like me, who had been in and out of sides, had a serious injury, and was also a well-known serious Class A drug addict, as everybody knows because they know someone who knows someone who's seen me at it.

I think underneath it all I had a problem with confidence, too. Maybe all players do, secretly, with the guilty doubts which gnaw away at them, but the young lads who came through after me, Becks, Scholesy, Butty, the Nevilles, had Eric Harrison drumming good habits into them. Many players have a mentor, a couple of years in the reserves or at a smaller club, where they build up their base of competence and confidence. Because I was thrown in, however well I did, I think I never quite believed in myself, that I was that good. I always felt that nagging sense underneath that I was a fake, about to be found out, that I was on a wing and a prayer.

On England trips, Ian Wright and Paul Ince used to take the piss: they used to call me the original Boy Wonder, because I'd played for England at nineteen, scored the hat-trick at Highbury. I'd run into them and Wrighty would go: 'Ah, it's the Boy Wonder! How you doing, Wonder?'

It used to burrow into me, the idea that it was all hype, that I was burning out, that I wasn't that good really. Maybe all players have that self-doubt, except Wayne Rooney, who's unlike anyone else, but now there are psychologists on tap, waiting to reinforce your creative subconscious with a barrage of affirmation. It's a shame there was never a manager who showed me that he believed in and wanted to get the best out of me. Except Graham Rix, who got sacked within a year. It's a shame management is such a lottery, a merry-go-round, that they're always covering their arses an inch from the sack. It doesn't make for nurturing talent. It's a shame the beautiful game can be so horrible once you're in it for a living. Throughout it all, I was determined to be me, that's all. When you look at what I did, the things I hit trouble for –

my clothes, hairstyle – they are so minor they wouldn't rate a mention in other walks of life; you'd stand out if you weren't a touch expressive. In football, I was never prepared to play that game, to suck up to a manager, suppress my personality, toe the line. Perhaps I would have got on better if I had, but I wouldn't have been me, so there'd have been no point.

When I finished at Bradford I did have a few offers but it was all lower-league stuff which I didn't fancy. I went to Exeter at the beginning of the 2002–03 season. Another dismal episode. The club had big debts; two blokes, John Russell and Mike Lewis, had taken over, and I was part of their PR, I suppose, along with them making Uri Geller the club chairman. I was the Beni Carbone, the crowd-pleasing promise of good times. I'm not sure quite what Uri's role was. The football wasn't too good, the club was in trouble, there was no way I was moving, with Jo and Ellis, down to the South-West to play for Exeter. I left after five games; Exeter went out of the League at the end of the season, and the club went into administration. Lovely.

Still, I honestly don't regret leaving United; I had to leave, for my sanity, even though I learned that outside United's gates were a load of two-bit, wannabe outfits dancing on the edge of ruin. It was awful, quitting, falling out of love with the game; it was like going out with a girl you love to bits, then it ending horribly with the two of you hating each other, but with neither of you feeling that's the way it should be. You're left with the sour memories, the introspection, the desolate feeling of bewilderment about what to do next. I'd still get offers, to resurrect my career at some godforsaken club which had fallen on hard times. I'd always feel a surge of temptation, to get fit again, get out there and knock the ball around, pin my ears back and run, then I'd remember the travelling, the managers, the being dropped and sitting on the bench, the petty rules around a football club, the way it's all so damn serious, and would decide it wasn't for me.

I spent some time in 2004–05 being the PR coup for Garforth Town, a local semi-pro club in the North-East Counties League, who had been taken over by Simon Clifford, a good, mad bloke, a bit of a guru who has run football schools all over the world based on Brazilian skills. He was the guy who had Socrates, the old Brazil World Cup captain, over playing for Garforth. Socrates was supposed to stay a month. I loved the picture of him sitting on the bench at Garforth wrapped in the thickest down coat you ever saw, with a look on his face which said he didn't know cold like that existed. He came on for a few minutes, looking every minute of his fifty-odd years, then went back to Brazil sharpish.

I played because I thought I'd enjoy the game at that standard; it'd be easy for me, I'd keep myself reasonably fit. But I didn't. It's a strange position to be in, as an ex-pro: you don't want to take the game too seriously because you've been there and done it, but for the players alongside you, it's everything, and the opponents want to kick you because of who you are. Everybody's fit, too, so you can't stroll around and take it easy, enjoy the outdoors. But because you've played at a higher level it's frustrating that players can't give and go, pass the first option, play the obvious ball to feet, perform at your level, so the game itself isn't enjoyable. We were training one time, just doing some stretches, the lads were having a bit of banter and the fitness trainer said: 'Oy, no talking! Serious!'

I thought: at every level of this game, people think you can only play it properly if you show no sign that you're enjoying yourself. Even here, Garforth Town, doing a few stretches on a Tuesday evening, we're not allowed to smile. Would that make your hamstring tighter, if you smile when you're stretching it? I suppose I could have played the politics more, done what Giggsy did, left the flash car at home, turned up quiet, serious, not smiled around a football club. But what kind of a recipe is that for working life?

I thought maybe I should really get back to basics, play with my mates in the pub team. That didn't work either. The football's awful, you play on mudbaths, the facilities in the public parks are appalling, and even at that level there are people for whom it's the be-all and end-all, who want to have a go at you if you're an ex-Man U or Leeds player. 'Kick the shit out of Lee Sharpe next time he gets the ball,' I heard one of the opposition's meatheads say when I played my second game, so I made it my last. Life's too short.

Simon Clifford texted me one afternoon. He'd been at a lunch – he's a heroic networker – and he'd met Alex Ferguson. 'He says he still loves you...' Turned out Simon had told Ferguson I was playing in his Garforth team, and Ferguson had leant back in his chair at this dinner, and said: 'He could have been the best left-back in the world.'

I imagine Alex Ferguson has this idea in his head that Lee Sharpe 'saw the stardust', and threw it all away. My take on that: I was at Old Trafford for eight years, and I don't remember him ever telling me then I could be the best left-back in the world. I remember arguments about me playing defensively, but I don't remember him ever presenting it in that sort of positive way. Now, I can see it making sense. I was a good all-round left-sided player with natural pace but without the brilliant skills of someone like Ryan Giggs. At first I was quicker than all the full-backs I was playing against, so I was good on the left wing, but by the time I was twenty-two, twenty-three, the game had speeded up around me and I wasn't getting a yard on as many defenders. I didn't want to move to left-back as a permanent slot. To me it was boring there, not what the game is about, but Alex Ferguson was thinking I could do everything there – tackle, pass, overlap, cross the ball, even head it if I really had to – and my pace would have given me something extra. Plus I was left-footed. Instead, United played all those years with Denis Irwin at left-back, and he's right-footed. If the manager had sold it to me, said I could have a long career, play regularly, be a Roberto Carlos, I might have gone for it. In fact, I'm sure I would. Maybe it shouldn't have, but it made me quite angry to hear that he'd leant back after a fine lunch, years after I was long gone, and said wistfully to the non-league manager I was playing for that I could have been a contender.

Gradually, I felt I was getting over it; I had to. Thinking it through, going over it in my mind, knowing I had made the right decision but cursing some of the reasons for it, I started to come out of the football blackness, tease out and remember what I loved about the game. Slowly, like someone in rehab venturing out, I edged into watching the odd game with my mates, at home or in the pub, and some of the old enjoyment seeped back in.

That didn't make things very much easier – there was still the small matter of what to do with the rest of my life. I had earned well in football: it wasn't quite in the time of really silly money where one Man U contract would now more than set you up for life, but it was a good wad. I invested it in property, loaded my pension, have some money put away; I wasn't Captain Sensible like Gary Pallister, but I didn't blow it all on coke as the rumour mill would have it. Still, financially, and by choice because you go mad otherwise, I have to work. My income just stopped immediately when I retired and I had to earn some money. I had a few plans, but they didn't all work out. I was involved in property development, which was fine, but hardly filled the empty days with thrills. Then I bought a pub, with my mate Ross – the same Ross who was my friend way back, in the days when at six or seven we'd take our bikes round our estate in Birmingham and imagine we were on a world tour. This time we parked up in a pub in Leeds, but we had a bit of a crash. Ross has trained as a chef, and with my investment and name locally, it seemed a great idea to buy a pub and build it up for food and drinking, but somehow we couldn't make it work. Some of the locals immediately decided to go elsewhere, and very quickly we were losing money and having to build it up from the back foot. What had been an exciting venture, which should have been a pleasure, turned into drudgery and pressure, dealing with brewery bills, staff problems and a barrel-load of niggles carefully measured out to make your head sore. I'd thought it would earn me a few quid, but we started to lose serious money and early in 2005 we just had to cut our losses and get out, so we sold it on, both taking a big hit on it. Now I know I wasn't ready. I have to take my share of any blame going: I didn't put the hours in, I didn't have a grasp of the detail, and I wasn't ready, in the state my head was in, for suddenly having a business with staff to pay and keep happy. It was a learning experience, but a bruising, troubling one, a headache, and a financial black hole that I really didn't need to land in at that time.

This was the culmination of two years of misery. It was hard on Joanne. They say nine out of ten married footballers get divorced within two years of retiring, and while that is a shocking statistic, I can understand it. It's a horrible, bleak time, as if the good part of your life is over; you have to start again, an empty future yawning ahead. You've finished your real career in your thirties, when most people are just beginning to master theirs, and have to find what you're going to do by trial and error, unless you're one of the few who is made for coaching or management, which isn't, let's be honest, my dream job. With the structure gone, and everything I enjoyed most in life, I was no fun to be with: a sodden lump of self-pity, quiet, withdrawn, brooding, depressed. I'd still get a lot of attention from girls, and I took refuge in some of that. Jo found some texts on my phone, she was hurt, she moved out, so now I was on my own in my big house. We spent weeks and months dragging it out, whether we were going to get back together or not, and eventually we split up. I will settle down one day, I do want that, but I know I have a problem trusting women and making that ultimate commitment.

Spring came and, little by little, break by break, shoots of new life popped to the surface. I had a call to play in a Man U veterans' team – sorry, they call it 'masters' to be polite to the old-timers – in Canada. Went over there; it was utterly freezing, but quite a few of the lads were together again. Lee Martin and Russell Beardsmore played for us. Lee has had his own troubles since retiring through injury, although he's doing OK now, and Beardo had a career playing for Bournemouth and other clubs in the lower divisions. It was good to see them. Schnozz had a chuckle when he saw us, three old lags washed up together in the masters: 'The fledglings,' he chortled. 'The fledglings are back together.' And we all smiled.

Frank Stapleton played, still utterly dedicated, and Frank McAvennie guested for us. He, we can safely say, isn't 100 per cent dedicated, and we had some good nights out. The football was brilliant, too, real quality, playing with great former players. Liverpool won the tournament, with Gary Gillespie, John Wark, Jan Molby, keeping the ball as of old, you couldn't get it off them. Molby was awesome. There were 10,000 crowds to watch it, and people were coming up telling me they were fanatical Man U supporters, that they'd loved what I'd done for them as a player, that I'd lit the place up, made them so happy, which put a smile back on my face and put some of it in perspective. There are more of those tournaments coming up, and they suit me fine; they're a better way for an ex-professional to play the game than dropping down too many levels in standard, or fetching up on the public parks with the pub teams.

Then, out of the blue, ITV called my agent to see whether there was any chance I could step in at short notice and be a contestant on a new show they were doing, *Celebrity Wrestling*. Why they thought of me, I don't know – they had a couple of standbys they didn't even use. They called on the Monday and by the Friday I was down there. I don't think I'd be hurting anybody's feelings by saying it perhaps wasn't the best show ITV have ever done – they pulled it after a week – and I came back with a broken rib, but it was TV work, something for me in the vague area where I wanted to be, and the producers told me they'd really liked my attitude, the way I got on with everybody, was easygoing, did everything with a smile on my face. Funny, they liked all the things which drove managers mad in football.

Kenny Dalglish called, inviting me to play in a celebrity golf tournament at La Manga with Alan Hansen and one or two other old stars, all expenses paid. I went over there with Leilani, a model who'd been another of the celebrity wrestlers, and all the old-timer footballers took the piss. My mates were laughing by now: I'm flying round the world to play for an ex- Man U players' team, doing TV work, playing golf all over the place, plenty of girls around for me. They just shook their heads: 'Lee Sharpe,' they'd say. 'Where did it all go wrong?'

Then ITV phoned again. What did I think about *Celebrity Love Island*? Celebrity what? Six weeks away, being filmed twenty-four hours a day with a bunch of celebs with agendas of their own? Er, not quite my scene, I thought. But it was a sign of where I was in life that, giving it some thought, I actually didn't have much to keep me away from it. OK, I said, still not sure; with three days to go, I very nearly pulled out. I'm glad I didn't. I know it took a panning by some TV critics at first, but it was an incredible experience for me. I had a great time when I was out there, and it was amazing when I got back. The experience was what I needed, something which dropped for me just when I needed it. I couldn't have scripted, imagined, spirited it into being any more perfect.

When I first arrived on the island, I was still wary. It wasn't really my world, the celebrity life, people needing to boost their profiles to keep their earning potential up, or because they're looking to get into acting, or whatever. I was different: I went with nothing to lose and no plan, except to be myself. My dad offered me some advice: 'Be the Phil Tufnell.' Tuffers had done so well on one of the celeb shows because he'd been normal, a sportsman used to a group situation, good banter, bit of a laugh, coming across as a guy you'd like to be mates with. So I thought: I'll just go over there and be me, be natural, see what happens.

They flew us out to Fiji, stuck the twelve of us, six blokes, six women, at a resort they'd built specially for the show, plied us with quality food and drink, sat us by the pool, and surrounded us with TV cameras to show the nation what would unfold.

For the first two weeks, I still wasn't sure it was my scene, and also I was conscious of Joanne at home, that we'd been dragging ourselves through the will-we, won't-we agonies of long-term relationship troubles. Then suddenly I was out in full view on prime time, half naked with a bunch of lovely women, encouraged to flirt and let loose. I did initially want to go home, melt back into the life of the ex-footballer, but two weeks in, the sun began to work into my bones, melt away some of the misery. I grew friendlier with Callum Best, who was a good guy, whatever the public perception of him is, and Abi Titmuss, who was cool and so different from her media image. And I thought: do you know what, I'm going to enjoy this; I'm going to relax. I'll deal with anyone I upset when I get home.

From then on, I had the time of my life. Literally. I may have had stardom and fame before, but from the age of sixteen it was in the regimented world of football. After leaving United I had six difficult years, and the last two after retirement had been awful. Now, by some miracle, here I was in the sunshine, on a beautiful resort on an incredible island, in a situation where, while you couldn't ever forget the cameras were there, you could at least get used to them, and suddenly I was in my element.

Some of the day trips we did were just awesome, once-in-a-lifetime experiences. I love boats anyway, and I was taken on a catamaran with Abi to an island, where we were given champagne and lobster. It was a beautiful, cloudless day, and we were put down in perfect little bays with lovely sandy beaches. Sitting on this boat in the clear turquoise sea with Abi Titmuss feeding me lobster, the sun beating down, was a true, ultimate, where-did-it-all-go-wrong moment.

I loved being away. Although the cameras were always there – and, yes, they captured me, drunk, declaring my love for Abi, which could have been quite embarrassing – we were in a glorious bubble: no newspapers, no TV, no phones or mobiles, no computers, nothing. At home, I was convinced I'd be getting panned, that girls from the past would be kissing and telling, the newspapers delivering their vitriol, but I didn't have to care because I couldn't see any of it. It was, in that unreal TV bubble, a strange kind of freedom.

At first I'd thought I'd be voted off quickly, but I lasted weeks, relishing it more as time went on. I felt more comfortable with the other people, who were mostly fine, and the sun, the bliss of it all, seeped into my being.

Some aspects of my life must have stood me in good stead. Most of the celebs hated the communal sleeping arrangements, the beds all lumped together, but I loved that. It helped me get up in the mornings because there was life around me, beautiful girls pottering about in bikinis –

no point lying around with a day like that stretching ahead of you. Also, I'd spent my career in group situations, in teams of footballers with endless time to while away, on tours abroad, so I could handle it. In fact, I'd missed it for two years and it was great to have whole days with nothing to do but laze and banter the time away. On one of those trips, sitting back in the boat with the sun in my face, I thought of my time in football. Briefly, Alex Ferguson flashed into my mind; I wondered what he'd think if he saw me. Probably despair: what the hell is that Lee Sharpe doing now? I had a realisation: for better or worse, everything that happened in football brought me to this. If I'd been a different kind of person, toed the line, allowed my personality to be suppressed, I would never be in line for a part in this growing brand of pure entertainment TV. All the characteristics which led me into trouble in football, which I stubbornly fought not to lose, had brought me this great experience and the chance of a new career, in which I really could be me.

Out there, though, we had no idea how we appeared to the watching public. There was liberation in that, but it was also worrying: was everyone gathered round TV sets chucking cans of beer at the unbearable annoyance of Lee Sharpe? Was I in for tabloid hell back in England? When, finally, I was the last to be voted off – out in the semi-final, not too bad – I saw Callum. 'You have got nothing at all to worry about,' he told me. 'The British public loves you.'

It was unreal. On the way back, we stopped off for two days in Sydney, and there were some British lads who'd been watching the show and recognised us straight away. What's this, worldwide fame? Then, stepping off the plane at Gatwick, it was mad. Forget playing for Man U, this was fame across men and women, young and old, of all types. A couple of middle-aged women walked past, then recognised me, smiled: 'Hey, you're that nice young man from *Celebrity Love Island*.' Girls were coming up to me, telling me I was lovely, I was so natural, I was such a nice bloke, I'd come across really well. Well, shucks, I was only being me. Men were telling me I'd been brilliant, I'd kept it real, been down-to-earth, they could relate to me.

When I finally got home to Leeds, my mates were waiting for me with plenty of piss-take about my Abi moment, but they were chuffed, said they'd watched every episode – I was like: get a life – and I'd done really well. Then we went out to my local and it really was like the prodigal son had returned: applause, warmth, girls coming up to me, a guy buying me a drink: 'You pulled Abi Titmuss. Fair play to you, mate.'

The great thing about it, the reason it feels like more than just a show which went well, is that I got this positive reaction thanks to simply being myself. People weren't responding like this because I'd put on a performance, which I'd then have to repeat every time I was on television. It really had been me up there. It was so weird; it was as if you go on holiday, and when you get back, everybody in the country suddenly knows you. It was a different kind of fame from football stardom. Fans don't really know you, they only see what you've done on the field. They find it difficult to approach you in a bar or social situation, and there is always the tribal part of it, that you're identified with one club or another, and the hint, not strong but always possible, of trouble. After *Love Island*, there was so much warmth: people had no reservations about coming to talk to me. They felt they knew me; they *did* know me. Suddenly I was being celebrated not for playing for a team, but for being myself.

It felt as if doors were opening for me and I hope they stay open. It landed me, almost miraculously, where I wanted to be. I did some presenting work while I was still playing football and I felt that if I was going to have an interesting second career, it would be in TV; not as a football pundit, criticising other players, which I never wanted to do, but as myself. Suddenly, from the phone barely ringing for two years, ITV wanted to talk to me about possibly having my own show. There were offers coming in to my agent from all over the place. The news was that I was natural, likeable, appealing to all ages but particularly to the sixteen to thirty-four range that advertisers crave. Where it will all lead, I don't yet know, but it has reawakened my life, made me more confident that I can thrive in another sphere, and also made me more ambitious.

In the trough of those two years, I was sinking into the idea that my time in the sun had gone, that my days of fame and fortune were over, I had to settle down into an ordinary humble existence, doing I'm not sure what. That show delivered to me the realisation that there is much more still out there, and I have to work hard to go out and do it, make another life and career for myself. Sitting out there in one of the most beautiful corners of the world, I felt the worries and strains, the depression and confusion, washing away, bringing me to some acceptance of who I am, that I have a great deal still to offer. I felt for the first time that I could close the chapter that was football, its glory and grief, the beauty and trauma, the good and the bad of it. Finished. Over.

And now, if all goes well, a new chapter of life is about to begin.